Movement Parties Against Austerity

D1615258

Movement Parties
Against Austerity

Donatella della Porta,
Joseba Fernández,
Hara Kouki and
Lorenzo Mosca

polity

First published in 2017 by Polity Press

Polity Press
65 Bridge Street
Cambridge CB2 1UR, UK

Polity Press
350 Main Street
Malden, MA 02148, USA

ISBN-13: 978-1-5095-1145-7 (hardback)
ISBN-13: 978-1-5095-1146-4 (paperback)

A catalogue record for this book is available from the British Library.

Library of Congress Cataloging-in-Publication Data

Names: Della Porta, Donatella, 1956- author. | Fernández, Joseba, author. |
    Kouki, Hara, author. | Mosca, Lorenzo, author.
Title: Movement parties against austerity / Donatella della Porta, Joseba Fernández,
    Hara Kouki, Lorenzo Mosca.
Description: Cambridge, UK ; Malden, MA : Polity Press, 2017. | Includes
    bibliographical references.
Identifiers: LCCN 2016033696 (print) | LCCN 2016052382 (ebook) | ISBN
    9781509511457 (hardback) | ISBN 9781509511464 (pbk.) | ISBN 9781509511471
    (Epdf) | ISBN 9781509511488 (Mobi) | ISBN 9781509511495 (Epub)
Subjects: LCSH: Political parties. | Social movements–Political aspects. | Financial crises–
    Political aspects. | Economic policy.
Classification: LCC JF2051 .D434 2017 (print) | LCC JF2051 (ebook) | DDC
    324.2/3—dc23
LC record available at https://lccn.loc.gov/2016033696

Typeset in 10 on 12 pt Sabon
by Toppan Best-set Premedia Limited
Printed and bound in the UK by CPI Group (UK) Ltd, Croydon, CR0 4YY

For further information on Polity, visit our website: politybooks.com

Contents

Acknowledgements

The idea for this book came to us, at the beginning of 2015, during a casual conversation over a lunch with colleagues in Berlin, in the observation of a relevant but unexpected dynamic of emergence of parties from within a social movement and, at the same time, a strange lack of, first, conceptualization of them and, second, comparative research on them. These gaps suggested not only theoretical thinking but also empirical investigations. In theory, our aim has been to build an ideal-typical definition of movement parties, locating it within social movement studies and party studies. In reality, we have triangulated various sources on party actors, who, while writing this book, became more and more visible and successful, achieving power at local and even national level. While their evolutionary paths are still developing, we thought that the time was certainly right for first analysis.

Ideas mature in context under favourable circumstances. First and foremost, our work was made possible by an Advanced Scholars Research Grant from the European Research Council for Donatella della Porta's project of 'Mobilizing for Democracy'. Some parts of this volume have been presented at a conference on Movement and Parties at the Centre for Social Movement Studies of the Scuola Normale Superiore in Florence. We are grateful to Daniela Chironi, Jonas Draege, Sven Hutter, Frank O'Connor, Martin Portos, Ken Roberts, Anna Subirats and Sidney Tarrow for their comments. We also wish to thank Sarah Tarrow for her careful editing.

The authors are listed in alphabetical order; they contributed equally to this book.

1

Movement Parties in Times of (Anti-)Austerity: An Introduction

1.1. Parties and movements: An introduction

During austerity policies and the cycle of protest against them, while the downward trend in party-movement relations had pushed towards an expectation of further separation between institutional and contentious actors, a new wave of parties emerged that took inspiration (and strength) from social movements. This first became visible in Latin America in the 1990s, with a parallel move in Europe (particularly in Southern Europe) more than a decade later. The stunning electoral success of movement parties like SYRIZA in Greece, Podemos in Spain, and the Movimento 5 Stelle (M5S) in Italy challenged expectations of an increasing separation of movement and party politics in social movement studies, as well as anticipation of a decline of the radical left in studies of political parties. This volume presents a social-science analysis of these topical socio-political phenomena, within a cross-national comparative perspective.

A first contribution of our research is in the bridging of concepts and theories developed in two quite successful subfields in the social and political sciences: studies on social movements and on political parties. In particular, focusing on movement parties that have been successful in electoral politics, we will address the relevant issues of social movement effects as well as party system changes. Bridging both traditions of study, we will reflect on the genesis of movement parties within broad transformations in social conflicts induced by the neoliberal critical juncture and contemplate the organizational changes that, from social movements, spilled over into party politics. Rather than searching for structural determinants, however, we will take a processual stance, considering the emergence and success of movement parties within an approach that is *relational*, as it looks at repeated interactions of various actors; *dynamic*, as it addresses these interactions through trials and errors; and *constructed*, as it considers those actors' construction of their social reality (della Porta 2014).

This introduction will review the existing research on relations between parties and social movements, setting the theoretical stage for the empirical analysis that will follow. First, we review existing literature on the relations developed between movements and parties in an attempt to *conceptualize* movement parties as based upon a specific type of relations with movements. Movements have developed special links with political parties or party families by targeting parties, allying with parties, founding parties. Movement parties are defined with reference to these different types of relations (Kitschelt 1989). Second, we will single out some *conditions* under which social movements are expected to influence parties, up to the foundation of movement parties (Tarrow 1989; 2015; Goldstone 2003; della Porta and Diani 2006). Following existing literature in social movement studies and party studies, explanations for movement party emergence will be located within the structure of political cleavages, the representative capacity of existing parties, the characteristics of electoral competition and party systems, the degree of electoral volatility and institutional trust as well as electoral laws. Third, we will address the evolution of party models *over time* – from parties of notables to personal/cartel parties putting particular emphasis on the characteristics of an emerging type of party organization: the neoliberal populist party. Hegemonic party models in specific historical periods play an important role in providing environmental imprints affecting newborn parties – such as movement parties – despite their aim to challenge and change the existing party systems. In particular, neoliberal populist parties tend to be organizationally thin, highly personalized, post-ideological and mediatized – characteristics that to a certain extent can also be found in contemporary movement parties. Fourth, we will focus on the evolution through time of movement party types that emerged from some social movement families (i.e. labour movements, environmental movements) focusing particularly on the Green parties. Our aim is to shed light on the relations developed between parties and movements in history and on the different ways some movements have interacted with the existing party system. We shall add to this analysis the characteristics of social movements that can lead to the foundation of a party. We will also reflect on movement parties' strategies (in frames, organizations, and forms of action) by mapping the *trade-offs* that a close relationship between movements and parties creates for both actors. The last part of this introductory chapter presents the *research* design of the book, including the case selection and the methods for data collection and data analysis. Building on the knowledge of party/movements relations presented above, we have chosen SYRIZA, Podemos and the M5S for in-depth analysis throughout the volume, as these political actors represent cases of movement parties that emerged during the crisis of neoliberalism and which achieved electoral success. We will finally present the structure of the *volume*.

1.2. Conceptualizing relations between movements and parties

While it has often been noted that parties are important for movements and vice versa, the literature on relations between the two is at best sparse. Reciprocal indifferences have been further fuelled as research on parties moved away from concerns with the relations between parties and society – focusing on parties within institutions – and social movement studies mainly framed them as a social phenomenon whose political aspects had to be located outside of the political institutions. Research on contentious politics has indeed become too movement-centric, dismissing the existing reciprocal relationship between electoral and protest politics (Hutter 2014). At the same time, literature on political parties grew more and more biased towards institutions, forgetting about the linkages with the society (della Porta 2015a).

Critiques of a vision of movements as outsiders have been voiced, however, within social movement studies. As Jack Goldstone suggested, institutional politics is permeated by social movements considered as 'an essential element of normal politics in modern societies', which do not necessarily institutionalize or fade away. Rather, 'parties and movements have become overlapping, mutually dependent actors in shaping politics to the point that long-established political parties welcome social movement support and often rely specifically on their association to win elections' (2003, 4). Relations between the two are various: 'Movements compete with parties. Movements infiltrate parties .... Movements become parties' (Garner and Zald 1985, 137). Social movements have often addressed programmatic challenges to parties, by proposing new issues; organizational challenges, by promoting a participatory model; electoral challenges, by raising support for some emerging topics in public opinion (Rohrschneider 1993), and even succeeded in changing parties' programmes and organization (della Porta 2007). In a recent contribution, McAdam and Tarrow (2010, 533) singled out six types of relations between movements and parties: 'Movements introduce new forms of collective action that influence election campaigns. Movements join electoral coalitions or, in extreme cases, turn into parties themselves. Movements engage in proactive electoral mobilization. Movements engage in reactive electoral mobilization. Movements polarize political parties internally.'

On the side of party studies, relations between parties and movements have been addressed as relations with interest groups, in particular within reflections on organizational linkages. A linkage has been defined as 'any means by which political leaders act in accordance with the wants, needs, and demands of the public in making public policy' (Luttbeg 1981, 3). A link between elite action and citizens' preferences provides a 'substantive connection between rulers and ruled' (Lawson 1980, 3). Particularly important have been considered the relations between parties and interest organizations, as linkages through organizations allow for a better selection and aggregation of 'relevant grievances into reasonably coherent packages of political demands which then become the object of negotiation between organizational and party elites' (Poguntke 2002a, 45). This could prove very effective for the party, since 'As long as organizational integration is high, organization members may cast their vote according to their leaders' recommendation even if they disagree with individual elements of the deal, because their prime loyalty is to the organization' (ibid., 46).

Relations between parties and interest groups are said to co-evolve, adapting to each other, through competition and cooperation as the two actors see each other as means potentially useful for their ends, and thus try to influence each other through overlapping leadership or other forms of pressure – but also provide each other with brokerage for reaching out of one's own networks as well as bridging identities (Heaney 2010). In fact:

> political parties strive to craft platforms that will draw the support of majorities of voters, while interest groups pressure the government to enact policies that advance the substantive agendas or ideological perspectives of narrower constituencies.... Groups sometimes prop up parties by supplying them with essential volunteers and financial resources, thus enabling a group to dictate key parts of a party's agenda. At other times, a group may find itself 'captured' by a party such that the group must accept a party's weak efforts on its behalf because the other major party refuses (or is unable) to bargain for its loyalty. (Heaney 2010, 568)

The definition of movement parties refers in fact to political parties that have particularly strong organizational and external links with social movements. In social movement studies, the political opportunities approach has linked parties' evolution to movements. When looking at party systems, a very first observation is that some social movements have *produced new parties (and party families)*: the labour movements arose from, or gave birth to, socialist parties; regionalist parties have been rooted in ethnic movements; confessional parties in religious movements and the Greens in environmental ones. As Tarrow (2015, 95) noted:

> Many parties begin life as movements. Think of the labor movement that gave birth to social democratic parties in Western Europe; or the abolitionist movement that was at the core of the Republican party during and after the American Civil War; or the indigenous peoples' movements that produced ethnically supported parties in Bolivia and Ecuador in recent decades. Movements frequently give rise to parties when movement activists transfer their activism to institutional politics.

In parallel, in party studies, influentially Lipset and Rokkan (1967) have located parties within social cleavages, in which they originate and which they contribute to perpetuate.

Movements have moreover developed special links with a political party or party family. Social movements have, more or less harmonically, *allied* with parties even beyond stable organizational linkages. Considering parties more broadly, external linkages have often been created with various types of interest groups and civil society associations, such as religious ones for confessional parties or ethnic ones for ethno-nationalist parties. Linkages to movements can be stressed in the very name of the party, in the opening of participation to movement members, in support for movement claims, in the shared use of protest. The presence of overlapping membership at grassroots and leadership levels as well as the presence of movement activists in party lists testify for these ties. Party members may 'engage in social movement activities themselves, thus promoting and leading to attitudinal changes in the party with respect to those themes at the core of the social movements' mobilizations' (Piccio 2012, 268). Indeed, 'for a social movement to be more likely to have an impact on a party, a certain degree of overlap must exist between the party and the social movements' identities' (ibid.).

The traditional allies of the progressive social movements have mainly been the leftist parties (Kriesi 1989; Kriesi et al. 1995; della Porta 1996), and the radical left is considered as by far the most relevant party in protest politics (Hutter 2014; Kriesi 1989, 296). From the Labour Party in Great Britain to the Social Democrats in Germany, from the French socialists to the Italian communists, the programmes and members of the institutional left have changed following interactions with social movements and in response to increasing awareness on themes such as gender discrimination or environmental protection. As mediators between civil society and the state, parties need to mobilize public opinion and voters, so that the programmes and membership of the institutional left have often been altered by interaction with movements (i.e. Koelble 1991; Maguire 1995; Duyvendak 1995; Koopmans 1995; Piccio 2012). Social movements have indeed been extremely sensitive to the characteristics of their allied political parties: they have often privileged action in society, leaving parties the job of bringing their claims into institutions. They have placed themselves on the political left–right axis, and have constructed discourses consistent with the ideologies of their allies.

Movements parties' relations have been addressed with reference to *political cleavages*. Comparative research has indicated that, in general, the 'old left' has been more disposed to support movements where exclusive regimes had for a long time hindered the moderation of conflicts on the left–right axis (della Porta and Rucht 1995; Kriesi et al. 1995, 68; Tarrow 1990).

Party divisions within the traditional left have also been cited as influencing attitudes towards social movements. In particular, divisions on the left between a social-democratic (or socialist) and a communist party are said to increase the relevance of the working-class vote, discouraging left-wing parties from addressing post-material issues (Kriesi 1991, 18). Differently, the global justice movement, stressing the traditional demands of social rights and justice, seems to have been more able to influence the institutional left in countries such as Italy, France, or Spain, where the moderate left feared the competition of more radical Communist or Trotskyist parties (della Porta 2007). More generally, electoral competition is an important variable in explaining the reaction of potential allies towards social movements as the propensity to support protest has been connected with electoral instability, which renders the winning of new votes particularly important. In fact, member-challenger coalitions are most probable in closely divided and competitive political situations (Piven and Cloward 1977, 31–2; Tilly 1978, 213–14). Alliances between parties and social movements can be facilitated when the electoral environment is more unstable (Piccio 2012). Additionally, the position of the left towards social movements is influenced by whether or not they are in government: when in opposition, social democrats take advantage of the push provided by social movements; when in power, on the other hand, they are forced by budgetary constraints or coalition partners to limit their openness to emerging demands (Kriesi 1991, 19; Kriesi 1989, 296–7). Finally, availability towards changes could be different for mainstream versus peripheral parties, the latter being those who have little to no chance of achieving power (Kriesi 2015a).

Whatever the reasons for alliances, we can speak of movement parties when relations with social movements are particularly close. Social movements are usually defined as networks of groups and individuals, endowed with some collective identification, that pursue goals of social transformation mainly through unconventional forms of participation (della Porta and Diani 2006). Political parties are instead, in Max Weber's (1922) influential definition, free associations built with the aim of achieving institutional power. This is mainly done through participation in elections – in democracy, 'a party is any political group that presents at elections, and is capable of placing through elections, candidates for public office' (Sartori 1976, 64).

Movement parties emerge as a sort of hybrid between the two, when organizational and environmental linkages are very close: to different degrees, they have overlapping membership, co-organize various forms of collective action, fund each other, address similar concerns. As organizations, they participate in protest campaigns, but also act in electoral arenas. As social movements are networks of organizations and individuals, movement parties can be considered as part of them, as testified for by overlapping memberships as well as organizational and action links. According to Kitschelt, 'movement parties are coalitions of political activists who emanate from social movements and try to apply the organization and strategic practice of social movements in the arena of party competition' (2006, 280). Additionally, even if in different formats, movement parties aim at integrating the movement constituencies within their organizations. Movement parties also represent movements' claims, by channelling their concerns in the institutions. As for framing, 'movement-based parties are more likely to be driven by ideological militancy than by pragmatic political considerations' (Tarrow 2015, 95). Moreover, even if using (also) an electoral logic, they tend to be supportive of protest, participating in campaigns together with other movement organizations, as 'in terms of external political practice, movement parties attempt a dual track by combining activities within the arena of formal democratic competition with extra-institutional mobilization' (Kitschelt 2006, 281).

1.3. The genesis of movement parties

A main question is, when do movement parties rise? In addressing this question, we can draw inspiration from social science research on both parties and movements, by singling out some sufficient, if not necessary,

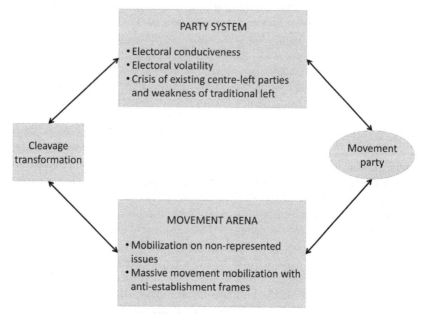

Figure 1.1.   Explaining the genesis of movement parties

causes at the level of the cleavage structure, the party system, and social movements. Bridging party and social movement research, we might build a model about the movement parties' genesis (see Figure 1.1).

Some main elements presented in the figure need to be briefly introduced by referring to relevant literature that indeed addresses the emergence of movement parties.

Transformations in the cleavage structures. Research on the rise of new parties has stressed the role of emerging cleavages, as they are likely to develop in response to neglected or new issues (although strength of post-materialism does not explain the appearance of Green parties), especially in times when economic or other problems become more visible and politicized (Kitschelt 1988; Müller-Rommel 1993). As economic competition erodes protected citizenship rights and also increases cultural diversity, globalization as a critical juncture has been related in Europe with the formation of a cleavage between winners and losers. While research in Europe had looked at the populist right-wing parties as mobilizing the losers in the electoral arena (Kriesi et al. 2008; 2012), research in Latin America (Van Cott 2005; Yashar 2005; Silva 2009; Roberts 2015) has focused instead on the ways in which the neoliberal critical juncture produced counter-movements towards social protection. In Southern Europe, too, neoliberalism and its crisis have transformed the cleavage structure that was at the base of the domestic party systems with the emergence of a precarization of labour as well as a proletarization of the middle classes. Movement parties have emerged where the crisis has been faster and where it more radically challenged everyday life.

Conducive conditions in the electoral field. Research on the political system has singled out the relevance for the rise of new parties of some institutional conditions. So, it has been noted that 'In some countries (e.g. the United States), ballot access requirements make it difficult for any but the few largest parties to gain the opportunity for electoral success. Plurality or majority electoral systems with single-member districts have sometimes (e.g. in France) been adopted specifically to deny electoral success to extremist parties, and have had the same effect on other small parties' (Harmel and Robertson 1985, 505). Studies on parties have discussed in particular the effects of the electoral system on the emergence and success of new parties, although with inconclusive results. While some opportunities must be available in terms of formal electoral access – institutional conduciveness having been linked to degree of decentralization, proportionality, reserved seats for minority, low barriers for registering parties, low threshold for earning seats (Van Cott 2005) – even more important is the level of electoral volatility.

Unrepresented claims and the delegitimation of bipolar party systems – especially of centre-left parties and the traditional left. As Kitschelt noted, 'movement parties are most likely to appear where (1) collective interests are intensely held by a large constituency, willing to articulate their demands through disruptive, extra-institutional activities, (2) established parties make no effort to embrace such interests for fear of dividing their own electoral constituency and (3) the formal and informal thresholds of political representation are low' (2006, 282). Movement parties emerged in bipolar systems of alternative coalitions or parties (Sartori 1976) where a relevant portion of the electoral perceived new grievances/interests/identities as not represented by the existing blocs. In this sense, the number of existing parties is expected to affect the coverage of demands, as a large number should increase the possibilities that new issues are addressed (Harmel and Robertson 1985; Hug 2001). New parties arise in a structured environment in which of highest importance is the behaviour of existing parties that are often unwilling to follow new movements, as they also think they will soon fade (Hug 2001). While the relevance of institutional thresholds is still debated, the emergence of new parties is clearly linked to the reactions by the other parties. The emergence and success of new parties is in fact embedded within relations inside the party system, as 'mainstream parties can undermine niche party vote with dismissive or accommodative tactics and boost it with adversarial strategies' (Meguid 2005, 347). This is the case as 'mainstream parties also manipulate the salience and ownership of the new party's issue. It follows that competition is not restricted to interaction between ideological neighbors, as the standard spatial theory claims; non-proximal parties play a critical role in the success and failure of Western Europe's niche parties' (ibid., 357).

Relevant characteristics of party systems that favoured the emergence of indigenous-peoples parties in Latin America are de-alignment, fragmentation, and the weakness of the left (initially, the channel of access for indigenous people) – especially the decline of a once strong left (Van Cott 2005).

Mobilization on non-represented issues. If these new parties emerge especially when movement entrepreneurs realize the need for a complex reorganization of the society, when they assume there is a constituency, and when there are low barriers to entry, they are successful 'only where an intensively felt, salient political interest harbored by a quantitatively significant constituency lacks representation in the existing party system' (Kitschelt 2006, 282). Looking at the Latin American experience, Kenneth Roberts (2015) noted that new parties emerged on the left in those countries in which centre-left parties had been leading forces in the implementation of neoliberal reforms. In this regard, research has looked at the loss of representative capacity that is linked to increasing exogenous constraints, such as responsibility towards international and market-related conditionalities, which thwarted established parties' capacity of representation, reducing their electoral support (Mair 2009; Streeck 2014). Neoliberal developments have jeopardized parties' ties with potentially disruptive effects as, as Peter Mair noted:

> parties should be seen not as being in complete control of the political agenda, but rather as sharing that control with other, non-electoral, organizations....This sharing of roles presents no problems for the parties as long as these latter organizations are linked to them in some way. A weakening of these links, however, and/or the emergence of new, non-party associated organizations, and/or a weakening of the agenda-setting role of those associated non-electoral organizations that do exist, could imply a challenge to the hold of party systems on the mass public. (1983, 420)

With the financial crises of the 2000s and 2010s, parties' conception of responsibility is challenged. If in the 1990s the mobilization on the right of the losers of globalization seemed a major phenomenon at the electoral level, in the 2000s the critique of globalization (especially in its neoliberal form) developed on the left as well, in this case more within contentious politics. Movement parties emerged in fact as established parties were most dramatically losing citizens' trust and the relations of cooperation of centre-left parties with social movements have been reduced as left-wing parties moved to the centre, while movements increasingly addressed social issues. Similarly to the Latin American cases, in Europe the movement parties seem therefore to have emerged and succeeded when centre-left parties were perceived as compromising with austerity policies. As we are going to see, during the economic crisis the PASOK in Greece, the Democratic party in Italy, and the PSOE in Spain all turned towards neoliberal policies based on structural reforms and privatization programmes which translated into cutting social spending, increasing the retirement age, reforming the labour market, reducing the public sector, and so on.

Massive movement mobilization with anti-establishment frames. The emergence of movement parties is also related to the characteristics of social movements themselves. In particular, movement parties tend to be successful when social movements mobilize new cleavages on which representation in institutions is perceived as weak. In fact, new parties have been successful when they have appealed to mobilized constituencies during waves of contentious politics, as has been noted in ethnonationalist parties and new left-wing parties in Latin America (Van Cott 2005; Madrid 2008; Roberts 2015). Strongly rooted and unitary movements, together with the configuration of power within the party system, had an influence on the formation and endurance of ethnic parties, to which organizers from declining left-wing parties brought frames of cultural recognition, autonomy and anti-neoliberalism (Van Cott 2005, 223). The main preconditions for the emergence of an ethnic party have been indeed singled out in the presence of a deep-rooted indigenous social movement, with dense networks of members, party fragmentation and harmony among indigenous groups, as well as the recruitment of former leaders of left-wing parties in decline (ibid., 223). In addition, ethno-populist parties are said to have succeeded, whereas traditional ethnic parties instead have failed, in conditions of low levels of ethnic polarization as well as fluid ethnic identification which allowed the broadening of the electoral appeal beyond specific other ethnic categories. In recent times, the legitimacy crisis of late neoliberalism has fuelled anti-austerity protests that have pointed at the corruption of an entire political class as the mechanism through which the profits of the few prevailed over the needs – the very human rights – of the many. In opposition to the corrupt elites, the protesters defined themselves as part of the large majority of those suffering from social and political inequalities. Social movements became in fact more and more critical of representative democracy. While these attitudes reflected a drop in trust in existing parties that was widespread in the electorate, however, social

movement activists remained convinced of the need for political intervention to control the market (della Porta 2015b). Anti-austerity protests in
particular have taken different forms – some more traditional, channelled
through existing organizations (including unions and parties), some more
innovative. In some countries, they brought about the – almost paradoxi-
cal, considering huge mistrust in institutional politics – choice to create
new movement parties; the widespread mistrust in the existing political
parties then favoured the electoral success of the new parties. Much
research has indeed indicated the role of massive waves of protest but
also of inclusive frames in the emergence of successful movement parties
in countries such as Greece, Spain and, to a minor extent, Italy.

1.4. Evolution of dominant party models

Apart from the genetic approach mentioned above, as far as movement
parties' evolution is concerned, literature on political parties has also
paid attention to the dominant models of party organizations. Within the
context of our research, we shall make reference to the organizational
strategies of political parties in an attempt to locate our parties within
evolving party systems, keeping, however, into account also the parallel
literature on transformations in social movement organizations. In fact,
the dominant party organizations as well as the movement parties have
changed in various periods adapting to but also promoting transformations in their environment.

Historical evolution of party organizational models. Party literature
has devoted much energy to singling out dominant organizational models
and their evolution in time. These reflections are also relevant to addressing movement parties in their historical evolution.

Looking at parties' internal characteristics along three dimensions –
organization, strategies, and culture – Panebianco's (1988) typological
approach pointed at the types of parties that are dominant (even if not
exclusive) in specific periods, linking them to contextual characteristics. Summarizing existing literature, Gunther and Diamond suggested a
typology based upon three criteria: (1) the nature of the party's *formal
organization* (thick/thin, elite-based or mass-based, etc.); (2) the *programmatic commitments* of the party (ideological/pragmatic, particularistic-
clientele-oriented/promiscuously eclectic electoral appeals, etc.); and (3)
the *strategy and behavioural norms* of the party (tolerant, pluralistic
and democratic versus proto-hegemonic and anti-system) (2003, 171).
Literature on political parties described, in fact, a double trend with initially an opening to civil society, with the development of the ideologic
mass party, but then a continuous approaching of the parties to state
institutions and distancing from society (see Figure 1.2). It is in this

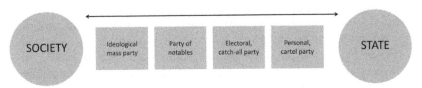

Figure 1.2.   *Dominant party models in history and their relation with state and society*

evolving context that movement parties emerge, as innovators but also in part adapting to existing institutional structures.

At the origins of political parties was what Max Weber (1922) called the *party of notables*, as party candidates were capable of devoting time to politics thanks to their economic conditions, and built upon their personal social reputation. Parties were organized in (informal) committees, made up of members of the social elite (Duverger 1951) and aimed at electing candidates who were supposed to represent the individual interests of those who voted for them (Neumann 1956).

In nineteenth-century Europe, there was indeed a move of party models towards the society as *mass parties* emerged, endowed with a stable bureaucracy (Weber 1922) in order to represent the collective interests of those who had hitherto been excluded. As these representatives did not possess individual resources that allowed them to devote themselves to politics, the parties (organized in party sections) built complex organizations in which politics became a profession (ibid., also Duverger 1951). Parties then assumed a function of social integration, allowing for the development of collective identification around common values and solidarities, with a growing influence on the everyday life of party activists (Neumann 1968). Ideological incentives became central for the development of party loyalties (Pizzorno 1981; 1997).

After the mass ideological party, defined as an invention from the left, started to decline, various labels were used to point at the autonomization of parties from their linkages with a specific social base (catch-all parties), a prevalent attempt at getting votes (electoral parties), an interpenetration of party and state based on inter-party collusion (cartel party). The *catch-all party* is defined by the watering down of the ideological appeals and the aim of representing specific classes with, at the same time, growing power of the leaders and declining influence of the rank-and-file (Kirchheimer 1966). The dominant aim for this type of parties is increasing electoral support, rather than socialization of members. In a similar vein, Panebianco (1988) described the *professional-electoral party* as characterized moreover by the presence of a bureaucracy that specializes in the relations with electors, through marketing and communication experts. Organizationally weak, this type of party focuses on the electoral moment, with a decline of organizational ideologies. The relations with the mass media also bring about a *personalization* of the leadership (Mazzoleni and Schulz 1999), often with personal conflicts as well. The *cartel party* represents the culmination of this trend, when parties collude with each other in order to get more and more state support, thus losing more and more the relations with their members (Katz and Mair 1995). In cartel parties, parties become mainly partnerships of professionals, not associations of, or for, the citizens.

These tendencies seem to peak in what appears as an emerging party model that we name as 'neoliberal populist party'; this is organizationally light, heavily personalized, split in non-ideological factions and characterized by heavy manipulative use of mass media but also by a power rooted in the occupation of institutional positions, often used for clientelistic or corrupt exchanges. This new party type has become mainstreamed in contemporary Europe during the last two decades following the evolution and decline of twentieth-century political ideologies. At the *organizational* level, the emergent party model displays a centralization of decisions in the hands of few visible leaders, which is intertwined with the merely formal involvement of the rank-and-file members (considered mainly as card-payers) and, especially, a reduced influence of activists, normally considered as more intransigent than either the leaders or the rank-and-file, and therefore as obstacles to moderate political choices (Crouch 2010). The centralization of decisions and the personalization of leadership – typical of neoliberal populist parties – have led scholars to speak of an Americanization of European parties, more and more oriented to an individualistic management of gains, and less and less to the creation of collective identities, progressively assimilated into the state (depending on the state for finances and profits) and less and less autonomous from public institutions (Calise 2000).

Crucial for our analysis of this newly emerging type of party, there is also a weakening of relations between parties and civil society organizations (Allern and Bale 2012). Party activists as channels of communication to potential voters tend to be substituted for by the mass media, particularly television, which facilitate direct identification of electors with leaders able to transmit a self-assured, confident and warm image, as well as appropriate some relevant themes (Barisione 2007), thus sidestepping the mediation of the party. At the same time, a decline of party members is seen as a permanent trend (van Biezen, Mair, and Poguntke 2012) and distinguishing feature of neoliberal populist parties. However, such parties seem to invest, but differentially, in the recruitment of new members (Kittilson and Scarrow 2003; Hazan and Rahat 2010; Cross and Blais 2012). 'Active members' became less important in terms of party financing as state subsidies substituted for membership fees, and changing lifestyles, post-materialist values and higher educational levels reduced the supply of membership (Scarrow 2009), producing rather calls for more participatory forms of political commitment (Montero and Gunther 2002). If organizational reforms tended to empower 'ordinary members' rather than activists (Mair 1994, 15) especially on the selection of candidates and legitimization of party programmes, party elites kept the power of veto (Scarrow, Webb, and Farrell 2000, 149).

As we shall see in the next chapter, the *framing* of neoliberal populist parties changed accordingly, becoming less and less ideological. In fact, the use of an 'anti-political' language by leaders, in contrast with parties and professional politicians (Campus 2006), also becomes an instrument for reinforcing personalized leadership by politicians that underlines, paradoxically, their estrangement from politics. Similarly, populist appeals (to the people against the elites) by these parties (prevalently, but not only from the centre-right) seek to utilize low party identification and mistrust in institutional politics to create an electoral following. In a vicious circle, the decrease in trust and identification in parties could further push for personalization as a strategy to win back consent (Diamanti 2007), above all (but not only) from the most socially marginalized and least politically interested voters.

In sum, the emerging model of party presents a shallow, weak, and opportunistic organization; ideological appeals are (at best) vague, with an overwhelmingly electoral orientation. Electoralist parties debouch into *personalistic* parties, whose '*only* rationale is to provide a vehicle for the leader to win an election and exercise power…an organization constructed or converted by an incumbent or aspiring national leader exclusively to advance his or her national political ambitions. Its electoral appeal is not based on any programme or ideology, but rather on the personal charisma of the leader/candidate, who is portrayed as indispensable to the resolution of the country's problems or crisis' (Gunther and Diamond 2003, 187).

It is within this evolution in dominant party models that we should locate the organizational choices made by movement parties emerged during the economic crisis.

1.5. Evolution of party/movement relations over time

While party literature has focused almost exclusively on dominant party models, one could examine this process in parallel with the evolution of the movement-sponsored, challenging party models. Some characteristics

Table 1.1. Party/movement relations over time

Dominant party type	Movement party type	Relation party/movements
Party of notables	Ideological cadres party	Party as vanguard
Interclass mass party	Class-based mass party	Organic relation
Electoral, catch-all, personal, cartel party	Left-libertarian (Green) party	Fragmented (dual) relation
Neoliberal populist party	Movement parties against austerity	Dialectic relation

of movement parties in fact have also changed over time. Looking at the Latin American case, Roberts (2015, 39) has distinguished the following model of party/movement relations:

- vanguard model – with party control of social movements;
- electoral model – with relations only mobilized at elections;
- organic model – with deliberately blurred distinction between party and movement.

Paralleling the evolution in mainstream party types, we could indeed single out specific movement parties that opposed and at the same time adapted to dominant party types (see Table 1.1); in what follows, we will discuss this dynamic process focusing in particular on the relations developed between parties and movements.

First of all, the party of the notables was contrasted by parties of (left-wing) *cadres* that, in conditions of limited representation, tended to defend the interests of the excluded, within a conception of the party as a vanguard of the proletariat. Similar to Duverger's cell-based 'devotee' parties (1951) and Neumann's (1956) parties of 'total integration' are Gunther's and Diamond's proto-hegemonic mass-based parties, which 'place greater emphasis on discipline, constant active commitment and loyalty on the part of party members for the conduct of political conflict in both electoral and extraparliamentary arenas. Thus, recruitment of members is highly selective, indoctrination is intensive, and acceptance of the ideology and short-term party line is demanded of all members' (2003, 178–9). This type of party emerged and survived where institutional opportunities for expression of left-wing positions were more limited. In these parties, there is

> …a closed structure based on the semi-secret cell (rather than the open branch, which characterizes pluralist class-mass parties). Membership

is highly selective, and the party demands strict loyalty and obedience on the part of members. Ideological indoctrination of party members is intense and uncompromising, and the party penetrates into key sectors of society....Decision-making within the party is highly centralized and authoritarian, even if 'democratic centralism' often allows for open debate prior to the taking of an official stand. (ibid., 180)

While challenging parties initially had a small organizational core, they often expanded into the *class-based, mass, ideological party*, characterized by a hierarchical relationship with the labour movement within an integrated interaction. Classic research on parties stressed in particular the strong linkages that since the late nineteenth century had grown between socialist parties and trade unions in Europe; linkages developed via 'liaison committees, leadership and membership overlap and interchange, and a wide arena of common collective activities' (Allern 2010, 37).

As mentioned, the ideological mass party was an invention of the working class. With different models in different countries, the left-wing parties developed an organic relation between the electoral (party) and the functional (trade union) representation of the working class. Born in Europe in the nineteenth century from within the labour movement, these parties raised claims for political and social rights, contributing to the development of the very conception of democracy (della Porta 2013, ch. 2). They mainly originated outside of parliament, with the aim of bringing the claims of the workers in institutional politics, working as the transmission belts of the workers' interest within a (dominant) class cleavage.

The developments on the left of the then-movement parties were influenced by the reactions by the elites. As Rokkan (1970) noted, in the Scandinavian countries and the United Kingdom, open elites refrained from repressing the workers, facilitating the growth of large and moderate labour parties. Deeper cleavages in Germany, Austria, France, Italy, and Spain, with related repression of the emerging workers' movements, pushed towards *soziale Ghettopartei* with radical ideology and a consolidated but also isolated membership. In general, the higher the obstacles to enter into representative institutions, the less appealing was a strategy of gradual reform (Bartolini 2000, 565–6) and the more divided the left (Marks 1989).

From the organizational point of view, in what Kirchheimer (1966) called the *class-mass party*, authority was located in the executive committee, which centralized power, even if the party congress was formally to act as the last legitimate authority and the parliamentary wing sometimes aimed at increasing autonomous power. These parties established bases within their class constituency through groups organized both geographically (the local 'branch') and functionally (trade unions). While they seek to proselytize prospective members or voters, indoctrination and the demand for ideological conformity are minimal. While social integration through the activities of party and trade union allies is a significant objective, the party is primarily concerned with winning elections and taking part in the formation of governments. Recruitment of members is quite open. (Gunther and Diamond 2003, 179)

Class-mass parties (particularly social democratic ones) have been characterized by collateral, ancillary organizations 'strongly tied to their party via partially or fully overlapping memberships and mutual co-determination rights' (Poguntke 2002a, 49) and capable of attracting members who would not be willing to join the party.

Class-mass parties have, however, transformed dramatically since their foundation. A crisis of the political parties of the left has been singled out as related to a decline in party linkages. In particular, relations between socialist parties and trade unions became less strict and collective membership rare. As Kitschelt observed, 'From the early 1980s to the early 1990s, socialist, social democratic, and labor ideologies underwent more change than in any decade since World War II. Parties everywhere began to withdraw from old programmatic priorities, yet the pace, extent, and direction of that strategic transformation have varied across countries...new priorities have begun to complement, if not eclipse, conventional social democratic concerns with social security and income equality' (1994, 3).

It was from the critique of the bureaucratization of the ideological class party that a new form of movement party emerged with the development of new social movements. As Hanspeter Kriesi summarized, 'the more recent left-libertarian new social movements which were responsible for the wave of protest that swept across Western Europe and North America from the late 1960s to the 1980s of the last century were highly critical of representative democracy and of parliamentary procedures in particular. They sought more participatory modes of mobilization, and engaged heavily in protest activities to push their claims onto the agenda' (2015a, 672).

A different type of movement party – the *Green* party – emerged from social movements when ideological mass parties were already in crisis and cartel electoral parties had grown (Muller-Rommel 1993). New social movements challenged in fact what they saw as a hierarchical model of relations between movements and parties, calling for a more horizontal relationship. Between parties and movements, tensions increased in fact on the relevant organizational format. Given increasingly bureaucratized parties, the democratic quality of participation has remained central in the visions and practices of social movements. Left-libertarian parties have reflected this mood, with attempts at developing more participatory conceptions of politics (Kitschelt 1989, 3). Grassroots democracy was quite central for Green parties, who defined themselves as anti-parties and were seen as alternatives to conventional parties. The Green parties' stress on internal democracy has been seen as part of a dialectic process in which 'each new party type generates a reaction that stimulates further development, thus leading to yet another party type, and to another set of reactions, and so on' (Katz and Mair 1995, 6). These movement parties have spread in particular since the 1980s, with a main focus on the defence of the environment, but soon extending their appeal to civil rights in general. From the organizational point of view, the German Green party was characterized initially by *Basisdemokratie* organizational features such as collective and amateur leadership, imperative mandate, rotation, open access to meetings, and gender parity (Poguntke 1993). More in general, in these parties, 'The strong commitment to direct participation leads to the weakness (even rejection) of centralized organization and leadership, and a sometimes chaotic "assembly" organizational style.... Organizationally, the movement party is based on loose networks of grassroots support with little formal structure, hierarchy and central control' (Kitschelt 1989, 66). Open membership and a heterogeneous clientele were additional characteristics of left-libertarian movement parties (Gunther and Diamond 2003, 188–9).

From the point of view of their identity, these parties generally hold 'a negative consensus that the predominance of markets and bureaucracies must be rolled back in favor of social solidarity relations and participatory institutions' (Kitschelt 1989, 64). Young and small, they have been seen as characterized by the adoption of thin ideology from movements (Frankland, Lucardie, and Rihoux 2008), with ambivalent relations with the state – they may take subsidies but distrust institutions, with frequent conflicts as members are ideologically motivated and critical of authority (Kitschelt 1989). At their origins, these parties have been characterized by a post-materialist ideology and a participatory organization, with low formalization and bureaucratization, large involvement from the rank-and-file, and a non-conventional repertoire of action, including forms of protest (Poguntke 1993, 81; also O'Neill 1997, 43).

Besides their call for a more horizontal politics, Green parties have been located at the basis of a new cleavage, which has also transformed existing parties and party systems. In fact, the emergence of Green parties has been linked to the behaviour of the other existing parties – first and foremost, those on the left. In Kriesi's assessment, 'In consensus democracies, the Green and right-wing populist challengers have partly given rise to new parties, partly they have been co-opted by mainstream parties that have been transformed in due course.... in majoritarian democracies, the rise of new parties coming out of social movements is much more difficult, which means that the transformation of existing parties by social movements is more likely' (2015b, 12).

Green parties emerged in particular when there were strong environmental movements, from 'problem push' (Rüdig 1990) but also 'opportunity pull'. Parties such as the Greens were, however, perceived as just one node in a (tendentially) horizontal network. With rather fragmented relations with the environmental movements, which never recognized them as true representatives of their struggles (Rootes 1995), Green parties developed an anti-party rhetoric, reflecting, however, the decline of bureaucratic machines and moving instead towards light structures. Interactions between parties and interest groups became more informal with new social movements, which indeed tended to protect their independence from political parties (Poguntke 2002a), with relations happening mainly at the individual level. In this direction, Kitschelt (1989) distinguished parties that followed a logic of electoral competition from those which, like the left-libertarian ones, privileged a logic of constituency representation.

The social movements of the late 1960s were in fact already interpreted as an indication of the widening gap between parties and citizens – and indeed of the parties' inability to represent new lines of conflict (Offe 1985). This is reflected in the growing separation between movements and parties, which had together contributed to the development of some main cleavages. Linkages between Green parties and new social movements are mostly informal, as a predominant lack of formal organization characterizes the latter. The establishment of formal ties to party organizations becomes very difficult, which means that 'such linkages are highly unstable and contingent upon cycles of protest mobilization' (Poguntke 2002a, 60).

A tendency towards institutionalization has also been noted in the Green parties, following changes at the systemic level (reform of the electoral system, financing of party or other legislation); in party competition (with the rise/decline of a competitor); at the party level (electoral defeat/victory, entry/exit from parliament, entry/exit from the executive); or at the intra-party level (leadership, factions, generational turnover, organizational size, social composition) (Frankland, Lucardie, and Rihoux 2008, 10). Green parties and environmental movements grew even further apart when the former were 'drawn into the normal party political game of negotiation and compromise' (Poguntke 2006,

402). Moving in the direction of a professional-electoral party, Greens become more diffuse or eclectic, with looser ties to movements, refusals to rotate as members of parliaments, declining participation, and professionalization.

Relations between left-libertarian parties (such as the Greens) and so-called new social movements are, however, by far less integrated – more dual – than those between labour movements and labour parties. Notwithstanding the obvious tensions between movements and parties, especially on the European continent, relations with parties (particularly those on the left) long continued to play a central role for movements (della Porta 1995; Tarrow 1998). In fact, social movements have continued to form alliances more or less closely with parties – and parties have sought to co-opt social movements, to absorb their identities, and to represent them in institutions. The global justice movement offers examples of more or less close interactions between movements and the radical left-wing parties that provided the social forum process with logistical support as well as directly participating in the protest (della Porta 2007; Andretta and Reiter 2009; Haug et al. 2009). Moreover, overlapping memberships are still frequent, even if coupled with activists' strong criticism of parties' oligarchic tendencies (della Porta 2009). The main modus of interaction was, however, a sort of loose division of labour between social movements and parties-as-allies.

As we are going to see in this volume, while the downward trend in party–movement relations had pushed towards expectations of further separation, a new wave of movement parties emerged during the anti-austerity protests. *The new organizational models of movement parties against austerity are influenced* both *by the dominant party type* and *by movements' characteristics*. Referring to some main concepts in social movement studies (della Porta and Diani 2006), we will suggest that contemporary movement parties reflect an evolution in movements' organizational structures, identity frames, and repertoires of action. This adaptation is not without its tensions, however, as movement parties have to balance the different logics and pressures present within party systems and social movement networks as main fields of intervention. In the movement parties we analyse, we will point out dilemmas and turning points on all three main dimensions (organization, frames, and repertoires of action). We suggest that movement parties' organizational models, framing, and repertoires are influenced by their relations with two fields of action: the party system and the social movement field (see Figure 1.3).

This process is not to be seen, however, in a deterministic way. In fact, movement parties – and the various actors that compose them – make strategic choices, which are to be understood as decisions within

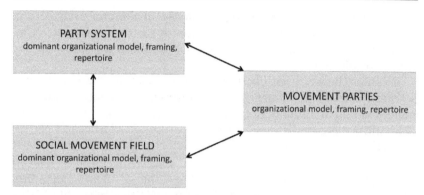

Figure 1.3.   Explaining movement party organizational choices

multiple available choices and antagonisms. Party literature has singled out trade-offs between seeking electoral supports, offices, or policies. Parties trade spoils for policy influence, or vice versa – or choose between vote seeking, on the one hand, and policy and office seeking, on the other, as the way a party behaves in office influences its future electoral performance (Strøm 1990, 573).

> Office-seeking (and policy-seeking) behavior may conflict with vote maximization to the extent that government incumbency is likely to have subsequent electoral costs....Governing parties have their reliability (consistency between promise and performance) more severely tested than the opposition. In addition, opposition parties can pursue coalition-of-minorities strategies against the incumbents, whose electoral strategies are more constrained by their very incumbency. Since votes are valued instrumentally only, the conflict between present office (and policy) seeking and future vote seeking boils down to a trade-off between short-term and longer-term benefits. (ibid.)

In their relations, parties and movements have to address several dilemmas (Jasper 2006; Chironi 2014). An *extension dilemma* contrasts the advantages of a watering down of identities in terms of expanding alliances with the benefits of maintaining defined clear collective identity. In a *Naughty or Nice Dilemma* more dialogic tactics, which are more fit to obtain some aims, enter in tensions with the occasional needs for disruption. And *Reaching out* versus *Reaching in* dilemmas also involves different tactics which can enter in contrast with each other. In addition to this, movement parties can opt for direct challenges or indirect persuasion, rely on continuity or innovation, connect or break ties with other actors.

Strategies are chosen in addressing these dilemmas. As Van Cott (2005) noted with reference to indigenous parties, among their positive effects for the social movements that support them are their promotion of non-exclusive, healthy society–party relations, values of recognition and respect for diversity, more transparency in politics, internal democracy, and increased participation. Potential negative outcomes are, however, present as well, since participation in party politics increases division in social movements – as Kitschelt (1989) noted, factionalism is normal in parties with grassroots participation. So, 'Successful new parties may reduce the effectiveness of indigenous social movements by distracting them from past priorities, such as the defense of territorial autonomy and the construction of new political institutions rooted in indigenous values and modes of self-government and participation' (Van Cott 2005, 234). There are also risks of contamination of indigenous culture by Western models of parties, as well as destabilization of collective identities.

As seen, this became visible, first, in Latin America in the 1990s, with a parallel move in Europe (in particular, in Southern Europe) more than a decade later. We can single out some expectations about some common characteristics of the emerging movement parties, as well as specific ones. We can, however, also hypothesize some differences, as movement parties have to address both long-lasting and recently emerged dilemmas.

We shall therefore single out the following characteristics, that we will further elaborate in our research:

- At the *organizational* level, emerging movement parties support a participatory vision, within a networked structure. While largely relying on digital media for the building of a decentralized organization, they also show trends towards personalization. If organizational structures tend to be diffuse, taking up the movement's claims for a horizontal, rhizomatic structure, a continuum can be singled out here between a structure more rooted in the territory and one more reliant on online communities.
- As for their *strategies*, while either developed within waves of protests or grown with them, several of these parties have had very fast access not only to parliament, but even to government. The disappointment of former voters of traditional parties has in fact often created large electoral opportunities for the emerging parties, thus increasing the tensions between the strategies on the street and the strategies inside the institutions. An innovative protest repertoire is a main strategy for these parties, although with different balances of investment in the electoral and protest activities.
- With reference to the *framing* of the self and the others, the analysed movement parties tend to reflect the movements' attempts to develop new subjectivities. The traditional definitions of the left enter in

tension with a perceived reshuffling of old cleavages and the emergence of new ones. Within a general tendency towards a redefinition of the constituency, through what Ernesto Laclau (2005) defined as 'populist reason', a continuum between the framing of 'the people' versus a more classical left-wing class definition can be detected.

During the research, we have focused on contradictions and cleavages within each party in relation with the three above-mentioned main dimensions so as to assess similarities and differences. We shall expect them to be influenced by two main fields of interactions to which movement parties belong: the movement field and the party field. In both, the movement party is expected to enter with a certain set of material and symbolic resources that filter external pressures in both environments.

1.6. The research

Departing from the above-mentioned theoretical considerations and historical analysis, we decided to use methodologies borrowed from social movement studies in order to examine the genesis and evolution of SYRIZA, Podemos and the M5S. As we will show in this book, the relationships between these three parties and popular, anti-austerity mobilizations in Greece, Spain, and Italy have changed over time. It was for a short period that the three parties have been experienced on the ground as hybrid political actors and as generating a dynamic process in between political parties and social movements. As such, the term 'movement parties' is not used in this book as a clear-cut definition to designate a static phenomenon, but it enables us instead to shed light on such complex and contingent dynamics developed when the field of party politics meets with protest politics with unexpected outcomes during critical junctures, in our case the one experienced in Southern Europe with the economic crisis. Movement party as an ideal type thus refers to a process embedded in time that may not last for long, but is crucial in revealing significant broader social transformations that other interpretative tools or social science methodologies might not grasp.

From the empirical point of view, we want to shed light on one of the ways in which the Great Recession has affected the political system: the emergence of new parties that have their roots in protest politics during the years of austerity. In particular, we want to understand cases of sudden and unexpected success, focusing on SYRIZA in Greece, Podemos in Spain, and the M5S in Italy. While we see all these parties as having special linkages with movements, the types of linkages varied, with Podemos developing from inside the anti-austerity protests and

SYRIZA inspired by the global justice movement, while the M5S has been related to local conflicts, initially focusing on environmental issues but later raising claims about public goods and social protection as well. Acknowledging the differences as well as similarities, for all three parties, we shall compare their social roots, organizational formats, collective frames, and repertoire of action, with a special interest in singling out the main dilemmas and trade-offs brought about by the relations between parties and movements. The research for this part is based on qualitative interviews with party and social movement activists, as well as an analysis of fundamental documents of parties and social movement organizations. A secondary analysis of electoral data and survey data is also carried out.

In a second step, we shall extend the analysis to unsuccessful cases (within the same countries, as well as in other countries in the European periphery such as Ireland and Portugal) that had been subjected to similar socio-economic pressures, which we will examine based on secondary analysis of existing sources.

On M5S, Podemos, and SYRIZA, we have collected information through analysis of fundamental documents and interviews with activists at different levels. As the focus is on relations between movements and parties, we analysed both party and movement documents that address these relations. As for the interviews (see list in appendix), we selected party activists, both with and without overlapping membership in movement organizations, as well as movement activists with no party membership. Databases are used from opinion polls with party voters and members, as well as electoral results and data on elected members. Data have been collected until the end of 2015.

Through these different sources, we collected information on the *organizational structure*, with reference to (a) the party on the ground, such as characteristics of members, members' rights, members' duties, recruitment, rank-and-file units, ancillary bodies, bodies open to non-members, overlapping members with movements; (b) the party in central office, including characteristics of decisional bodies, their relations with the party on the ground as well as with social movements, staff, financing, communication; (c) the party in public office, including electoral results, candidate selection, relations with the party on the ground and with the party in the central office. Additionally, we looked at the *framing*: in particular, framing the self (identity), framing the opponent (opposition), framing the field (totality), framing democracy inside the party, framing democracy outside the party. Finally, we looked at the *action*, with a focus on participation in protest campaigns, participation in parliamentary activities and participation in government. We also collected information on relations with movements such as thematic proximity (position on movement issues), overlapping membership as well as the position of movement organizations.

For the Greek case, we studied the evolution of SYRIZA throughout the crisis and up to 2015, when the party came to power: after consulting background literature on the evolution of parties and movements in the country since the establishment of the Third Republic in 1974, we collected information on the organizational structure, the framing and the repertoire of action of SYRIZA that are published or/and available online. The rise of SYRIZA is a very recent phenomenon that has just started to be scrutinized by researchers (Katsampekis 2015; Panagyiotakis 2015; Stavrakakis 2015); this applies to the recent wave of social movements that has lately attracted the attention of scholars (Psimitis 2011; Kousis 2012, 2013, 2016; Rüdig and Karyotis 2014; Kousis and Kanellopoulos 2014; Diani and Kousis 2014; Kaika and Karaliotas 2014; Kavoulakos and Gritzas 2015; Kanellopoulos et al. 2016). Still, there is no overall quantitative and comprehensive mapping of the anti-austerity mobilizations or an analysis of the interplay between the two.[1]

Given the limited availability of material, thus, a fundamental source of information was the ethnographic research conducted, which included qualitative interviews with both SYRIZA members and activists. Within the scope of this book, interviews' transcripts functioned as primary sources and served for reconstructing both the timeline of social movements and the development of SYRIZA in relation with these. Twenty-nine interviews were conducted between June and September 2015, in Athens, in Thessaloniki, the second major Greek town, in Halkida, a town of 60,000 people, and at Halkidiki, a region in the north of Greece, where an important movement against the creation of an open gold mine has developed during the last few years. Regarding SYRIZA members, fifteen interviews (four with women and eleven with men) were conducted with people from different layers of the party, representing different factions and with varied socio-demographic features, such as with party members from local branches, from centralized administrative organizations, with overlapping identities as members of movements, members of the Youth Section and others forming part of the euro-communist left since the 1970s. For the social movements, we interviewed fourteen members (six women and eight men) of movements preceding the crisis (anti-fascist mobilizations, neighbourhood assemblies, trade unions), of mobilizations that emerged during austerity (workers' collectives, mobilizations concerning electricity, base unions) and of ad hoc movements that have acquired a special symbolic role within the country (the self-managed Vio.Me. factory and the Water Movement against privatization in Thessaloniki; the mobilization of the 'Cleaning Ladies' and the self-managed ERT movement against the closure of the national broadcasting organization; and the Skouries movement against the opening of a gold mine in Halkidiki).

Regarding the case of Podemos, the data included in this volume have been collected relying on secondary sources and original texts published by the party. We have analysed several official Podemos documents and statements, including electoral programmes and the official documents of the party related to the organizational structure, funding model, and political manifesto. These documents were mostly approved in the Constituent Assembly of Podemos in 2014. On the other hand, we have analysed articles and interviews with the main leaders of Podemos, where the major issues and political ideas on the party strategy are developed. At the same time, between May and July 2015, we conducted fifteen in-depth interviews with activists representing different profiles of Podemos. Some are elected representatives at the local, regional, or European level, while others were local participants in different Circles (local assemblies) of the party. The interviews have taken place in different territories of the Spanish State (Madrid, Bilbao, Cantabria) in order to provide a more balanced description of the situation of Podemos and the diverse experiences of its militants.

Regarding the Italian case, information on the organizational structure, the framing, and the repertoire of action of the M5S have been collected both relying on secondary sources and by gathering original materials. We have extensively analysed official documents of the M5S: the 'non-statute', the statute, the M5S regulations, the national M5S MPs' code of conduct, the statute of the M5S parliamentary group in the low Chamber, the statute of the M5S parliamentary group in the Senate, the M5S MEPs' code of conduct as well as the statute of the Europe of Freedom and Direct Democracy group (EFDD) in the European Parliament. Besides European, national, regional, and local electoral programmes, Grillo's blog has been a core reference for analysing the discursive production of the leader and Meetup groups before, during, and after the official birth of the party.

Differently from the cases of both Podemos and SYRIZA, empirical studies on the M5S have been ongoing for years (Lanfrey 2011). Most of them were based on in-depth interviews and participant observation of local groups, as well as interviews with elected representatives at the local, regional, and national levels. We made reference, in particular, to two edited books (Corbetta and Gualmini 2013; Tronconi 2015a), based on forty-seven interviews conducted between the summer of 2012 and the beginning of 2014, with activists and representatives elected to local and regional assemblies covering regions as diverse as Veneto, Lombardy, Liguria, Piedmont, Emilia-Romagna, Campania, and Sicily. Another useful edited book has focused specifically on the party on the ground covering sixteen cities (Turin, Milan, Como, Genoa, Parma, Florence, Carrara, Viareggio, Pisa, San Giuliano Terme, Piombino, Rome, Bari, Lecce, Catania, Palermo) between 2013 and 2014 (Biorcio 2015a). Moreover, a particular attention has been dedicated to the case of Parma where, between the summer and the autumn of 2012, we conducted eight interviews on the relationship between the Indignados movement and the electoral success of the M5S. During the summer of 2014, interviews were also carried with the M5S mayors of Pomezia and Ragusa and with a regional councillor of the Lazio region in charge of developing interactive online platforms. Data on online participatory tools have been collected on the digital platforms used by the Movement (Grillo's blog and Lex).

1.7. This volume

In what follows, we will address both the genesis of movement parties and the evolution of movement–party relations during the evolution of the parties of reference. With a focus on the empirical research on SYRIZA, Podemos, and the M5S, we shall look at the origins of these parties (Chapter 2), their choices in terms of organizational and action repertoires (Chapter 3) as well as their framing (Chapter 4). In doing so, we will problematize the conceptualization of movement parties, reflecting on both the differences and the similarities among those parties. In Chapter 5, we aim at strengthening our analysis by, first, introducing some negative cases for both parties – by looking at movement parties that failed in our three countries – as well as the non-rise of movement parties in countries of the European periphery which were heavily hit by the crisis, such as Ireland and Portugal. Second, we will look at the interaction between movements and parties in Latin America during the neoliberal critical juncture. In Chapter 6, we will conclude by summarizing our results and extending our reflection on the interaction between contentious and institutional politics during the Great Recession.

2

The Genesis of Movement Parties in the Neoliberal Critical Juncture

This chapter locates the genesis of the analysed movement parties within a neoliberal critical juncture that has deep effects, both socially and politically. In Southern Europe, as in Latin America (see Chapter 5), the crisis of late neoliberalism has been combined with the crisis of traditional parties (particularly the social-democratic ones), with consequences for both conventional and contentious politics.

2.1. The crisis of late neoliberalism in Europe

A first question of obvious relevance for an attempt to understand the parties we are studying concerns the socio-structural conditions in which they develop. While social movement studies have paid limited attention to this dimension, political economy has recently acquired more and more relevance in its attempt to single out both broad common trends in capitalist development and internal regional differences within global dynamics. What we additionally address in this volume is in fact the role of the protests that developed in the EU – especially in its periphery – as the financial crisis spread from the United States to Europe.

In Europe, the crisis started as a financial one, linked to bank difficulties related to reduced liquidity. After the deregulation of the financial markets had brought about highly speculative and risky investments in the United States, the financial crisis it generated reverberated in Europe, especially at its periphery. Here, financial bubbles had developed in the years of expansion as capital moved from countries like Germany – in which there was a positive balance between exports and imports – into, among others, the European periphery, whose countries instead had a negative balance.

After some attempts to develop counter-cyclical policies, the crisis was aggravated as it was addressed as merely a debt crisis, derived from the public debt of peripheral EU countries. In reality, in 2007, while Greece had a public deficit exceeding 6 per cent and a public debt of 107 per cent, the other GIIPS countries (Greece, Ireland, Italy, Portugal, and Spain) met the parameters of the Stability and Growth Pact (Armingeon and Baccaro 2012). For them, public debt was not a cause of the crisis but rather a consequence of it, as it increased due to policy decisions to bail out banks and cut taxes, as well as some attempts at addressing growing unemployment. What started, thus, as a bank crisis spiralled into a crisis of public debt and then a crisis of investments; a related social crisis then affected the European periphery (Varoufakis, Holland, and Galbraith 2015), reflected in high degrees of unemployment, home-lessness, health or poverty rates. In the critical evolution of the crisis, political institutions indeed played an important – and far from posi-tive – role.

The economic crisis of the Eurozone has overlapped in time with the long-term and multi-dimensional crisis of political parties. In this sense, literature on political parties had often pointed to increasing signals of crisis, especially for parties rooted in civil society. In sum:

> ...studies of party change have highlighted that the party types which tend to prevail since the 1980s are characterized by (a) a more and more marked lightening of their organizational structure and ideo-logical baggage; (b) the progressive estrangement from their social classes of reference, of which in the past they tried to organize and protect the interests; (c) a growing permeability to lobbies representing particular interests; (d) the reduction of participatory spaces and of the membership influence on the party line. (della Porta and Chironi 2014, 64)

As mentioned in Chapter 1, since the 1980s, researchers have observed a rapid decline in the capacity of political parties to function as mediators between civil society and political institutions (della Porta 2015a). Not only has the attachment of citizens to parties been dramatically falling (Gunther and Diamond 2003), but the trust of voters in the competences and abilities of their own parties has also decreased (Dalton 2004, 28 and

149). Party membership has also declined steadily, along with electoral participation.

In this situation, the economic crisis acted as a coagulant for discontent with the party system. With increasing exogenous constraints, such as the (unregulated) markets and international conditionalities, parties have been considered to be trapped between the representation of the citizen and the responsibility towards various external actors, including 'the market' and international institutions. With the financial crises of the 2000s and 2010s, parties' conception of responsibility as implying capacity for economic growth was moreover challenged, as was legitimacy based on effective results.

Furthermore, as economic competition has eroded protected property rights, while also increasing cultural diversity, globalization has brought about the formation of a cleavage between the winners (endowed with exit options) and the losers (without exit options) (Kriesi et al. 2008). According to Kriesi et al. (2012), this situation gives rise to four further cleavage coalitions: interventionist cosmopolitan (greens, social democrats, unions); neoliberal cosmopolitans (liberals, Christian democrats and conservatives, business); neoliberal nationalist (right-wing populist), interventionist nationalist (left-wing populists: communist left socialists). While right-wing groups are more oriented to the electoral arena, left-wing ones privilege the protest arena. By the early 2000s, participation in protests on economic issues started to rise to the level of cultural campaigns, with growing mass protests against retrenchment of the welfare state (Kriesi et al. 2012, 171). The financial crisis then represented a turning point in the relationship between parties and movements.

Available Eurobarometer data clearly show that a process of disenchantment with traditional politics and institutions is at work in all member states of the European Union (EU).[1] Data display an evident trend of declining trust in national parliaments, national governments, and domestic political parties (Figures 2.1–2.3). When confronted with average levels of trust in the EU, the drop of institutional trust in Mediterranean countries appears as even more dramatic.

The peak of distrust in parliamentary institutions in the three countries we analyse was reached between 2012 and 2013, a time when the economic crisis deepened and the effects of austerity policies hit very hard. In fifteen years, distrust grew from 33–68 per cent to 86 per cent in Greece and Spain, and from 45 per cent to 84 per cent in Italy (May 2012). In the most critical period, the distance from the European average reached almost twenty percentage points.

Similarly to what we saw concerning distrust in legislative assemblies, the peak of no confidence in the national government in the three

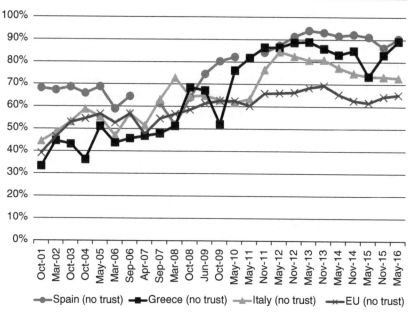

Figure 2.1. Distrust of parliaments

countries was reached between 2012 and 2013. In the considered period, distrust increased from 46–47 per cent to 91 and 79 per cent in Greece and Italy, and from 39 per cent to 83 per cent in Spain (May 2012). In the most critical period, the distance from the European average reached almost ten percentage points in Italy and twenty in the other two countries.

The trend of distrust in parties does not differ significantly from those concerning parliaments and national governments. The peak of no confidence in parties in the three countries was reached in 2013. In fifteen years, distrust rose from 68 per cent (it was 52 per cent in 2008, after confirmation of the centre-left government of Zapatero) to 94 per cent in Spain; from 72 per cent to 94 per cent in Greece; and from 78 per cent (it was 64 per cent in 2006, after the victory of the centre-left coalition led by Romano Prodi) to 87 per cent in Italy (May 2013). During the most critical period, the distance from the European average reached almost ten percentage points in Italy and fifteen in the other two countries.

During the crisis of neoliberalism, distrust towards existing political institutions was accompanied by a global wave of protest. The

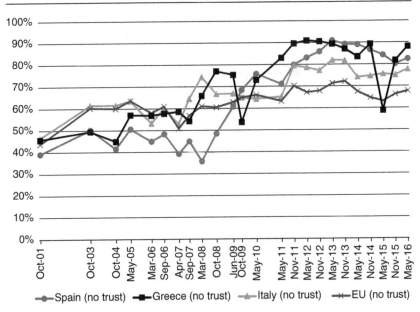

Figure 2.2.   Distrust of governments

mobilizations that occurred in Egypt and other MENA countries, in Spain and Greece, and in the United States, as well as later on in Turkey and Brazil, took place in different times and spaces, but had common characteristics (della Porta and Mattoni 2014). In the many events over these five years, 'two trends in particular seem to constitute a context in which all these movements are situated: a crisis that is not only economic, but also political, and that has affected to varying degrees many countries in the world. For this reason, these have been called 'movements of the crisis' (della Porta and Mattoni 2014, 2), with the label 'crisis' covering the economic and political crisis from which these movements originated and which they targeted, revealing the increasing inequalities even in those countries where the economic crisis seemed to have hit less intensely. While recent protests across the world have also maintained a transnational stance, national governments and policies appeared as the first target.

Protests followed, in fact, the geography of the emergence of the economic crisis – quickly transformed into a crisis of political legitimacy – which hit the different European countries with different strengths and at different times. In a similar way to Latin America, a moral call for

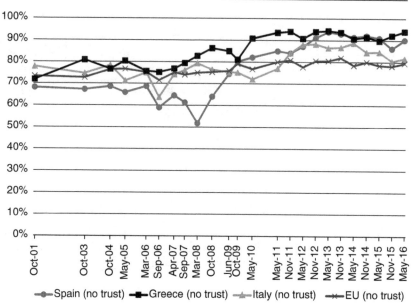

Figure 2.3.   Distrust of political parties

recognition has been expressed in the 2010s anti-austerity protests (della Porta 2013). The framing of neoliberalism as immoral has indeed been linked to a framing of the self, with the appeal to morality as the common basis of a broad, and broadly different, mobilization base. Calling for recognition of the injustice of their conditions, protesters expressed their indignation against the loss of dignity imposed by authoritarian and democratic regimes alike. Invoking 'old rights', they contested the corruption of the political class, in its collusion with the big corporations. Migrating from South America to Europe and back to North America, the slogan 'we do not pay for your crisis' targets the increasing (and increasingly arrogant) power of the 'one per cent'.

Anti-austerity protests have been, to a certain extent, backward looking. In their framing there is in fact an appeal to better previous conditions, which badly deteriorated during neoliberal capitalism and, especially, during its crisis. From this point of view, some of the claims of the movements against austerity can be seen as moderate and reformist – a restoration of old rights. At the same time, there have also been many innovations in the ways in which democracy and citizens' rights are conceived. The struggle against the corrupt one per cent is conducted in the name of the citizens suffering from the corruption of democracy, with the aim of deepening democracy through a participatory management of the commons.

As we will see in what follows, Greece, Spain, and Italy are characterized by the mentioned trends, as well, but also by some specificities that affected differently the development of movement parties in each country.

2.2. On the genesis and evolution of SYRIZA

On 6 May 2012, parliamentary elections were held in Greece. These were the first elections since 2010, when the debt crisis exploded and a 'Troika' of lenders (the International Monetary Fund, European Central Bank, and European Commission) imposed austerity measures of unprecedented ferocity on the country. These led to much more than a serious economic crisis: since then, the country has been experiencing the most severe recession faced by any established democracy in the post-war era (Eurostat 2015), one that has taken a horrendous toll on Greek society. These were also the first elections after the eruption of a massive, multi-faceted anti-austerity movement that enveloped Greece: the level of nationwide mobilizations has been unusually high, even by Greek standards, engaging thousands of citizens in protest and solidarity actions. The results saw the rise of SYRIZA (Coalition of the Radical Left), as a contender for government, jumping from 4.6 per cent of the vote in the 2009 elections to 16.8 per cent in May and 26.9 per cent in the new, June 2012 elections. SYRIZA, once a fringe party, came into power in January 2015, securing 36.3 per cent of the vote and becoming the only left-wing party to win the government in Europe, in a country that had by then become even poorer.

2.2.1. The society in the economic crisis

The failure of the implemented structural reforms to improve the country's fiscal position had been revealed already before SYRIZA took power: in 2013, Greece became the first developed nation to be downgraded from a developed to an emerging economy, as austerity measures led to one of the biggest fiscal consolidation processes among developed economies during peacetime. Beyond the mere economic figures, this recession has had detrimental consequences upon the Greek people's everyday lives. The official unemployment rate skyrocketed between 2008 and 2014, from 7.7 per cent to 27 per cent, whereas youth unemployment escalated to a record 58.6 per cent in 2013 – figures that do not even take into account those under flexible, unregistered, or short-term contracts. Adding to this, a large proportion of the country's younger and university-educated people seek employment abroad: almost three out of ten have already emigrated, most of them overqualified (Lambrianidis 2011; Tsilimingra 2011).

Moreover, the austerity measures implementing cuts in salaries and pensions have led to significant reductions in household incomes, which dropped by more than one third between 2007 and 2013, representing the biggest decrease in the OECD countries and four times as big as the loss recorded in the average Eurozone countries. This shift took place not just in terms of disposable income, but also in terms of quality and access to basic social services due to severe public spending cuts in health and social security as well as other social benefits (ibid.). Since 2008, broad segments of the Greek population have been threatened with exclusion and poverty, as severe deprivation increased from 11.2 per cent to 21.5 per cent between 2008 and 2014, and child poverty jumped from 23 per cent to 40.5 per cent between 2008 and 2012 (Kalogeraki et al. 2014). In addition, there has been an unprecedented rise in suicide rates: since 2009 there has been an annual increase of up to 22.5 per cent (Chalari 2015) while, at the same time, new socially excluded groups have emerged – for example, the 'neo-homeless', referring to a new genera-tion of homeless people who in many cases are well-educated and lived in the very recent past under satisfactory conditions (Theodorikakou et al. 2013).

It was against this catastrophic context that the radical left party SYRIZA managed to achieve a huge victory in 2015, building an anti-austerity profile against the Memorandum of Understanding (MoU) that echoed the social and political opposition to the country's relentless austerity policies over the last five years. Attracting much international coverage, the complex and variegated 'anti-austerity movement' did not draw from a particular sector of society, but rather crossed all ideological divides, professional backgrounds, and age cohorts (Rüdig and Karyotis 2013; Kanellopoulos and Kostopoulos 2013): already in 2010, 66 per cent of the Greek adult population was supportive of protests against the austerity measures, with about one in four actually taking part in demonstrations (Rüdig and Karyotis 2014). Even if this overwhelming protest turmoil along with changing voting behaviour seemed focused on economic issues, recent analyses suggest that the degree of perceived deprivation is important but not decisive in terms of actual protest (ibid.), and the same seems to apply to evaluations of the economic situ-ation and their effect on partisanship (Teperoglou and Tsatsanis 2014a; 2014b). While, of course, these phenomena are both by-products of the sovereign debt crisis, which affected Greece more than any other country in Europe, at the same time there is no automatic relationship between a worsening economic situation and the growth of protest movements or/and the total realignment of the political system. This is also reflected in the different (re)alignments of the party systems of other Southern European countries in crisis. Contextual factors, political opportunity structures, and longer-term processes and divisions in Greek society should also be taken into account.

In order, then, to explain the emergence of SYRIZA, we look on the one hand at how the post-1974 party system developed so as to enter into deep crisis, and on the other how the anti-austerity mobilizations unfolded.

2.2.2. Party system in the crisis

(a) The electoral collapse of bipartisanism

Since the 1970s and up to the early 1990s, the Panhellenic Socialist Movement (PASOK), allegedly on the centre-left, and New Democracy (ND), allegedly on the centre-right, competed in a polarized bipartisan political system, gradually converging towards a neoliberal centre and reaching consensus on key economic and social policies after the mid-1990s. Both mainstream parties are run in a top-down fashion and operated a modernized version of the patron–client system, creating a tradition of a 'clientelistic social contract' (Teperoglou and Tsatsanis 2014a). During the 1990s, under Costas Simitis' leadership, PASOK had already abandoned its socialist–populist leaning to embark upon a modernization project that would 'Europeanize' the Greek society and economy (Lyrintzis 2005). Until the early 2000s, the two mainstream parties predictably rotated in power, together gathering well over 80 per cent of the national vote. By the time the crisis hit Greece, the two former political rivals had converged to the point where forming a coalition to govern the country in 2011 – two years after the signing of an emergency bailout agreement with European institutions and the International Monetary Fund (IMF) – did not come as a surprise.

Soon afterwards, however, this two-party system came to a dramatic end. In November 2011, the PASOK government was replaced by a coalition between PASOK, ND, and the right-wing populist LAOS party, with its leader George Papandreou to be replaced by former ECB Vice-President Lucas Papademos. Continuing its steep downward trajectory, PASOK saw its support collapsing to 13.2 per cent in May 2012, when not even a coalition between the two major parties could form a majority and a government (Verney 2014). With ND facing severe losses, both parties received an aggregate of 32 per cent of the votes. The (until then

Table 2.1. Election results, 2009–2015 (including only PASOK, ND, and SYRIZA)

Party	2009	May 2012	June 2012	May 2014	Jan 2015
SYRIZA	4.6	16.8	26.9	26.6	36.3
New Democracy	33.5	18.9	29.7	22.7	27.8
PASOK	43.9	13.2	12.3	8.0	4.7

Source: Author's edit of Election Results by Ministry of Interior, www.ypes.gr

small) left-wing SYRIZA rocketed into second place and refused to join a coalition that would adopt a pro-austerity programme. In the new June 2012 elections, the pro-austerity (*mnimoniaka*) parties ND and PASOK gained a majority of seats and were initially supported by the new centre-left party 'Democratic Left' (DIMAR), which had split in 2010 from SYRIZA, opposing its leftist turn (Kousis and Kanellopoulos 2014). The May and June 2012 elections also saw the emergence of an extremist right-wing party, Golden Dawn, which entered the Greek Parliament for the first time with about 7 per cent of the vote (Ellinas 2013). Against this background and a looming recession, the antagonistic relationship between the once major mainstream parties was turned into a symbiotic one that defended and imposed upon the citizens a bailout programme, thus securing a steady breakdown for both of them. In the elections of 2014 and then in January 2015, the national bipartisan party system was totally de-aligned: while the two former major parties collapsed, SYRIZA received more votes than any other party associated with the traditional left in Greece has ever received (Teperoglou et al. 2015) becoming the ruling party.

(b) Electoral volatility and shifts in political identification

While the May and June 2012 legislative elections have been already termed as a 'double electoral earthquake' (Voulgaris and Nikolakopoulos 2014), the 2015 party system bears little similarity to the two-party system dominating public life in the country for almost forty years; it lacks any stability and predictability as to what it will bring forward. Almost one in two voters chose a different party in 2015 than in 2012 (42 per cent). From being the most influential political actor of the post-authoritarian period, PASOK was transformed into one of the smallest parties represented in parliament, while ND collapsed and is in search of new leadership and identity. New parties have also emerged, such as the anti-austerity right-wing ANEL (*Independent Greeks*) and Golden Dawn, which has formed an electoral base polling around 7 per cent. As for SYRIZA, after its spectacular rise in 2012, it consolidated much of its electoral base and has replaced PASOK as the main party for left-of-centre voters (Teperoglou et al. 2015).

These changes in the party system coincided with a collapse in institutional trust. In Greece, public confidence in political institutions, both national and European, had until recently been high in comparison with other countries in Southern Europe, as were the levels of party identification. Even if PASOK's social democratic rhetoric had already been receding since the mid-1980s, the party had managed to frame and articulate at a parliamentary level the claims of the post-1974 social movements and dominate the centre-left, capitalizing on a durable right–left polarization; this was done by systematically satisfying 'the corporate interests of all those who could be identified as potential supporters of the party...coupled with a rhetoric that praised the people and advocated radical policies while avoiding major confrontations' (Lyrintzis 2005). Since the early 1980s, clientelistic ties built on existing strong political identities have given rise to very high levels of party attachment (Teperoglou and Tsatsanis 2014a), with the two main parties reaching 80 per cent of the national vote.

Yet, a series of corruption scandals (2007–09) accentuated feelings of political alienation, until the explosion of the sovereign debt crisis in 2010 generated a complete collapse of citizen trust in the government and parliamentary politics in general. Citizens' dissatisfaction with national and supra-national institutions – including the Greek and European Parliaments, parties, government, and the EU, but also the role of the media – grew to remarkably high levels. Confidence in the functioning of democracy has fallen to historically low levels during the last five years (ibid.), while the crisis turned cynicism into open hostility towards the political elites. Partisanship receded, especially among the youth, while voters became unwilling to place themselves along a left–right axis (ibid.). The dramatic shift in the economic landscape was coupled with a massive loss of confidence in the once prevalent major parties and the broad delegitimation of the national political establishment and the European Union idea (Teperoglou and Tsatsanis 2014b; Verney 2014). It was within this context that huge numbers of citizens became involved in contentious politics.

2.2.3. Anti-austerity mobilizations: from nationwide protests to localized solidarity actions

When the crisis erupted, Greece found itself at the centre of the storm. Greek citizens 'suffered the equivalent effects of a war, indeed a class war' (Panagyiotakis 2015) that deepened the rupture between the governing and the governed. Democratic accountability was challenged, as were labour rights, as workers were increasingly exploited, unpaid or, in massive numbers, fired; pension cuts undermined the health of the elderly; reductions in public health, tax increases, and cuts in welfare benefits were not accompanied by national social security programmes; and police violence and impunity escalated – while fascist violence was tolerated, if not protected, by the establishment, and press freedom suffered as all major media channels supported austerity policies and silenced oppositional opinions. Faced with such a shock, Greek citizens responded promptly, as testified by the interviewees' reconstruction of the 'anti-austerity' mobilizations unfolding from 2010 to 2015 producing a distinct cycle of protest in the country (Serdedakis and Koufidi 2016).

The start of this wave of protest can be located before the actual eruption of the crisis, in the early 2000s when neoliberal policies started to be implemented (ibid.); resisting the collapse of the welfare state, the privatization of public goods and the abuse of social and political rights, this protest wave was reflected in the mobilizations against the 2004 Olympic Games, the 2006–7 student protests and, especially, the December 2008 youth rebellion. The latter made particularly visible a looming crisis that was far from just economic (I18G), anticipating some characteristics of the protest events that would follow: police violence, youth alienation, delegitimation of the political establishment, massive participation, the mingling of different groups of people (like migrants, unionists, and students) (I20G) in the streets, and the emergence of a novel repertoire of action as urban self-organized initiatives spread across the country (I5G).

After these incubating moments, all of our interviewees observe that the 'anti-austerity' movement unfolded in two distinct periods, from 2010 to 2012 and from 2012 to 2015, as it is also testified in the literature (Diani and Kousis 2014; Serdedakis and Koufidi 2016). The first phase saw an extensive and massive eruption of the so-called conventional forms of protest, which was more intense than in any other European country: general strikes, protests, marches, and demonstrations dominated public life during the first two years of the crisis, 'dragging everyone to the streets' (I3G). The Greek General Confederation of Workers (GSEE) and the Union of Public Employees (ADEDY) organized seventeen 24-hour and three 48-hour general strikes between 2010 and 2012 (Kanellopoulos and Kostopoulos 2013), with forty-two general strikes in the first five years of the crisis alone. Even if participation rates were often low and both union confederations perceived as clientelist, bureaucratized, and strongly tied to PASOK, in some cases those 'routinized' events managed to articulate popular anger through massive participation in the demos: 'people attributed to strikes their own meaning, beyond unions' aims' (I15G). During this first phase, there were also sit-ins, building occupations, and confrontational protests, during which large crowds (from 40,000 to 500,000) expressed their discontent, often in synchronized actions across the country (Kousis and Kanellopoulos 2014).

While the general public became a more visible participant in all protest events, those organizing such mobilizations were the actors regularly active in Greek street politics: the official trade unions, the left-wing parliamentary parties Kommounistiko Komma Elladas (KKE, Greek Communist Party) and SYRIZA, the coalition of extra-parliamentary left-wing organizations ANTARSYA and other political organizations of the radical left, as well as anti-authoritarian and anarchist groups – all part of an informal and polycephalous protest coalition against austerity (Kanellopoulos and Kostopoulos 2013). But this period also saw a steady increase in the types of participating groups and organizations, while ordinary people of all educational backgrounds and ages (Psimitis 2011) took part in and contributed to the formation of a contentious political culture (Teperoglou and Tsatsanis 2014a). This also generated novel forms of protest (Kousis 2013) of a disruptive nature, such as activist actions taking place in supermarkets and public transport, or of a direct democracy character, such as open public assemblies and neighbourhood committees resonating with the December 2008 events (I18G). Moreover, a series of intense, often violent outbursts of public anger against traditional mainstream politicians could not be predicted or, often, controlled (I3G, I11G, I25G, I27G) (for a detailed analysis of this first period of protest, see Diani and Kousis 2014).

The geographical diffusion of protests and the mobilization of social and professional groups that were previously not part of collective action were combined to activate a new repertoire of action that engaged the totality of the resisting population (Serdedakis and Koufidi 2016): in the summer of 2011, the feeling of rejection of the political establishment peaked in the Greek version of Indignados at central squares in all urban centres of the country (I18G). These spatialized protest events were calling for a rejection of austerity, for direct democracy and self-organization. There were massive assemblies all over Greece: a June 2011 poll showed that 52 per cent of respondents (2,700,000 adults according to the polling company) would either 'surely participate' or 'probably participate' in the 'movement of the squares' (Panagyiotakis 2015). Notwithstanding the diversity and complexity of demands and modes of protest present in the square, respondents testify that those few months of *indignados* politicization had an impact on people's consciousness: many citizens became familiar with libertarian ideas and 'learnt not to be afraid of the movement and of the left' (I9G). The 'squares' created a new mode of protest that 'was not only about denouncing and expressing discontent, but about constructing something new' (I24G).

All respondents agree that after 2012, a different kind of mobilization emerged. On the one hand, while the more confrontational and massive protest events seemed to fade out, the country saw the eruption (or continuation) of specific ad hoc movements that acquired a symbolic role as struggles against different aspects of austerity. These included the 595 female cleaning workers fired from the finance ministry, who camped outside the ministry building for nearly two years fighting with police; the 'I'm Not Paying' movement, which reflected a collective refusal to pay increases in ticket prices; the self-organized Vio.Me. factory in Thessaloniki and the self-managed ERT movement, which organized against the closure of firms and the national public broadcasting organization; the local movement in the small town of Keratea that opposed a planned toxic landfill, and another in Skouries (Chalkidiki) that disputed the opening of a gold mine. Together, other localized forms of protest took place in urban neighbourhoods or workplaces, and numerous important initiatives of counter-information emerged, along with a broad anti-fascist mobilization against Golden Dawn and the police forces colluding with it. Extremely important was the emergence and consolidation of a rich and multi-faceted solidarity movement that spread across different cities. In many cases, protest was transformed into collective and self-organized social support to socio-economically deprived individuals through soup kitchens, social groceries and social clinics, educational services and community networks; in other cases, workers' collectives were set up and grassroots unions were established, all functioning within this mentality of collectivity and horizontality.

Serdedakis and Koufidi (2016) argue that despite the widespread feeling of retreat of collective action after 2012, protest events continued unabated, even if losing much of their dynamic and impact upon austerity policies. In line with this, most respondents observe that from 2012 to 2015, there was a decline in what is considered as a conventional pattern of mobilization. Notwithstanding the (often conflicting) explanations offered, interviewees agree that social movements in Greece have traditionally been dominated by politics due to 'a predominance of the political over the social' (I13G, I24G); departing from PASOK's post-1974 trajectory, they observe that mobilizations have been in many cases related with, dependent on, or even co-opted by, political parties including, of course, SYRIZA. However, as hundreds of thousands of people took part in protests, 'the barriers between those already politicized and those deemed as a-political disappeared' (I2G), as people experienced that police repression and impunity made no distinctions among protesters (I19G). While protest was escalating in terms of numbers of participants, repertoires of action, and geographical diffusion, collective action had a tremendous impact upon institutional and party politics; but it was also the definition of the movement itself that was changing: this became evident in the squares during the summer of 2011, when ultra-leftists met with SYRIZA party members or anarchists with (ex-)PASOK voters, all of them opposing the same political establishment and asking for a more fair and equal world. At the same time, people realized on the ground and after exhausting all the resources they deemed available to them that 'demonstrating is over' (I3G) and that nothing could be achieved through the post-1974 protest tools at hand (I5G) – 'what else could people do?' (I2G). 'Movements were defeated in 2012' (I9G, I28G, I30G), not only as they were violently crushed by the political establishment, but also because they could not respond to the actual material needs of the people (I3G). This is when solidarity started to emerge, building upon the self-management culture and the social networks that had been developing in the country since 2008 (I20G). This solidarity was 'the politicization of everyday life that provided an alternative political imaginary of the crisis' (I24G). Following the first phase of the cycle of protest, numerous alternative political and economic spaces emerged around the country (Kousis et al. 2016) – what Kavoulakos and Gritzas name as a 'new civil society' (2015, 2016).

2.2.4. The evolution of SYRIZA (2004–2015) and its electoral base

It was within this context of a volatile electoral background and shifting protest mobilizations that SYRIZA increased in popularity (see Table 2.2). In terms of the party's evolution over time, as will be accounted

Table 2.2.   Electoral evolution of SYRIZA (2004–2015)

Parliamentary Elections	Seats Won	%	Votes
2004	6	3.26	241,714
2007	14	5.04	361,101
2009	13	4.59	313,231
May 2012	52	16.79	1,061,929
June 2012	71	26.89	1,655,042
January 2015	149	36.34	2,246,064
September 2015	145	35.46	1,925,904

Source: Author's compilation from www.hellenicparliament.gr

in detail in the two following chapters, SYRIZA was formed in 2004 as an electoral coalition of left, radical left, and ecological movements, networks, groups and individuals. Its major constituent is Synaspismos (1988), a party whose origins can be traced back to the euro-communist faction that split from the Greek Communist Party (KKE) in 1968. A 'lesser' pole within Greek politics (Panagyiotakis 2015), the party had traditionally struggled to pass the three per cent threshold in elections and was considered as part of a delegitimized party system. SYRIZA, on the other hand, represented a 'radical' left turn in this history: operating in a consensus-based mode, the party allowed for the existence of internal factions, participatory internal politics, and loose partisanship. Aspiring to address the precarious youth and the mobilized strata of the society, its aim was to create a political space between the already corrupted PASOK and the orthodox communist party and to gain, thus, an electoral presence. From 2004 onwards, SYRIZA participated indeed in transnational and domestic social movements, mainly through its younger cadres, while electing in 2008 the 33-year-old Alexis Tsipras as its president – the youngest-ever leader of a parliamentary party in Greece. SYRIZA's electoral gains, however, remained limited until 2009.

After the eruption of the crisis, things changed radically: building on this 'left turn', SYRIZA adopted an 'anti-mnemoniaki (against MoUs) agenda' considering austerity policies not as resolving, but on the contrary as deepening a long-lasting crisis (Teperoglou et al. 2015), gradually endorsing fully anti-austerity claims and grievances. In 2011, all the left-wing parties (DIMAR, KKE, and SYRIZA) gained support in opinion polls, as citizens were disappointed with the pro-austerity coalition government. In the June 2012 elections, however, and against an orchestrated attack by both mainstream media and pro-austerity actors, SYRIZA became the main opposition party to a coalition government composed of ND, PASOK, and DIMAR. Since then, the party was 'in the waiting room for power' (I8G): in 2013, in its Founding Congress, SYRIZA was transformed from a coalition into a unitary party, reached first place in the 2014 European Parliament elections, and after the legislative January 2015 elections took government.

Electoral results reflect a class polarization underway in the Greek society: those self-defined as belonging to the 'lower social class', who perceive themselves as 'not able to deal with austerity measures', voted for SYRIZA. SYRIZA's electoral success derived indeed from a capacity to attract the support of those who were most hit by the social butchery brought about by the austerity policies. Given its clear anti-austerity platform, it is no surprise that since 2012 it has been, by a considerable margin, the most popular party among the unemployed, while business classes and employers overall support the right (Mavris 2012). Moreover, SYRIZA tends to be voted for by women (43.2 per cent, against 28.2 per cent of men in 2015) and to dominate in urban centres (ibid.). Most importantly, it is the most popular party among the young: the 18–24 age group brought the party to the second position in 2012 (45.5 per cent), with instead a very low 13.8 per cent among those aged sixty-five and over. In the 2012, 2014, and 2015 elections, voters for the once major parties tended to be disproportionately the more elderly, with lower qualifications, employed in the primary sector and out of the labour force altogether (retired and homemakers) (Teperoglou et al. 2015) – in particular, ND received 49.4 per cent among those over sixty-five years old in 2012. The bipartisan system survived in the oldest age group but collapsed among the youngest of the working population, testifying to the high level of class-based voting in SYRIZA's electorate (Mavris 2012) or, as an interviewee noted: 'the class and generational aspects cannot be differentiated...we are young and, thus, precarious, they are neither of the two' (I6G). However, in the latest 2015 elections, SYRIZA's strength has been much more evenly distributed across the age groups, while it also has a clear lead among salaried and self-employed professionals. The party also managed to gain access to homemakers and farmers, groups that traditionally voted for those who promised to guarantee stability and the status quo. While ND maintained its predominance in the pensioners' group, SYRIZA attracted individuals belonging to the 'waged labour' group and the youth – that is, the more productive and dynamic strata in Greek society (Teperoglou et al. 2015).

2.3. The genesis of Podemos

The economic crisis that hit the Eurozone had enormous consequences for the Spanish economy as well as the political system. Since the irruption of the 15M and the related wave of anti-austerity protests, the social and political consensus established in the political transition was broken. Triggered by a neoliberal critical juncture, what looked like a stable political regime and party system entered into a deep crisis. This juncture opened the opportunity for new discourses and the emergence of new political options, which were also favoured by a series of corruption cases that affected the two main parties. This caused a loss of trust in the country's major institutions and a crisis of representation for the two mainstream parties (PP and PSOE), while creating a favourable environment for anti-establishment political actors. It was in this context that Podemos emerged via the strategic use of mass media and the charismatic figure of its leader, Pablo Iglesias.

2.3.1. The context: The interaction of social and political crises

The emergence of Podemos has taken place in a particular historical context in Spain, in which a double (economic and political) crisis is combined in what can be considered as a neoliberal critical juncture. This multi-dimensional crisis and its social impacts have stimulated a cycle of mobilizations which have also contributed to change in the Spanish political system.

After the Spanish political transition, political parties grew through state structures rather than by expanding their organizational bases in the society. The 1978 Spanish Constitution embodied a representative government model based on the central role of parties, favouring a two-party system, political alternation, a decentralized territorial structure, and an electoral system that supported the formation of parliamentary majorities and strong and stable governments (Gunther, Montero, and Botella 2004). Until the political crisis following the economic collapse, the Spanish party system had followed predictable patterns (Linz and Montero 1999), with low levels of party fragmentation and inter-bloc volatility and a bipolar structure of competition (Gunther 2005). Spanish voters remained moderate, showing weak party identification and low levels of party membership (Mair and Van Biezen 2001) but high political disaffection, cynicism, and anti-party feelings (Torcal 2006).[2] With the emergence of Podemos (and Ciudadanos at the national level), the Spanish party system experienced a deep transformation as the crisis of bipartisanship in Spain led to a more fragmented political scenario and to political polarization, with a deep transformation of the party system.

The 2007–9 global financial meltdown was met with a set of austerity-ridden policies that several national governments and international institutions implemented at different levels. In the Spanish context, these policies were first adopted in 2010, under Rodríguez Zapatero's social-democratic government – relatively late, in a comparative perspective. These policies implied reforming the pension system and the labour market as well as slashing salaries and worsening conditions of civil servants and public employees. Most remarkably, the planned Labour Law reform would bring about precariousness, increase job-market instability, and facilitate dismissals; likewise, it would weaken the collective bargaining power of employees. This led to a new cycle of social protest that started in September 2010 with the first general strike in eight years (the sixth in recent Spanish democratic history), called by the main unions and other small organizations.

Overall, political parties have faced a generalized crisis of legitimacy in Spain in the shadow of the recession, which opened the opportunity for the entry of new parties (Subirats 2015a).[3] Lack of trust in the two major parties in Spain has led to a weakening of party loyalties, which is another feature of political party transformations in the age of austerity (della Porta 2014), a trend fuelled in part by protest. Negative appraisals of parties were especially acute around 2013, when political class and political parties became the third most common concern among citizens (Feenstra and Keane 2014). This loss of confidence has punished the two major parties in particular.

This increasing mistrust in the mainstream parties was first felt on the centre-left. During the neoliberal crisis, centre-left incumbents in general suffered more severe electoral punishments than did their right-wing counterparts (Bartels 2014). One central reason behind this failure has been their inability to implement traditional leftward policies. Before 15 May 2011, the centre-left PSOE government supported neoliberal policies – exemplified by the harshest collection of austerity measures being implemented three days before the 15M events began, or by the reform of Article 135 of the Spanish Constitution, destined to guarantee the payment of the debt's interest. Notwithstanding the dispersion of electoral preferences on the left (Lobera and Ferrándiz 2013), many (left-wing) citizens, unhappy with PSOE's performance, felt that there were virtually no alternative forces with potential for winning, most obviously in the 2011 general election.[4] This crisis of representation affecting PSOE was reflected in high electoral volatility, which is a general condition for the emergence of successful new parties (Rashkova and Van Biezen 2014). The declining electoral support for PSOE (from 43.8 per cent in 2008 to 22 per cent in the 2015 general elections) testifies to 'a breach of trust of PSOE with its own electorate – and, by extension, with the rest of the citizenship – that is twofold: first, at the level of the "ideological contract" and, second, related to the confidence in their effectiveness in overcoming the crisis' (Lobera 2015, 101). Thanks to its anti-austerity position, Podemos could then take electoral advantage of the PSOE's structural crisis in the last years. Not by chance, as Pablo Iglesias himself recognized, the 'political space of social-democracy was empty and we have occupied it' (Iglesias 2015c).

2.3.2. The anti-austerity cycle of movements in Spain: From extra-conventional participation to the ballot boxes

The social and political crises did not automatically produce party changes; rather, the political opportunities for the emergence and success of Podemos were created by a long wave of contentious politics. On 15 May 2011, marches called by the digital meta-organization Democracia Real ¡Ya! [DRY; Real Democracy Now!], under the slogan 'We are not goods in the hands of politicians and bankers', gathered tens of thousands all across the country. This gave rise to the Indignados movement, which delivered the most massive protest performances beyond traditional institutions of representation in Spain's recent history. However, the impact of the 15M in terms of mental schemata, political agendas, activist culture and the like took some time to leave a mark on the electoral arena.

The transition from unconventional forms of action to conventional participation through the emerging new parties might be explained by a combination of three crucial aspects: (1) institutional closure, which led to the exhaustion of activists and repertoires of protest while grievances persisted; (2) presence of windows of political opportunity, given the inability of majoritarian parties to channel citizens' demands and the neoliberal turn of PSOE; (3) organizational resources, especially in terms of leadership and the symbolic capital gained by some activists.

The wave of protests against austerity and 'for a real democracy' prepared the terrain for Podemos. Through a sustained critique of the existing parties and party system and the definition of party divisions as fictitious, it contributed to undermining the political and cultural consensus established during the democratic transition (Sampedro and Lobera 2014). According to a Podemos leader, the 15M movement 'constituted a new political identity by articulating heterogeneous and dispersed demands in a basic narrative frame, which is massive to the extent that is transversal and with extremely ideological porous borders' (Errejón 2015, 128). This construction of a new transversal dissent during anti-austerity protests is at the core of Podemos' 'populist hypothesis'. Institutional closure and the start of a demobilization process provoked a turning point in the contentious cycle: from a destituent process (based on protest and unconventional repertoires) to a constituent process (based on the 'assault on institutions'); and from a more movementist pre-15M cycle to a post-15M cycle with more electoral connotations (Subirats 2015a, 164).

Some authors have pointed out the blockage of movements' potential and their incapacity to stop neoliberal and post-democratic forms of governance and crisis management, accounting for the emergence of Podemos and other new actors at the local level (e.g. Arribas Lozano 2015). In short, anti-austerity protests developed in a political framework with restricted opportunities for movements. However, the movement itself created opportunities by weakening the position of central actors in the political system and thus creating space for the emergence of new ones. The irruption of new actors, such as Podemos and other oppositional slates of candidates at the local level, gives continuity to a twofold challenge for anti-austerity movements: the opposition to the economic crisis, but also 'the political crisis with which it is strictly intertwined' (della Porta 2014; see also Zamora-Kapoor and Coller 2014). In this sense, Podemos is rooted in the evolution of protests during the preceding years. It rises when protests decline, not as its immediate consequence. At the very same time, new party actors (Podemos, Partido X as well as local lists such as Guanyem in Barcelona) emerged. Hence, Podemos might be considered as a deliberate attempt on the part of movement actors to build up electoral tools, which causes them to leave the extra-conventional arena in the background. The very evolution of the frames and core claims of the anti-austerity movements mirrors this strategic shift within the cycle.

2.3.3. New issues, new cleavages

Social science literature states that new parties emerge as interests are neglected by existing parties (Harmel and Robertson 1985; Hug 2001), thus filling representational needs and responding to dissatisfied voters. In the democratic history of Spain, the two major parties have reached consensus with regard to the most important economic issues, with a lack of real policy conflict between them over the size of the welfare state in the last decades (Fernández-Albertos and Manzano 2012; López 2012; Sampedro and Lobera 2014). Accordingly, a closed structure of opportunities developed which minimized social and political conflict (see Aguilar Fernández 2008). Pressures from financial markets and international institutions to adopt pro-austerity measures have strengthened this political closure at the top; but it was broken by movements, which created opportunities to introduce new issues and set a new political agenda. The politicization of social problems thus left gaps for new parties to fill (Lucardie 2000).

   In particular, the wave of protests allowed for the emergence of a new cleavage based on an anti-establishment dividing line, pitting 'new politics' against 'old politics'. This distinction was also used to transcend the classical left–right cleavage ('we are neither leftist nor rightist' was stated during the 15M protest), building a new one based on the distinction between those below (the ordinary people affected by the crisis) and those above. Podemos aimed at reorganizing the political map around this new axis and promoting a new double and mixed cleavage: 'the caste' against 'the people',[5] and 'the old' against 'the new' politics.

While parties are easy to form in Spain, given weak regulation (Rashkova and Van Biezen 2014), the electoral system makes new entries in national parliaments difficult. The success of Podemos (and Ciudadanos on the centre-right[6]) results, however, from the perceived crisis of the mainstream parties, which spread the belief that successful participation in the electoral arena was possible, especially in the European elections. This sort of self-fulfilling prophecy spiralled, thanks to the encouraging results of participation in the European elections. In fact, as second order elections, the European polls (Reif and Schmitt 1980) facilitated protest voting for small or new parties (Ramiro and Font 2012). Additionally, the absence of barriers in the electoral law for these elections[7] stimulated the decision to participate in the European contest (Galindo et al. 2015).

2.3.4. The evolution of Podemos: A periodization

According to interviewees, in the short life of Podemos we can distinguish three different phases: (a) an initial one, with the launching of the party as an initiative oriented towards building a tool for empowerment and a method for the creation of popular unity; (b) a second one, in the weeks before and immediately after the European elections (May 2014), led by the process of territorial extension of the project based on a massive self-organized and grassroots initiative around the 'circles'; (c) a third one corresponding to the process of the constituent assembly and the transformation of Podemos into a regulated party.

(a) The origins: Podemos as a method for self-organization
Podemos is a top-down endeavour initially launched by, on the one hand, a group of activist-scholars with a prior record of involvement in the Global Justice Movement and in anti-austerity protests and, on the other hand, by a small but active political group of the Spanish radical left (Izquierda Anticapitalista, now Anticapitalistas[8]).[9] The public launch of the party occurred on 17 January 2014, when Podemos' spokespersons promoted the collection of 50,000 signatures in support of the initial manifesto 'Mover ficha: convertir la indignación en cambio político' (*Making a Move: Turning Indignation into Political Change*), which had been promoted by twenty-eight social activists.[10] This manifesto contained radical leftist programmatic proposals and explicit critiques of the 'two-party regime of the PSOE and PP'. Since its public presentation, Podemos was conceived as a case of a contender party (Harmel and Robertson 1985), as its goal was electoral success and not just becoming a vehicle to bring attention to particular issues or causes. In that sense,

more than a defined model of a party, it was presented as a 'method' for a 'popular unity' candidacy and for self-organization. In the words of Errejón (2014), Podemos was born 'as a tool for "popular and civic unity" understood as the articulation of floating discontent and for the popular activation oriented towards recovering sovereignty and democracy, kidnapped by the oligarchical "caste"'.

(b) The European elections (May 2014): The success of a movement party

The rooting of Podemos in the territory was extremely successful. In the four months prior to the European elections, more than 400 Circles (territorial and sectorial assemblies) were organized. Completely open to participation and horizontally structured, they involved thousands of citizens in the electoral campaign, with evident similarities to the spreading of the 15M movement. The person responsible for the organization of Podemos at that time talks of 'a kind of 15M of politics' (I6G). At the digital level, there was growing success on both Twitter and Facebook. During these months, Podemos was thus able to achieve a critical mass, enabling extensive spread of its Circles through the main social media (Toret 2015). Podemos' strategy combined two elements: on the one hand, the leadership of Iglesias and, on the other, a huge process of citizen participation. The process of self-organization and grassroots participation driven by Podemos allowed an unexpected result (7.98 per cent and five representatives). At the same time, the punishment of both the ruling party and the main opposition party reached extraordinarily high levels: both lost 2.5 million votes when compared to the previous EP elections. The results of the EP election were therefore read as 'a sign of a very possible electoral and party-system de-alignment in forthcoming elections' (Cordero and Torcal 2015).

During the weeks following the elections, Podemos increased its popularity exponentially. The number of followers in social media grew considerably: in just one week following 25 May, Facebook followers increased from 200,000 to 610,000 and Twitter followers from 60,000 to 200,000. There was similar growth in participation in the Circles. As the new political scenario that opened up after the EP election put Podemos under the pressure of the mass media, the need to organize the party led to a Constituent Assembly to clarify its structure, political orientation, and strategy.

(c) The constituent process (October 2014–November 2015): The configuration of a party structure

In the Citizens Assembly between October and November 2015, 107,488 people elected the members of the various organizational bodies. Ethical, political, and organizational documents were also voted on by 112,070 people between 20 and 26 October 2014. Thus, the Assembly approved an organizational model and defined a political strategy. In both dimensions, the proposals supported by Iglesias and his close collaborators achieved a majority.

The long process of the Constituent Assembly meant the election of the various party officers at the national, regional, and local levels. During this Process, different ideas and visions emerged, especially about the organizational model of Podemos. As noted by Bouzek (2009), during a party's formative phase, factions often represent different communities of interests, subcultures, and distinct cleavages (political, socio-economic, ethnic, geographic, or ideological). In Podemos, internal differences started to be explicit during the Constituent Process, as two different organizational models faced each other. The first one, promoted by Iglesias and his close collaborators, proposed a more conventional party model (with a general secretary, an executive and a central committee, and a majority system with open rolls in which the winner takes all) (Rendueles and Sola 2015). The other, supported by MP Pablo Echenique, promoted a more horizontal, experimental structure, including the 'allocation of some of the positions of responsibility by drawing lots and giving more of a leading role to grassroots activist circles' (Rendueles and Sola 2015).[11] These two models were linked in the debate on Podemos' broader strategy, with some stressing efficacy and the construction of what was called 'a machinery for electoral war', and others defending a more democratic innovation in terms of repertoire and organizational structure. An online ballot, open to all members of Podemos, gave an overwhelming victory to Iglesias' model, with 84 per cent of the votes.

2.3.5. The electoral base of Podemos

The emergence of a new party like Podemos signified a change in the electoral preferences of the voters. Since its launching, Podemos attracted both activists with previous experiences (either in leftist parties or in social movements) and others for whom Podemos was their first activist experience (I9S, I13S). The coexistence of these two groups (experienced activists and neophytes) has not been easy. Podemos' leaders have indeed tried to support the engagement of less ideological and less experienced sectors, but internal recruitment processes *de facto* privileged experienced activists from movements and parties (including many cadres of the United Left) (I6S).

Podemos' constituency is generally characterized as young, urban, well educated, and actively using new technologies (Galindo et al. 2015).

Its potential voters are those who (by far) show more distrust towards politicians, parties, judicial system, EU, banks, and unions (Cordero and Torcal 2015). While one of the main explicit goals of Podemos has been to achieve transversal support – following the idea of overcoming the left/right axis and trying to create a kind of 'catch-all party' – the voters often came from the centre-left and the left (PSOE and IU) and defined themselves as leftists (Galindo et al. 2015). Specifically, 32 per cent came from PSOE and 26 per cent from IU, while 10 per cent had voted for other parties and 10 per cent had abstained in 2011 (Galindo et al. 2015). The PP voters in 2011 constituted only 5 per cent of Podemos' supporters. Podemos' voters tend to consider this party as far leftist (scoring 2.3 on a scale from 1 to 10), even more than IU. In fact, despite the pretended 'transversality' of its discourse, Podemos has 'managed to position itself at the centre of the left, and to scrape off votes from non-ideological sectors' (Rendueles and Sola 2015).

Podemos emerged, then, as an alternative for the social-democratic electorate disaffected with the Socialist Party, becoming a real competitor for PSOE (Galindo et al. 2015). In the European elections, it won the votes of activists and people with high levels of political information, but with its increasing popularity, it also began to attract voters in a more vulnerable economic situation (Fernández-Albertos 2015). In this way, Podemos has progressively consolidated 'as a party less and less of activists, and more and more supported by social groups punished by the economic crisis and frustrated by the lack of opportunities' (ibid., 100). Thus, Podemos is said to have moved from a party of political renewal to a class-based party (ibid., 102). In this sense, Podemos' electorate seems to be more and more composed of social sectors of what can be considered as the 'losers', or those 'excluded' from neoliberal development.

Podemos' voters also reflect the social composition of the anti-austerity protests: young, often well-educated, unemployed, and precarious workers (della Porta 2015b). The profile of the people supporting Podemos is not the one traditionally associated with social movements. Its voters are active politically, but not as active as the voters of other leftist parties such as IU or Esquerra Republicana de Catalunya (Cordero and Torcal 2015). However, various surveys show that Podemos' support is particularly high among voters of specific age cohorts (Galindo et al. 2015). Specifically, Podemos is the most preferred party among young people (those aged 25–34), with 20.6 per cent of support, and even more among the very young (18–24 years), with 27 per cent. This has reinforced the vision of a 'new' versus 'old' division as also a generational phenomenon.

2.4. The genesis of the M5S

The unexpected rise of the M5S since 2012 was related to a particularly favourable context characterized by the formation of a bipartisan government, the economic crisis, and widespread corruption scandals involving all parties, including the former supporters of the moralization of politics.

2.4.1. A favourable political context

The corruption scandals of the early 1990s (*Mani Pulite* – Clean Hands) had already spread ample hostility towards representative institutions and decreased trust in traditional political parties (della Porta and Vannucci 1997). Several cases of widespread corruption emerging in early 2012 generated even more aversion to political parties, including those in opposition, with an anti-establishment rhetoric and harshly contrasting corruption (Fella and Ruzza 2013; Mosca 2013).

Despite efforts to reform institutions, the parliament's inability to revise the electoral law and to reduce significantly the costs of politics – something that was commonly expected by the bipartisan government – brought further discredit to the political parties, creating an extremely favourable context for challengers. This situation opened up opportunities for outsiders in the political arena, which were effectively pulled in by Grillo's party.

2.4.2. A structural but worsening economic crisis

The Italian crisis had started well before 2008 as a structural crisis, mingling stagnation and inflation (Allern, D'Ippoliti, and Roncaglia 2011). As in Spain, the Italian crisis, which was exacerbated after 2008, was more related to low productivity than to public debt. Over the past decade, Italy's real GDP growth per capita has been among the weakest in the OECD, which reflects very low underlying growth in productivity (Goretti and Landi 2013), with the real GDP growth rate at 1.3 per cent per year on average between 1995 and 2008. The effects of a very high public debt were, however, buffered by high private savings. Nevertheless, in Italy as well, when fears of contagion rose, structurally low growth even before the Great Recession and policy stalemate (with the Berlusconi government paralysed by internal cabinet disputes and a split majority) did nothing but contribute to the flight from Italy's sovereign debt. In 2011, from April to July, Italian credit default swaps tripled; in June, the European Council asked for specific measures to reduce the budget imbalance, which was passed by the parliament a few weeks later (Sacchi 2015).

In early August 2011, when the Italian bond spreads surged to 390 points against the benchmark German *bund*, the Berlusconi government received a 'strictly confidential' letter from the ECB explicitly calling for 'fiscal sustainability and structural reforms', including 'the full liberalization of local public services and of professional services', 'further reform [of] the collective wage bargaining system', and 'a thorough review of the rules regulating the hiring and dismissal of employees'. The letter also asked for 'ensuring the sustainability of public finances' by 'interven[ing] further in the pension system', 'reducing the cost of public employees', introducing 'an automatic deficit-reducing clause', and placing under tight control 'commercial debt and expenditures of regional and local governments'. Moreover, the ECB urged the Italian government to pass such reforms 'as soon as possible with decree-laws, followed by Parliamentary ratification by the end of September 2011'.[12] According to Giannone, 'the text of the Italian letter can be considered as the *manifesto* of the neoliberal restructuring of European democracies' (2015, 114). Even without having signed a MoU, similarly to Spain, Italy was subject to heavy conditionalities, 'as the ECB was setting the policy agenda, alternatives and instruments to be adopted in exchange for its support' (Sacchi 2015, 83). Since the Berlusconi government failed to pass some of the agreed measures, 'members of the ECB governing council discussed (and disclosed) the possibility of stopping the purchase of Italian paper if the Italian government failed to implement the promised reforms' (ibid., 84).

After Berlusconi resigned, the grand coalition government led, as in Greece, by a so-called technocrat, Mario Monti, implemented all the requests included in the ECB letter, with particular emphasis on labour market flexibility and pension system restructuring. Reforms included transformations of the collective bargaining system, institution of a minimum retirement age of sixty-seven by 2019, as well as the abolition of seniority pensions, which the Monti government implemented moving from (traditional) negotiation to unilateral action (Sacchi 2013). The EU sided with premier Monti on an intransigent line. In particular, 'The labour market reform is monitored at every juncture, its contents thoroughly scrutinized, warnings are issued in a way that could easily make defenders of old-school democracy raise an eyebrow, and the parliamentary process is followed day by day' (Sacchi 2015, 89). While initially unions maintained some influence over the process, European institutions have been said to have encouraged national governments to go ahead with austerity measures even without their approval, unions being stigmatized as conservative.

The alignment to European Commission (EC)'s requests penalized parties of the centre-left as well as of the centre-right. After one year of grand coalition supporting Monti's government, the 2013 general elections brought about heavy electoral losses for both the right-wing People of Freedom,[13] which fell from 37.2 per cent in 2008 to 21.6 per cent, and for the PD, which dropped from 33.1 per cent in 2008 to 25.4 per cent. The M5S, however, in its first experience of national elections, obtained the second best results in the lower chamber, with 25.6 per cent of the votes. Indeed, there was the higher vote-swing of the Italian Republic, with aggregate volatility at 39.1 per cent (Bellucci 2014). In parallel, the indicator of trust in parties (measured on a 0–10 scale) fell from 3.2 in spring 2011 to 2.1 a year later (ibid.).

After Monti's bipartisan government, the subsequent large coalitions – first under the left-wing Democratic Party (PD)'s Prime Minister Enrico Letta, including Forza Italia (FI), and then under PD's Prime Minister Matteo Renzi, supported by a splinter FI faction – proceeded rapidly to the implementation of EC requests.

After the collapse of Berlusconi's government in the autumn of 2011, the role played by the PD within the succeeding governments became continuously more prominent, discouraging protest and reducing resources and opportunities in the movement arena. Moreover, the M5S occupied the political space in between the protest arena and the institutional arena, also appropriating movements' resources such as activists, struggles, and ideas (Mosca 2015a) and impeding the emergence of an anti-austerity collective identity able to transcend individuals, groups, and organizations.

2.4.3. The anti-austerity protest arena during the Italian crisis

Contrary to the anti-neoliberal protest wave of the early 2000s (Smith et al. 2007) and differently from other Southern European countries during the crisis (as seen in previous sections), the anti-austerity protest arena in Italy was dominated by established actors, which made coalition building extremely difficult. As such, 'although protest mobilization has been relatively high against anti-austerity measures, an anti-austerity movement failed to emerge' (Andretta 2016).

According to a protest event analysis on the newspaper *La Repubblica*, 1,140 events were covered between 2009 and 2014 (della Porta et al. 2015; Andretta 2016). The protest cycle peaked in 2010 during Berlusconi's centre-right government, when the crisis became manifest in Italy. Seventy per cent of protest events included anti-austerity related claims such as references to the economic crisis, budget cuts, privatization, labour issues, and cuts in welfare. Demonstrators addressed particularly the austerity policies imposed by European and domestic institutions, criticized as being implemented without citizens' agreement and as intensifying the crisis instead of solving it. Protest events during the crisis focused particularly on the three topics of labour, environment, and housing.

Regarding the social profile of protesters, the research found that workers (being present in 62 per cent of protest events), students (15%), precarious workers (8%), and to a lesser extent unemployed (2%) and immigrants (5%) tended to be more visible in the protest arena. In terms of collective actors, the research confirmed the role of established trade unions (such as the leftist Cgil and the metalworker union Fiom), rank-and-file unions, student collectives, local committees, squatted social centres and other informal groups, as well as formal associations. Also documented was the declining presence of political parties. During the period under scrutiny, the most visible form of action was the strike, also re-invented by rank-and-file unions in the form of the 'social strike', as a means of addressing structural changes in the working class and aimed at involving any kind of atypical worker in road blocks.

During the Italian anti-austerity cycle of contention, despite the mushrooming of protest events, any effort to unify the different sectors of mobilization in creating broad coalitions failed because of tensions between individual actors, organizations, and practices that hindered the emergence of new forms and actors (della Porta and Zamponi 2013). According to Andretta (2016), the most intense anti-austerity mobilization 'has been produced under the last Berlusconi government, when the main centre-left party (the PD), with its traditional links with the biggest trade union (Cgil), supported the protest. But, as the centre-right government was substituted by a grand-coalition in support of the self-defined "technical" government led by Mario Monti, the implementation of anti-austerity measures found weak opposition from unions and associations that had traditionally developed near to the center-left parties.'

2.4.4. Foundation and evolution of M5S

Beppe Grillo is a well-known Italian comedian who became famous with his television shows at the end of the 1970s. Banned from public television during the 1980s because of satire against the governing Socialist Party, he decided to move his shows to squares and theatres (Vignati 2015). His performances have always been a mix of political satire, social and environmental campaigns, consumer defence, and other topics.

Before establishing his own party, Grillo had supported countless events, initiatives, and social campaigns, as well as groups, associations, and political forces. He has subsequently acted as spokesman for several social movements, referendum campaigns, and campaigns for consumer protection (Mosca 2013). Environmental protection is one of the themes to which Grillo has always been chiefly committed. After meeting with the communications expert Gianroberto Casaleggio in 2004, he realized the importance of the internet and started a blog in 2005 that became very successful. Initially, the blog represented an important hub for his fans all over the country. In July 2005, Grillo suggested that his supporters create local groups using the Meetup platform.[14] Politics rapidly moved from the background to the foreground of Grillo's discourse and his fans were quickly transformed into activists (Biorcio and Natale 2013) who could easily meet in person and define a local agenda (Lanfrey 2011). These groups were the basic cells that facilitated the emergence of the M5S a few years later.

As such, the Movement's history can be roughly divided into four phases: (a) latency (2005–7); (b) visibility (2007–8); (c) entry into the electoral arena (2008–11); (d) electoral boom and institutionalization (since 2012).

(a) Phase 1: Latency on the web (2005–7)

The latency phase started when Grillo set up his blog in January 2005 and invited his fans to create groups on Meetup called 'Beppe Grillo's friends' (*Amici di Beppe Grillo*) in the same year. While the blog was the Movement's unique voice, the Meetup groups served as its territorial backbone (Lanfrey 2011). In this phase, Grillo gradually put aside his role as a comedian and became a political entrepreneur (Biorcio and Natale 2013). At the same time, supporter groups started to form on Meetup and get to know each other. Meetup provided a locus for the aggregation of Grillo's fans, for staying in contact, and for promoting projects of active citizenship in the local domain. Public visibility and media coverage of the Movement were extremely limited at this stage, and the new (pre)political creature was mostly known to the limited circuit of supporters and activists. According to Passarelli et al. (2013), the role of Meetup changed considerably from the first to the second phase: while it acted mostly as a platform for online discussion throughout the former, during the latter it facilitated activists' face-to-face meetings.

(b) Phase 2: Visibility through mass protests (2007–8)

Before considering the option of creating a political party, Beppe Grillo tried to find interlocutors within the existing party system. In the 2006 general elections, he supported the centre-left coalition headed by Romano Prodi against Berlusconi's centre-right, as the lesser of two evils. Following the formation of the new government, Grillo met with Prodi, bringing him the results of what he called 'the primary of citizens' – a consultation held during the previous months on his blog on topics such as economy, information, health, and energy.[15] He argued that since the centre-left coalition did not have a programme, he was willing to donate to them what citizens had elaborated from below. Soon after, however, Grillo expressed his disappointment with Prodi's inertia; throughout the legislative sessions, he repeatedly criticized members of the government and their reforms.

During this phase, Grillo's fans moved from the web and the local domain to the squares, and their mobilization acquired national resonance. Two massive public events were organized through the internet, mobilizing hundreds of thousands of people. These protest events served to define and provide a concrete reference to the Movement's fluid identity and to build a sense of solidarity among participants beyond the local level, also by pointing to the 'enemies' of the Movement: above all, traditional parties and the mainstream media.

On 8 September 2007,[16] a first public demonstration called 'V-day' against the 'caste of politicians' was held in Bologna and other Italian cities to collect signatures for a popular law initiative demanding a 'clean parliament'. It called for a ban from parliament of all convicted persons; electoral system reforms, allowing voters to express preferences for individual candidates; a two-term limit in parliament; and the prohibition of holding two elected posts at the same time. On 25 April 2008,[17] a second 'V-day' against the 'caste of journalists' took place in Turin and in other Italian squares, collecting signatures for three abrogative referenda: to abolish subsidies to the publishing industry, cancel the Gasparri Law (regulating the media system) via a referendum, and eliminate the official journalist register. In both cases, the initiatives collected hundreds of thousands of signatures, delivering them to the parliament and expecting reactions from political parties that never arrived. After the success of the first V-day, Grillo proposed that his supporters set up civic lists 'certified' by him and his staff to participate in local elections.[18] This decision paved the way for the creation of the M5S and its entry into the electoral arena.

(c) Phase 3: Entry into the electoral arena (2008–11)

On the occasion of the election day in 2008, Grillo adopted a double strategy: endorsing 5-star civic lists in local elections, while repeatedly stressing the similarities between the main competitors in general elections and defining abstention as the only possible answer and 'the only democratic weapon left'.[19]

Following the experiment of local elections, it became evident that in order to expand its electoral appeal, a common symbol and a common name were needed to create a unique reference for Grillo's supporters and to avoid the creation of fake lists evoking the leader's name in their party symbols.[20] The creation of the M5S – until then a 'meta-organization' networking autonomous local groups under the coordination of an organizational core of limited size (Lanfrey 2011) – was preceded by some important events. First, there was the approval of the 'Carta di Firenze', a common programme drafted in a meeting held in Florence on 9 March 2009 by people drawing up the certified electoral lists, Grillo's supporters, and members of Meetup groups. The charter identified the main issues expected to drive local government's action – the so-called five stars: water, environment, mobility, development, and energy. Second, after its defeat in the general elections of 2008, the PD announced primaries for the selection of a new secretary. In July 2009, Grillo provocatively proclaimed that he would run in PD's primary. Although it is not clear if he really wanted to participate in the primaries of the centre-left party, the PD's board did not accept his candidature. Very telling was the reaction of a former secretary of the party, who claimed, 'If Grillo wants to do politics, he is welcome! He should create a party, stand for elections and we will see how many votes he will take!' (Piero Fassino, interview with Repubblica TV, 13 July 2009).[21] The (encouraging) results of the first tests of local lists, as well as what appeared as a political system extremely closed to outsiders, facilitated the decision to create a political party.

On 10 October, the M5S was officially born, and two months later a 'non-statute' regulating its functioning was made public (Fornaro 2012). Initially, however, the M5S participated only in local elections, in areas where local groups of supporters were already present and able to form a list.

(d) Phase 4: Electoral boom and institutionalization (since 2012)

The real turning point in the Movement's electoral results came with the local elections of May 2012, when it elected four mayors and obtained more than 10 per cent of votes in many northern areas (Pinto and Vignati 2012). After that 'electoral boom', the Movement's rise seemed unstoppable: the feat was repeated and even overtaken in the Sicilian regional elections in October 2012 and in the general political elections in February 2013.

With the entry into the national parliament of 163 representatives in February 2013, the Movement entered a phase of 'institutionalization' (Gualmini 2013), characterized by tensions mostly related to its fast growth and the unsolved question of the relationship between Grillo (the

unelected leader) and the Movement's representatives. The cohesion of
the parliamentary group has been bedevilled by Grillo's brusque refusal
to enter into any kind of political alliance (that is, a coalition government with the PD), and dissent and/or criticism have been punished with
expulsion. In addition, the issues of cuts to the salaries of the Movement's
own members of parliament (cuts to the salaries of all MPs was part of
the party's platform) monopolized the M5S political agenda for a long
time, offering an image of internal conflict.

2.4.5. The electoral performance of the party over time

As we have already seen, the electoral fortune of the M5S started with the
municipal elections held in May 2012. Although the party only presented
candidates in some municipalities, the average votes it gathered almost
doubled compared with those collected only one year before (from 4.7
per cent to 9.1 per cent – see Figure 2.4). Furthermore, on that occasion
the party elected its first mayors, one of them in the provincial capital
of Parma – soon labelled by Grillo as 'our little Stalingrad' to stress

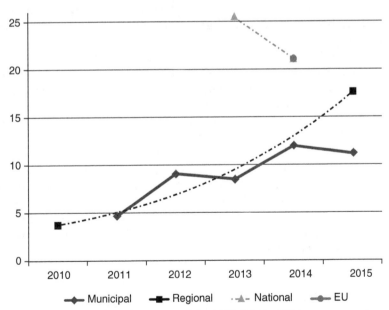

Figure 2.4.   Electoral performance of the M5S (2010–2015, percentages)
Source: Author's elaboration on data of the interior minister (http://elezioni.
interno.it)

the symbolic relevance of the victory.[22] The unexpected results of the municipal elections galvanized Grillo and his supporters to the point that they became the most voted-for party in the Sicilian regional elections of November 2012 and the first party (excluding the votes of Italians residing abroad) in the lower chamber of parliament in the general elections of February 2013 (Figure 2.4). The European parliamentary elections of 2014 represented an important test after the massive entrance into the Italian parliament. Though the final result was considered a defeat on the basis of the expectations raised by Grillo's campaign and polls (with a clear drop compared to the general election of 2013, in both absolute and relative terms), the M5S was still the second most voted party, gathering 21.1 per cent of the valid votes (Biancalana and Tronconi 2014; Bordignon and Ceccarini 2015).

Although comparison among municipal results must be made with great caution because in most cases the same municipalities cannot be compared, the trend in votes for the M5S in such elections has been quite steady over time, reaching a peak of 12 per cent in 2014 (Figure 2.4). In relation to national outcomes, however, the M5S has been generally less attractive and less competitive in municipal elections because of: (a) Grillo's more modest role in the local campaigns, especially after 2012; (b) a different issue at stake; (c) the great variance in terms of mayoral candidates and local political contexts. Nonetheless, in 2016 there have been victories in important municipal contests such as Rome and Turin.

As Figure 2.5 shows, the 2013 national elections represented a turning point in Italian politics. The critical juncture relating to the mingling of economic, political, and moral crisis has clearly unfrozen Italian voters, generating a tripolar party system. In the 2013 elections, volatility increased fourfold compared to the previous elections in 2008. It reached 39.1 per cent, almost doubling the standard threshold and indicating high volatility (Chiaramonte and Emanuele 2014). Most strikingly, volatility in 2013 was even greater than in 1994, when the collapse of an entire party system followed the 'Tangentopoli' corruption scandals (Figure 2.5). According to Chiaramonte and Emanuele (2014), the 2013 Italian elections were the most volatile in the history of Western Europe after the 2012 Greek elections (48.7 per cent) and the 1982 Spanish elections (40.5 per cent).

2.4.6. The electoral base of the M5S

The profile of voters of Grillo's party has changed notably since its entrance into the electoral arena. According to opinion polls, before the

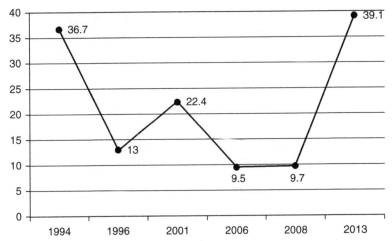

Figure 2.5. Total volatility index (Low Chamber, 1994–2013, proportional values)
Source: data from Chiaramonte and Emanuele 2014

'electoral boom' of 2012 the average M5S voter was relatively young (mostly belonging to the age cohorts 25–34, 35–44, and 45–54), mostly male, residing in the north or in the 'red zone', in medium-small, medium-sized, and medium-large cities (with populations between 10,000 and 250,000) (Pedrazzani and Pinto 2015, 81–2). Regarding social characteristics, the typical profile of M5S voters at that time was one of well-educated, regular workers and self-employed, hired as employees (white-collar, blue-collars and farmers) or active in small businesses (craftsmen and retailers) – also including, although to a lesser extent, students, teachers, and the unemployed. Voters' profile changed drastically in the year between the local elections of May 2012 and general elections of 2013, displaying a 'normalization' of the Movement's electoral base and 'getting support from a rather heterogeneous base' (Pedrazzani and Pinto 2015, 76).

After the 2013 national elections, the profile of M5S voters became more similar to that of the average voter: while the disproportion in terms of gender has almost vanished, the appeal of the Movement has greatly increased among those under 25, the gap between northern and southern areas has been filled, and differences have reduced regarding city size, as people residing in smaller and larger urban centres turn out to be more supportive of the Movement. Regarding education and working conditions, the M5S became more attractive to less educated groups and for unemployed and temporary workers.

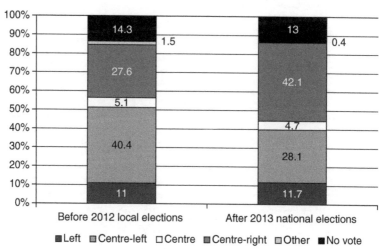

Figure 2.6. M5S voters' distribution by coalitions voted in 2008 general elections
Source: data from Pedrazzani and Pinto 2015, 92

The growing social and demographic heterogeneity of M5S voters over time has been paired with increasing heterogeneity in past voting behaviour and political positioning. In the beginning, in fact, Movement supporters came mostly from disillusioned voters of left and centre-left parties as well as from abstentionists (Corbetta and Gualmini 2013; Biorcio and Natale 2013). Former centre-right voters instead joined the M5S between 2012 and 2013, balancing the political composition of its electoral base (Figure 2.6).

The above mentioned changes are also reflected in M5S voters' political positioning: they in fact appear in between centre-left and centre-right parties. However, compared to other parties they show higher ideological heterogeneity, being an aggregate of opposite preferences where the average value has to be interpreted in light of the high level of standard deviation. Moreover, the M5S also displays the highest number of voters (27.7 per cent) that refuse to self-collocate on the political spectrum (Pedrazzani and Pinto 2015, 97).

The European elections have further highlighted the fluid nature of the Movement's electorate. According to a pre-electoral survey, the centre-left had in fact re-conquered a relevant part of voters lost in 2013 in favour of Grillo. Only 55 per cent of those who voted for Grillo in 2013 confirmed their choice: 13 per cent have moved to Renzi's PD and also fed abstention (22 per cent). The M5S has lost younger voters, while categories more hit by the crisis such as self-employed and unemployed confirmed their loyalty to the Movement. Compared with the 2013 general elections, M5S voters tended to be mostly male and to display middle levels of education. The M5S was also the most appealing party for non-religious voters (Ipsos PA 2014).

2.5. Conclusion

The origins of our case studies are quite different. Whereas SYRIZA is more connected to the euro-communist left and M5S is linked to the charismatic leadership of Grillo, in Podemos we can find the direct influence of the anti-austerity mobilizations. But despite the evident differences in the origins of each party, we can also find common elements to explain their electoral success.

First of all, support for all three parties was fuelled by the intertwining of the socio-economic and political crisis. Indeed, the parties took advantage of the structural conditions provoked by the deep economic crisis in their countries, especially as it fuelled a crisis of responsibility of the traditional parties, reinforced by the lack of trust in those parties. The main political institutions also facilitated the electoral growth of new (or previously marginal) parties. In countries characterized by longstanding weaknesses in the economy (with low productivity and high public debt) and in the political system (with widespread clientelism and corruption), the global financial crisis had particularly dramatic effects. Party systems that appeared as increasingly dominated by two mainstream parties in fact suddenly broke down. Furthermore, corruption has also meant a crisis of legitimacy for the traditional political parties in countries such as Greece, Italy, or Spain. Hence, new issues have emerged that found no representation in the institutional system (real democracy and anti-corruption, but also social and economic rights).

Second, in all three cases the space for new parties opened up as the traditional centre-left party dramatically lost support, perceived as no longer alternative to the centre-right. In particular, in all three cases (most dramatically in Greece), the centre-left parties' commitment to austerity policies triggered their own crisis, with losses of members and voters. Thus, the high electoral volatility in the three cases affected mainly the relationships on the left of the party system (especially in Greece and Spain), becoming the main factor to explain the collapse of the traditional ruling two-party systems. At the same time, the crisis of centre-left parties (such as PSOE or PASOK, but also PD) was a cause and a consequence of the electoral success of the anti-austerity parties as, in some moments, these parties filled the empty political and electoral space of the old centre-left parties (less so in the case of the M5S). This element is quite clear in their electoral genesis when they gained the support of traditional voters of the left, even if movement parties, electoral base tended to become more heterogeneous. The three parties, however, display important differences regarding the relationship with the left: while SYRIZA explicitly aimed to unite and represent the left (see Chapter 4), Podemos abandoned a rhetoric typical of leftist parties despite its leaders clearly emanate from such political milieu, the M5S catch-all identity and the ambiguous positioning of its leaders made the political profile of Grillo's party much more ambivalent.

Third, in all three cases, the new parties exploited some relational, cognitive, and affective resources that were generated by the waves of protests against austerity policies. These mobilizations were capable of developing new frames, identities, and repertoires that increased the opportunities for anti-establishment parties. Moreover, these movements succeeded in connecting the economic crisis to the crisis of representative democracy, transforming the economic crisis into a political crisis as well. The massive protests against austerity (or the environmental and local conflicts in Italy) also offered some organizational resources and political opportunities particularly useful for the success of these new parties.

Fourth, in all three cases, initial electoral success empowered the parties, giving them visibility and increasing the perception that the electoral path could be successful. In this sense, we have pointed out how the financial crisis in Europe signalled a turning point in the relationships between parties and movements. On the other hand, the trend of decreasing trust in parties and representative institutions has meant a crisis of responsibility that allowed for the emergence of new contender parties in different political systems.

Fifth, in all three cases, after the party's first successes, panicked reactions in the establishment favoured, rather than hampering, new victories. In a sort of legitimation by stigmatization, the harsh attacks by mistrusted elites gave visibility and sympathy to those who were under attack.

3

Organizational Repertoires of Movement Parties

3.1. Introduction: Organizational models between agency and context

In this chapter we will illustrate and compare the organizational strategies of the movement parties that emerged as a reaction to the critical juncture in Southern Europe. In this introduction, we depart from the vivid discussion on organizational agency and environmental influence that has been particularly relevant in social movement studies.

Attention to social movement organizations (SMOs) has been at the core of the resource mobilization approach, whose proponents have stressed that 'The entrepreneurial mode of analysis includes both the rational-economic assumptions and formal organizational thrusts of our approach' (McCarthy and Zald 1987, 45). Movement parties, like SMOs, must mobilize resources from the surrounding environment, whether directly in the form of money or through voluntary work by their adherents; they must neutralize opponents and increase support from both the general public and the elite (for examples, McCarthy and Zald 1987, 19). Beyond this instrumental understanding, organizations have also been conceived as sources of identity for the movements' constituencies as well as their opponents and the public (della Porta and Diani 2006). They play in fact an identification function, being defined as 'associations of persons making idealistic and moralistic claims about how human personal or group life is to be organized that, *at the time of their claims making*, are marginal to or excluded from mainstream society' (Lofland 1996, 2–3, italics in the original).

In our research, we have looked at organizations as both mobilization agents and spaces for value construction. In the social movement literature, the instrumental approach has been dominant. As Clemens and Minkoff (2004, 156) have noted, with the development of the resource mobilization perspective, 'Attention to organization appeared antithetical to analysis of culture and interaction. As organizations were understood instrumentally, the cultural content of organizing and the meanings signalled by organizational forms were marginalized as topics for inquiry.' In recent approaches, however, SMOs have been considered more and more as 'contexts for political conversation', characterized by specific etiquettes (Eliasoph 1998, 21).

We found some of the proposals of the neo-institutional approach useful to go beyond an instrumental understanding. First of all, we consider organizations as socialized agents and norms producers that 'do not just constrain options: they establish the very criteria by which people discover their preferences' (DiMaggio and Powell 1991, 11). Organizations are therefore understood not just as means of mobilization, but also as arenas for experimentation. Second, we look at formal as well as informal practices. Within the neo-institutional approach, 'The relevance of relationships was no longer defined by the formal organization chart; forms of coordination grounded in personal networks as well as non authoritative projects of mobilization were made visible, as were influences that transgressed the official boundaries of an organization' (Clemens 2005, 356). Thus, our analysis goes beyond the formal models to look at the practices and ideas that are embodied in each organization. Third, the environment in which an organization develops is considered as being particularly relevant for its organizational choices.

However, rather than assuming a rigid relationship between the form that movement parties give to their organizations and the characteristics of the institutional system in which they operate, we recognize that multiple organizational forms may be accommodated within the same political context. This underlines the margins of choice that movement parties have when trying to adapt creatively to their environment, instead of being determined by it – even if these margins are constrained by historically specific organizational repertoires (Clemens 1996). In any given country and at any given time, that repertoire is restricted; although it can be expanded by borrowing ideas from other countries or domains, such transformations are slow. The adoption of a particular organizational model becomes more likely 'to the extent that the proposed model of organization is believed to work, involves practices and organizational relations that are already familiar, and is consonant with the organization of the rest of those individuals' social worlds' (ibid., 211).

The movement parties under study tend to present some common characteristics. Even if in different formats, they tend to be loosely structured, they aim at integrating movement constituencies, they display overlapping memberships with movements, their programmes resonate with those promoted by movements, and they tend to be supportive of protest and to engage in common campaigns. Some characteristics of movement parties, however, have changed over time, challenging but also adapting to the characteristics of domestic political contexts. In particular, the organizational repertoires of SYRIZA, Podemos, and the M5S were influenced by those social movements to which they referred, as well as by the overall characteristics of the party system. While they were shaped to different degrees by the legacies of collective action in each country and the presence of social movements emerging during the neoliberal juncture (anti-austerity campaign in Greece, Indignados' movement in Spain, and environmental and local conflicts in Italy), movement parties in Southern Europe have also incorporated some dominant tendencies of party evolution, as described in the first chapter.

In the following sections, we will briefly describe the organizational structure of SYRIZA (§3.2), Podemos (§3.3), and the M5S (§3.4), and their more recent evolution during the last crisis-ridden years. In presenting our cases we will make particular reference to three main features of movement parties, as discussed in relevant literature: (a) the lack of a formal structure; (b) a peculiar system of interest aggregation; and (c) a political practice combining conventional and unconventional forms of action (Kitschelt 2006). We will start with a general overview of the formalized organization of each party by illustrating how the main official documents (statutes, codes of conduct, regulations and so on) define their organisms and internal rules. Then, we will discuss how interviews conducted with party members and activists from the social movement field reveal organizational dynamics that are at play beyond, or even against, official regulations illustrating the ongoing relations among the different levels and faces of the parties. We will look in particular at the presence and role of different bodies and their formation mechanisms, diverse models and practices of membership, varying sources of funding, and participatory instruments, as well as the role of the leader vis-à-vis other formal counterweights within the party. We will also briefly discuss the repertoires of action of the three parties and their proximity (or lack thereof) to more or less conventional forms of participation and protest, as well as their performance within representative institutions. In the conclusion (§3.5), after summarizing our findings as presented in the previous sections, we will compare the main organizational dimensions of the three parties.

3.2. SYRIZA's organizational repertoire

As discussed in the previous chapter, SYRIZA was formed in 2004 as a coalition of the parliamentary party of Synaspismos (SYN), itself a coalition of the remnants of the euro-communist party, a large faction of KKE, some ecologists, and some small extra-parliamentary political organizations and networks of the left and radical left. SYRIZA functioned from 2004 to 2012 as an electoral coalition with a consensus-based decision-making process which was led in principle by SYN's leader, while its constituent organizations retained their autonomy. Below we will examine the coalition's evolution from its foundation in 2004 up to its rise to power in 2015.

3.2.1. The organizational model: Too old to be new

The creation of SYRIZA as an electoral platform in 2004 was an organizational response to the need to address younger cohorts and mobilized strata of society in order to broaden its electoral appeal and create 'a vital space between the center-left PASOK and the communist KKE' (I3G), but also to attend to SYN members' disappointment with the internal functioning of the party (Tsakatika and Eleftheriou 2013). Especially under the leadership of Alekos Alavanos (2004–08), SYN's identity crisis was addressed by opening up through SYRIZA to movement activists and non-members' participation. It was within this context, in 2008, that Alavanos suggested the then very young Tsipras for SYN's president.

One fundamental aspect of SYRIZA that refers especially to the period before the 2013 founding congress concerns its loose organizational structure. Lacking organizational density and firm rooting in local spaces and trade unions, it differed from other parties and appeared strangely incoherent and always close to dissolution. However, surprisingly enough, after 2010 and for a period of time this weakness turned into a clear advantage. It appeared as a 'coalition in progress', where different opinions could be introduced, strengthening the profile of a pluralistic and open party. Even if not a deliberate goal, SYRIZA's public image of disorder as promoted by its opponents may have functioned as an inclusive model for young activists and movements (I5G). Moreover, this participatory linkage, or the 'lack of it' (I13G), made it easier for the party to adapt to a rapidly changing electoral landscape.

Nonetheless, from 2012 onwards, it was exactly this pluralism and incoherence in terms of organizational strategy that favoured the party's proximity to conventional institutionalized actors, at the expense of its relations with the grassroots movements (I3G; I25G). The interviewees problematize the issue of 'looseness' as referring to the lack of qualitative and quantitative participation of the base in party decisions. According to one of them, 'I think there is a considerable lack of democracy in SYRIZA, that is important, while there is much work being done at grassroots level, the participation of members in the decision-making process is allowed only through some intermediate organs (the Congress, regional committees), but, still, local branches have no actual role in the decision-making process' (I4G).

Even if SYRIZA was founded and functioned as a coalition, and maintained ties with less hierarchical and more horizontal groups at least until 2012, it has developed a static top-down and hierarchical structure. Notwithstanding the aspirations of the 'left turn' of the early 2000s, SYRIZA remained an alliance only at the leadership level (Tsakatika and Eleftheriou 2013), strongly dominated by SYN, which never actually developed into a true coalition of autonomous organizations. After 2013 and despite its image as a 'members' party', SYRIZA retained its pyramid-like structure and underlying logic (I2G) and became a more and more centralized party, tuned by its closed leadership and detached from its membership and, more importantly, from its electorate. In the words of a member, 'There is a considerable concentration of power in the leadership around Alexis Tsipras, as he becomes elected directly by the Congress and not via the much broader Central Committee...delegating its authority to the leader granted him with an increasing autonomy and executive power' (I7G).

After its great electoral advance in the 2012 parliamentary elections, it was transformed into a unified political party in its first and founding congress in July 2013. According to its founding Statute (SYRIZA 2013a),[1] SYRIZA functions in a democratic and collective way and, according to the majority's opinions, 'that is why it is transformed into a party with "tendencies"' (SYRIZA 2013a) – which in practice meant that the autonomous parties and organizations of the coalition were called to dissolve and be transformed into factions in favour of a unitary party. Apart from SYN, which has always been the dominant tendency of the coalition, there were eleven other constituent groups ranging from orthodox Marxist positions to social-democracy and ecology.

As for the internal organization (Figure 3.1), as described in the Statute, the core of the party are local 'member' branches, which are entirely sovereign, autonomous, and free to decide on candidates to local elections, with the exception of large urban centres and regions. Moreover, the local branches elect representatives every two years for the prefectural congresses, which in turn elect the Regional Committees:

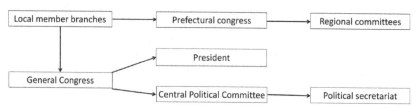

Figure 3.1. SYRIZA's organizational structure based on its Founding Statute

these are responsible for political planning at the regional level, coordinating the activities between the national and the local levels. Local sections also elect representatives for the general Congress, which is actually the supreme body of the party, meeting every three years (art. 13.1); approximately 3,500 members participated in the founding Congress. This group elects the party's president (art. 14), the Central Political Committee (CPC), and an organism responsible for economic auditing (art. 13.2). The CPC, the highest political organ, is constituted by approximately 200 members and is responsible for implementing the decisions adopted by the Congress. The Committee elects the party's executive – Political Secretariat and his/her Secretary (art. 13.1), which is a considerably smaller (less than ten members) and, thus, more effective organ for coordinating political actions and accountable to the CPC. The CPC also hosts 'departments', which are specific bodies responsible for party policy-making on particular issues concerning health, environment, local administration, and other topics, which are open to both members and non-members (art. 20). Internal party referenda are envisaged for major issues (art. 17). As for the Youth Section, this functions according to its own statute and retains considerable autonomy vis-à-vis the party, also in terms of organization (Transition Articles, II).[2] However, its organizational structure resembles that of SYRIZA, being based on similar organisms (Congress-Council-Secretariat) and, thus, imbued with a top-down rationale.

As quoted in SYRIZA's statute (art. 29), the party's financial resources include members' and friends' subscriptions and support, MPs' and salaried members' regular contributions, crowd-funding campaigns and ad hoc initiatives, as well as state subsidies. In the Greek party system, political parties are funded by the state depending on electoral results; in practice, however, dependence on private interests has grown parallel to the growth of state financing (Vernardakis 2012), while most parties are currently greatly indebted to private banks. SYRIZA's impressive electoral breakthrough in June 2012 provided the small coalition with significant funding, as its members' contributions have been very small. At the same time, since 2012, SYRIZA's MPs have been asked to provide a significant percentage of their salary to the party (20 per cent), as well as to a 'solidarity repository' (20 per cent) that funds the 'Solidarity4all' initiative described below. In any case, no particular innovations related to transparency or social funding have been suggested or adopted by SYRIZA to promote an image of 'autonomy from the state'.[3] Within the same context, no alternative forms of participation (online or offline) in the party's life and decision-making have been put forward: the lack of such a need, from both its members and its electorate, testifies to the fact that the party does not want or need to present itself as an alternative actor to the mainstream party system, but represents itself as distinctive *within* the already existing system.

Beyond the organizational structure and internal democracy described in the party's statute, SYRIZA has developed a hierarchical structure, especially after becoming the main opposition party in 2012, as testified by several interviewees. Even after the 2013 Congress that called for factions' formal dissolution, these remained strongly institutionalized in practice, sectarian and inward-looking, still defining the party dynamics at the local level. That was also the case regarding the party's engagement with unionism (I13G) but has even influenced the internal life of the Youth Section, which has also been divided into groups according to different factions (I2G). This organizational structure had generated a complicated and sectarian approach to politics that looked parochial, especially at a time when social needs and movements' practices have been moving to a different direction, striving for common, horizontal struggles beyond conventional politicization. As observed by one interviewee, a member of the party: 'New people attending the local meetings could not understand what was all that about, they were asking for convergence and found themselves faced with all this debating' (I8G).

More generally, individual members' initiative and energy were frustrated as SYRIZA 'draws from the Leninist tradition of party organization' (I7G; I24G). The underlying logic of its functioning was 'still part of the nineteenth-century organization of left-wing parties', which trusted the experts and those higher up in the hierarchy rather than the ordinary members (I3G). The party platforms, such as for instance the 'Thessaloniki Programme' (2014a) upon which SYRIZA took power, are most often drafted by 'specialists' or those participating in centralized organisms and not by ordinary members through participatory or democratic processes. Since 2012, most of these have not been debated or ratified by local branches or regional committees but just presented *a posteriori* in order to confirm a decision already taken elsewhere and absorb any dissenting voices (I3G, I5G, I6G). Even if local assemblies are indeed autonomous and have the opportunity to function as their members wish, their decisions, innovations, or disagreements cannot have any impact on the policy-making and the line adopted from above.

This has been reflected in levels of participation that were extremely low before 2009, and did not change strikingly after the eruption of the crisis – even after 2012, when the electoral power of the party increased immensely and beyond any expectation. Membership increased from 10,000 to approximately 30,000 members from 2009 to 2013, while the Youth's membership rose from 1,000 to 2,500 members.[4] Although an impressive rise, it certainly does not reflect the electoral growth of the party in numbers and does not concern the younger cohorts, among whom SYRIZA is mostly popular. According to those party members interviewed, young voters could not really fit into the party's patterns of action and internal procedures, which have been dominated since the outset by factionalism and excessive introspection (Tsakatika and Eleftheriou 2013, 10). Far from being deliberative and inclusive, internal decision-making processes became routinized and ineffective. 'There were so many people calling us daily at Koumoundourou [party's headquarters], especially after the 2012 elections, but also after the 2015 ones, asking for ways to help, to offer support.... But we didn't know how, we never called them back...and that kept happening', says a young party member (I2G). People wanted to join and contribute to what they perceived as 'new', but there were no available or new party structures to make use of these emerging resources (I5G).

Although SYRIZA members changed up to 2015 due to their osmosis with social movements and anti-austerity struggles, the pyramid-like structure impeded people from taking responsibilities and influencing the party, while at the same time no new forms of organization or structures were created (I11G). There is still, even in implicit form, 'a lack of trust from the non-members, to those coming from outside, to bottom-up processes' (I3G). SYRIZA, even if different from other parties in the country, is still considered as part of the old political system: activists participating in movements, no matter how supportive of it they may be, consider as given that they would never join as members (I18G, I25G).

As discussed above, some SYRIZA members were already part of social movements when the crisis erupted; it was due to this encounter on the ground that the party met at some point with the anti-austerity mobilizations and listened to their demands. However, it never allowed a movement-like mentality to run through its organization or a different paradigm of doing politics to be created. The looseness from which the party paradoxically benefited also reflected the lack of strategic planning for a different organizational model. Notwithstanding its great electoral victory, when SYRIZA took power in 2015 it remained part of the old establishment in terms of organization, membership, and decision-making structures.

3.2.2. SYRIZA's repertoire of action: A SYRIZA beyond SYRIZA

As stated above, SYN's 'left turn' and the establishment of SYRIZA in 2004 aimed at the creation of a 'radical left' actor, which also entailed a different strategy concerning the party's relationships with social movements. In practice, this was translated into its involvement since the early 2000s in the emerging new social movements and activism.

On the one hand, then, SYRIZA took part in a new wave of transnational contention: through its young cadres, the party engaged in the Global Justice Movement, participating in the Genoa anti-G8 protests in 2001, contributing to the formation of the Greek Social Forum, and coordinating the 4th European Social Forum (held in Athens in 2006), while also participating in the anti-war movement of the early 2000s (Panagyiotakis 2015; Papanikolopoulos and Roggas 2015; I1-7G, I10G, I18–20G, I24G). On the other hand, party members also became involved in the student movement that shook the country during 2006–7 against planned government reforms. All interviewed members of the Youth of SYRIZA had joined the party throughout or due to this wave of university protest, as this was how 'what was created in Genoa was introduced in the domestic context' (I2G). Moreover, in 2008 SYRIZA was the only parliamentary party that did not condemn, but on the contrary stood by the youth uprising following the killing of a fifteen-year-old boy by a police officer in the centre of Athens. At that time SYRIZA lost much of its support, being targeted by a whole apparatus as an 'accomplice of violence'. However, it gradually acquired the role of the political representative of social and especially youth struggles, which progressively became focal points in SYN and SYRIZA's political discourse, acting as symbols of a broader anti-neoliberal profile (Katsampekis 2015).

What has, then, been fundamental about SYN's building of a radical left profile through SYRIZA were the 'secondary' and most probably unintended consequences of such a strategic choice – namely 'the process of learning and training of a younger generation of members into activism' (I3G). Many of the 2000s movements had been characterized by the notoriously heavy-handed treatment of demonstrators by the police (Karamichas 2009; 2012), while mainstream parties and media outlets strongly condemned collective protests and accused SYRIZA – although it was insignificant at that time – of fomenting, or even coordinating them (Eleftheriou 2009). Accordingly, young members became familiarized with confrontational politics – both in the streets and in terms of political debate – a mentality that started to run through the party bottom-up, as those young cadres became members of the CPC in the early 2000s to gradually acquire key positions.

It is telling that Alexis Tsipras, the current political leader of the party, or Tasos Koronakis, the Secretary of the CPC until August 2015, participated in the 2001 Genoa protests and were both secretaries of the youth organization in the early 2000s. During that period, a significant overlap between movement activists and party members started to take place (Spourdalakis 2014), while SYRIZA Youth was becoming active in anti-racist festivals, political prisoners' committees, and urban movements (I1G, I3–4G, I10G): the idea that was gradually growing was that 'being members of the party does not mean we are different from other movement collectives' (I2G), something that was in sharp contrast with the strategy adopted by other left-wing parties. As a result, when the crisis erupted in 2010, even if there was no official line defining the party's strategy towards anti-austerity mobilizations, numerous party members (especially the younger ones) were already part, more or less actively, of resistance initiatives.

From 2009 onward, Greece saw the intensification of protests, with general strikes, massive demonstrations, and building occupations alongside violent attacks against politicians, supermarket lootings, anti-fascist mobilizations, open public assemblies and Indignados square gatherings, alternative information and solidarity networks and workers' collectives. In general, SYRIZA was there, through its (mostly young) members and several MPs, who were open to broadening its own repertoire of action along with society itself. However, the party's resources and experience in the social movement field were comparatively limited and, as a result, SYRIZA did not launch any mobilizations itself, conventional or novel, nor did it independently organize any protest events and contentious space or invent forms of action. SYRIZA had not even been a decisive part of any significant movement (I2G, I10G) – for instance, the squares movement, which was not and could not have been a product of SYRIZA's steering (Tsakatika and Eleftheriou 2013). Exceptions were a series of original events staged during 2010–12 in public by the Youth Section, traditionally the most radical and movement-oriented cohort of the party.

The sole innovation introduced by SYRIZA during the crisis was the 'Solidarity 4 All' platform created in 2012. This was an umbrella organization that aimed at facilitating the development and networking of solidarity structures across the country. It functioned as a rather autonomous horizontal assembly providing financial support and resources to thousands of small initiatives across the country, linking the party with social movements (I1G, I5G, I10G).[5]

One interviewee, a member of the party, when asked about SYRIZA's engagement with protest events during the crisis and until its rise to power (2015), gave a revealing answer:

> [I]n reality Syriza grew by constructing around it a series of networks with other political groups, individual activists, grassroots initiatives, movement-like things.... This created a Syriza beyond Syriza, a broader Syriza, a socially-oriented Syriza, something much bigger than the actual local branches of its members, than the actual sum of its members and organizations...and this network had a much bigger impact on the development of the party than the actual work of its organized members. (I10G)

As Kanellopoulos and Kostopoulos (2013) have aptly demonstrated in a quantitative analysis, SYRIZA has managed to create a very open alliance strategy both to its left and to its right: on the one hand it has officially participated in the administration of the General Confederation of Greek Workers (GSEE/ADEDY), and, especially, has attracted many defected PASOK MPs and rank-and-file social democrats; while, on the other, it has developed relations to grassroots trade unions, has established strong ties with social justice groups, and has fully embraced the squares movement.

As for its institutional role, adopting a broad *'anti mnemoniaki'* (against MoUs) agenda since the eruption of the crisis and especially when in opposition (2012–15), SYRIZA brought into parliament almost all movement claims heard in the streets (concerning labour rights' abuses, fascist violence, cuts in healthcare, education, and welfare provisions, and political corruption), demanding through the rejection of the MoUs an overall change not only of political personnel, but also of the functioning of democracy in the country. However, since the party took power and signed the third MoU (July 2015), most of these claims have been removed, at least in terms of overall demands.

To conclude, notwithstanding its proximity to grassroots practices, SYRIZA has been since the outset a parliamentary party mostly familiar with institutional proceedings and mechanisms, alliances, and contradictions. As such, it is not a party emerging from the movements, nor did it grow according to a movement-like strategy (I1–2G, I4–5G, I10G); on the contrary, it needed the movements in order to move forward. It has been common sense for almost all interviewees that the reference point to and the driving force for the anti-austerity movement in the country was not to be found in SYRIZA, as, moreover, a considerable part of activists remained hesitant towards the presence of a political party in the mobilizations and accused it of adopting co-optation strategies for electoral gains. Nonetheless, as a result of its 'left turn' in the early 2000s, some of SYRIZA's members have been consistently part of mobilizations, by being committed, sensitive to grievances, and open to adopting and serving activist initiatives. It was through associating with social grievances that the party looked radically different from the ruling ones and managed to gain the trust of (part of) the people during an era of severe legitimacy crisis and become a governing party.

3.3. The organizational repertoire of Podemos

Among the three movement parties discussed in this book, Podemos is by far the youngest one. Its funding processes preceded the first electoral test of just a few weeks. The Constituent Assembly was organized some months after the 2014 European elections. Despite its political identity based on common sense and beyond traditional political categories, the legacy of leftist organizations emerges in the organizational structure of the new party. Classical elements of leftist parties are, however, mingled with original features in terms of membership, funding, and participatory instruments.

3.3.1. Podemos' structure: A peculiar mix of innovation and tradition

At the organizational level, Podemos combines a participatory rhetoric and vision, although with a networked structure that is highly centralized (Rendueles and Sola 2015). Some authors have described it as a combination of verticality and horizontality (Galindo et al. 2015). On the one hand, the party originated from a top-down strategy elaborated by a group of political entrepreneurs (Iglesias and his collaborators) and presents clear personalization trends. On the other hand, the organizational model adopted during its Constituent Assembly (November 2014) also relies on digital media and tools for facilitating a decentralized and participatory organization and combines elements of movement parties with features of traditional parties. According to the lengthy document (sixty pages) on organizational principles (OPP 2014) (approved in the Constituent Assembly), the organizational structure of Podemos pursues three goals: participation, transparency, and democratic control (art. 6).

In order to join Podemos, the only requirements are filling in a form on its website and being older than fourteen (art. 12).[6] The online registration allows participation in the various decision-making processes of the party with a permanent voting code. No payment of membership fees is requested, and any monetary contribution is voluntary. This helps

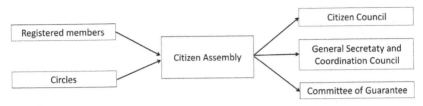

Figure 3.2.   Podemos' organizational structure

in creating a 'liquid' involvement in Podemos, drawing nebulous borders between the inside and the outside of the party. This is very similar to the kind of belonging established by the Indignados movement (I6S) and is intended 'to add a greater number of citizens to the analysis, the decision-making and the management of the public' (art. 6). Currently, there are more than 390,650 people registered in Podemos, according to its website.[7] However, this number is not adjusted to the organizational reality of the party and therefore the census is now under check and control.[8]

Participation is something that might be purely instrumental or circumstantial, not necessarily related with direct ties to the organization or to a strong political identity. In fact, many people have simply registered to participate in any of the internal processes (I14S). This leads to a distinction between registered and effective participants, causing recurrent problems. As such, the feeling of belonging to the party is extremely diverse among participants. In the words of a feminist activist in Madrid: 'I do not really know if I am actually a member of Podemos. Some days I feel I am, but others I feel myself very far away from the project' (I11S).

According to the OPP, the main organisms of the party are: the circles, the Citizen Assembly, the Citizen Council, the General Secretary and the Coordination Council, and the Committee of Guarantee (Figure 3.2).

The OPP defines the Circle as 'the basic unit of organization in Podemos' and as 'the tool that can promote participation, debate and active linkages with society' (art. 6). The role of linkage of the Circles with civil society and social movements is underlined in Article 58. During the months following the launch of Podemos, hundreds (around one thousand) of sectorial and territorial Circles (including those outside Spain) were created following a self-organized model and promoting a new kind of 'liquid' militancy (Galindo et al. 2015). Since the Constituent Assembly, these Circles have been undergoing a process of official sanctioning through a ratifying protocol.[9] They have suffered a dramatic decrease in their activities and functions relegated by the current prominence of the Citizen Councils. The emergence of local candidatures has also provoked the migration of many activists to these political spaces (I10S).

The Citizen Assembly is the highest decision-making body of Podemos and exercises its functions continuously (art. 10). Everyone who is registered is entitled to participate and vote in the Citizens' Assembly decision-making processes, using all the available tools (Circles, meeting places, polling stations in squares and parks, and so on), including the digital instruments. According to Article 11, this assembly should be consulted in order to take decisions on every relevant issue, such as strategic orientation, electoral lists, programme elaboration, election/recall of members of different internal bodies, agreements with other political forces, statutes amendments, and so on.

The Citizen Council is the executive body of the party (art. 17), composed of eighty-one members: the General Secretary, seventeen regional General Secretaries, a member elected by the registered people outside Spain, and sixty-two members elected directly by the Citizen Assembly. During the Constituent Assembly, all of the members elected by the assembly belonged to the team presented by Pablo Iglesias. This unanimity has led to some internal critiques regarding the lack of plurality and pluralism of this body (I11S, I14S). According to a member of the party in Madrid: 'We have spoken out much about transversality and inclusiveness but inwardly I think we have had a problem in managing the internal plurality and incorporating it into the spaces of decision' (I5S).

The General Secretary is also elected by the Citizen Assembly, which also has the functions of selecting the members of the Coordination Council. This body supports the daily tasks of the Secretary (internal coordination and public requirements). It is formed by between ten and fifteen members elected by the Citizen Assembly but proposed by the Secretary (art. 25). During the Constituent Assembly, the figure of the General Secretary was the object of controversy. The main alternative organizational model supported a collective body rather than an individual one, considered alien to the tradition of social movements and excessively personalistic.

The Committee of Guarantee is expected to safeguard the rights of registered people in Podemos as well as the fundamental principles and rules of the party (art. 26). Formed by ten people (five permanent, five substitutes) – at least half of them lawyers – it is elected directly by the Citizen Assembly (art. 27). The current members belong to a list supported by Iglesias and his team; criticisms have been raised because of a potential lack of political independence. Regarding the territorial structure of Podemos, the organizational model described above based on Citizen Assembly, Citizen Council, and General Secretary has been replicated in cities or villages, with more than one hundred people registered in the party (art. 30).

Podemos has defined and developed some participatory instruments, putting them at the core of the party's decision-making (OPP 2014, 6). These include open primaries, digital tools, and citizens' inquiries. The organization of open primaries to select the candidates was understood as a strategic resource to overcome the apparatus of traditional parties (mainly, leftist ones). According to the leader, primaries would serve to avoid 'militant nuclei to isolate us from the wishes of society, to hijack the organization' (Iglesias 2015a). Primaries were first introduced for the election of the candidates to the European election. Since then, they have been used several times. Although this mechanism is quite innovative and participatory, it has also provoked negative outcomes in the internal life of Podemos, generating a logic of competitiveness within the party (I9–10S, I13S) between one group supported by party's leaders (called 'Claro que Podemos' – Sure We Can) and several internal critical groups at different territorial levels. Many of these internal opposition groups survived over time with generally weak institutionalization. This has engendered fragmentation and polarization (particularly in relation to organizational issues) at both the national and the regional and local levels. However, factionalism also mirrors the plurality and diverse ideologies, interests, and subcultures existing within the party. The management of this plurality is considered as one of the main challenges for Podemos (I4S, I8S, I13–14S).

Interestingly, a declining tendency in the level of participation in the primaries can be noted. For instance, those organized to form the electoral list for the general election (July 2015) mobilized only 15.7 per cent of the people enrolled in the party (Figure 3.3). The broad feeling among many citizens that Podemos' primaries are really non-competitive might explain this trend (I11S, I13S).

Podemos has experimented with existing commercial online platforms that have seldom been used by social movements (Romanos and Sádaba 2015). The most intensively used tools have been *Plaza Podemos* and *Appgree*.[10] The first has become an enormous agora displaying 'hot news' related to the party and has been defined as a digital square, 'with collective life which thinks, debates and cooperates socializing information and generating debates and processes of collective intelligence' (Toret 2015, 132). In Plaza Podemos, 'the community of participants feels that they are deciding what the most relevant topics are, expanding some threads and closing others' (Romanos and Sádaba 2015). In November 2014 (coinciding with the debates around the Constituent Assembly), it reached its highest level of participation with more than 2,400,000 page views and more than 280,000 unique users (Ardanuy and Labuske

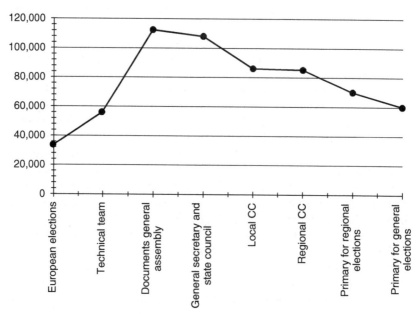

Figure 3.3.   Evolution of the participation in Podemos' primaries

2015, 102). Since then, there has been a decrease in the level of participation. Currently there are over 11,000 registered users[11] and the tool has also been used for other territorial levels of the party. *Appgree* is a communication tool useful for organizing massive gatherings and protests. This app 'allows quick opinion polls to be carried out, and the opinion of participants can be viewed at a glance' (Romanos and Sádaba 2015).

Other participatory tools implemented by Podemos are the Citizens' inquiries. This instrument is used for relevant issues apart from the ones considered as the exclusive competency of the Citizen Assembly. Inquiries – whose results are binding – can be called at the national level by the General Secretary, by the absolute majority of the Citizen Council, by 10 per cent of the registered members,[12] or by 20 per cent of the Circles. At the national level, just one inquiry took place to define the potential electoral coalitions for the general election.[13] The turnout was very low (only 44,792 people participated, just 11.6 per cent of the total registered), and 84.6 per cent of participants supported the option defended by Iglesias. At the regional level, inquiries have been organized to determine the formation of electoral coalitions and to confirm Podemos' support for the regional socialist presidents.[14] Finally, at the local level, dozens of Citizens' inquiries have been organized, most of them with the goal of making a decision about the form in which to participate in the local elections.[15]

The intensive use of all these participatory tools does not preclude a plebiscitarian relationship between leaders and members. As some interviewees have stated, the digital platforms might favour participation, but they are not intrinsically democratic. The main critical aspect of such procedures concerns who defines the issues on which members are consulted. Until now, apparently, citizens have been consulted top-down on a set of questions defined by the leaders and generally oriented to ratify their previous decisions (Galindo et al. 2015).

The charismatic leadership of Pablo Iglesias has been built over time through his frequent participation in political talk shows. Although contested within the party, this has been considered as an essential factor to do politics in the party field (Errejón 2014). Moreover, the personalization around Iglesias has been seen as functional to develop a direct link between the leader and the people. Personalization also represented an important resource for a political party that was officially founded only a few weeks before the European elections and was practically unknown to most Spaniards.

Regarding funding, Spanish parties have historically been dependent on the state (Casal et al. 2014). This situation created disincentives to building large membership parties (Méndez Lago 2007) or establishing a more structural relationship with civil society (Van Biezen 2000; Vergé 2012). The party finance regime has historically penalized small parties and has made it more difficult for newcomers to enter the system due to state reimbursement of electoral expenses (Van Biezen 2004). This method has reinforced the disproportional tendencies of the electoral system (ibid.). Moreover, the main Spanish parties have increasingly become indebted with private banks in order to finance electoral campaigns.[16] The purple party adopted a very innovative model to finance its activities, in order to distinguish itself from traditional parties. Its funding model seeks three different goals: independence, transparency, and innovation.[17] According to one of the party founders, 'If people did not support us, if they did not give money, then nothing would be possible. But people supported us also economically' (I6S).

The current funding model of Podemos is based on: (a) state funding, through the public subsidies to parties depending on electoral results; (b) crowd-funding, for specific campaigns and initiatives; (c) micro-credits,[18] subscribed with the party in order to support economically the electoral campaigns, which are returned once Podemos receives the reimbursement; (d) economic contributions of participants (non-mandatory); (e) salaries of the representatives in public institutions.[19] According to the Ethical Code[20] of Podemos (EC 6, XI a), all representatives earn three times the Spanish minimum salary (in total, around 1,880 euros). The rest of the salary is devolved to the party and part of it assigned to the 'Impulsa' (boost) project.[21] This initiative – which seeks to establish links with civil society groups – is a public competition among different social projects. The winners get a grant from Podemos in order to finance their proposals. This original funding model is probably the most innovative and supported element developed by the party, as even the most critical activists tend to appreciate it. As one member of the 'critical faction' of Podemos explains, 'It is clear that although I think that Podemos has been increasingly becoming a traditional party, the funding system makes a difference' (I7S).

The innovations related to the funding also include some elements of transparency. In this sense, all of the finances of Podemos are open (entirely available on the website quarterly), extensively detailed,[22] monitored and audited by external groups.

3.3.2. A 'reliable' actor: Podemos' strategies and repertoire of action

Pablo Iglesias has referred repeatedly to the main goal of Podemos as 'assaulting the skies'. The focus on this goal has translated into turning the party into 'an electoral war machinery', in the words of party strategist Íñigo Errejón. As such, the new party has mainly adopted conventional forms of action, especially since its entrance into the regional representative assemblies. However, this general tendency is not opposed to taking part, whenever considered appropriate, in unconventional actions.

On 31 January 2015, Podemos organized 'The March of Change'.[23] The rally brought together between 100,000 and 300,000 people from all over the country and ended with a crowded final meeting at the symbolic Puerta del Sol. The demonstration was called as an attempt to show the strength of the party, but without defined political goals. However, the march was articulated on three axes: sovereignty, democracy, and rights. Even if this type of demonstration (framed as a party-event) was alien to the tradition of socio-political mobilizations in Spain, Podemos used the march to 'maintain the idea that they are a hybrid movement/party that primarily seeks to give expression to popular feelings and needs' (Flesher-Fominaya 2015). This has been the only demonstration with such characteristics organized by the purple party.

Despite the decreasing trend of mobilizations in Spain, Podemos has been involved in different protest activities, actively supporting various protest events organized by diverse platforms involving several social and political organizations. Among them, we could cite the campaign against the 'Transatlantic Trade Investment Partnership' (TTIP), the active participation in some traditional events of social movements (such as the feminist protests around 8 March or the LGBT pride day on 28 June). The party has also been actively involved in the protests supporting the refugees or in the campaign of the 'Euromarches 2015'.[24] At the local level, it is also involved in campaigns and protest events launched by social movements (I10S, I12S).

The strategy of Podemos in the representative assemblies is mainly oriented to present itself as a challenging opposition and an alternative to bipartisanship. However, parliamentary activity is useful to the party in order to spread a public image of 'accuracy and reliability'.[25] According to an activist from Madrid: 'For us, institutional work is a big challenge because there we cannot fail; our adversaries are really looking forward to seeing us making evident mistakes at the institutional level. So we have to show much rigour to appear as a solid alternative' (I5S).

Regarding the relations with other parties at the institutional level, Podemos has refused to establish alliances with the PSOE. The strategic orientation followed by the party has been to support the investiture of PSOE's candidates in order to unseat the PP, but not to participate in the regional governments.

The main issues held by Podemos in the institutions are threefold (I6S): (a) human rights defence (i.e. support to migrants); (b) anti-austerity and defence of public services; (c) anti-corruption and political renewal. After its entrance into several regional parliaments, there was an ongoing effort to coordinate the tasks in such institutions. Two of the main initiatives driven by Podemos' elected representatives were: a coordinated institutional campaign against the TTIP,[26] and the prioritization of the payment of social benefits instead of other institutional expenses.[27] Activity in regional assemblies has also focused on public audits, emergency plans, anti-eviction laws, and cuts to the salaries and expenses of the institutions and representatives.

Finally, Podemos' elected representatives have also participated in protests and events launched by social movements at the international level. For instance, MEPs have actively supported various initiatives such as the Blockupy protest in Frankfurt (March 2015) or the last edition of the World Social Forum in Tunisia (I6S).

3.4. The M5S' organizational repertoire

Compared to the other movement parties analysed in this book, the M5S is very loosely organized, building its very identity on a distinct organizational model very far from traditional political parties in terms of membership, funding, and participatory instruments. The party label is even rejected in the very name of this political force, which self-presents as 'a movement'. Despite this, however, lack of formal organizational processes and bodies makes Grillo's creature extremely dependent on leaders' resources and decisions, while the organizational evolution appears as a sudden (often incoherent) reaction to internal or external shocks.

3.4.1. The peculiar organizational structure of the M5S: A 'non-party'

In September 2009, Beppe Grillo announced the birth of a national movement based on the 'charter of Florence', which had been agreed upon in a public assembly a few months before.[28] The charter would serve as a kind of manifesto for virtuous municipalities and should work as a common programme based on '5 stars' – environmental protection, public water, renewable energy, public transport, and sustainable development – for the 'certified lists' endorsed by Grillo in local elections. In October, the M5S was officially funded in Milan, presenting a detailed political programme and the rules for joining the Movement. An important document shedding light on the nature of the party is the so-called 'non-statute', issued in December of the same year. It resembles a constitution, although its very short length (only seven articles) and its name clearly indicate the difference with conventional statutes of traditional parties.[29]

According to Article 1, describing the nature of the Movement, the M5S is a 'non-association' and has to be understood as 'a vehicle for discussion and consultation which originated from the www.beppegrillo.it blog. The location of the M5S fits in with the web address www.beppegrillo.it. Contact with the M5S is exclusively through email.' Differently from traditional parties, the M5S headquarters is Grillo's blog, and any kind of communication is supposed to take place online. Physical places are not contemplated at all – as such, the M5S appears as a paradigmatic case of post-bureaucratic organization (Bimber 2003).

The peculiar nature of the Movement is further clarified in Article 4, describing its scope and goals: 'The internet is recognized as a prime tool in the process of consultation, deliberation, decision and choice for the movement itself. The "5 Stars Movement" is not a political party nor does it have the goal of becoming one in the future. It seeks being an avenue for achieving an effective exchange of ideas and democratic debate using the internet as the means of communications normally assigned to political representatives.'

In terms of membership, the 'non-statute' clarifies in Articles 5 and 6 that joining the Movement is no different from subscribing to a website, as it simply requires registration on Grillo's blog and no payment of membership fees is needed. However, in order to complete the registration and become a member with voting rights on the blog, one must send a digital copy of one's ID to Grillo's staff. Article 7 confirms the pivotal role of the internet, defining the blog as the place for the presentation and discussion of the Movement's candidates.

Another important aspect of the Movement's nature is illustrated in Article 3, claiming that 'The name of the M5S is connected to a trademark registered on behalf of Beppe Grillo, the sole owner of the rights of use.' This article illustrates the proprietary nature of the Movement and clearly identifies Grillo as the sole leader. This provision makes the M5S close to a business firm model, an exemplary case of a 'franchise party' (Carty 2004).

Regarding the distribution of power and the relations among the different faces of the party, decisions at the local level are generally made autonomously by territorial groups (Biorcio 2015a; Tronconi 2015b), while the national leaders (Grillo and Gianroberto Casaleggio,[30] the co-founder of the M5S passed away in April 2016, a seasoned tech-entrepreneur who normally remained behind the scenes) make the most important strategic choices at the national level (I1I; I2I). At the top, around the leaders, there is what everyone calls the 'staff', which has never been clearly described in terms of members and tasks (I3I), although it manages the blog, checks documents sent by supporters to become members, certifies local lists allowing or denying the use of the symbol in electoral consultations, and takes care of the party's communication at the national level.

Lacking any intermediate structure between its different faces, in order to create a linkage – or a whip, according to some critical observers (Biancalana and Tronconi 2014, 131) – between the party in central office and the party in public office, the leaders imposed the presence of 'communication groups', both in the two chambers of the national parliament and in the European Parliament. As clarified in the codes of conduct signed by MPs before their election, the members of such groups are indicated by the leaders, ratified by the MPs, and funded with the resources of the parliamentary groups.[31] According to the codes, MPs are explicitly prohibited from coalescing with other parties as they can only support specific proposals made by other groups in parliament. Spokespersons and coordinators of the parliamentary group change every three months. The rotation principle – inspired and adapted in a much lighter form from Green parties[32] – is supposed to counteract professionalization (Poguntke 1993).

Financially, MPs have to report on monthly expenses for their parliamentary activity. The exact amount of their stipend is also specified in the code of conduct (5,000 euros gross). Recalling a tradition from socialist and communist parties, part of the salary is to be given back. However, the money is not supposed to maintain the party but is used to provide micro-credits to small and medium enterprises. Electoral campaigns are self-funded through 'micro-donations' that amounted to 774,000 euros for the 2013 general elections.[33] The M5S entirely refused almost 43 million euros that were due as electoral reimbursements, whereas the ordinary contributions to parliamentary groups have been used for hiring collaborators and funding communication groups. The same model of funding also applies to other types of elections.

Concerning relations with the media, MPs are advised to avoid participation in political talk shows, and they have to refuse the title of 'honourable', opting instead for the term 'citizen'. MPs are obliged to resign in case of conviction. In cases of violations of the code of conduct and the 'non-statute', they can be expelled from the M5S group. The expulsion must be ratified by an online vote on Grillo's blog.

Over time, tensions between leaders and MPs have been solved with massive expulsions of 'dissidents' or voluntary exits from the parliamentary groups: almost one fifth in the Chamber of Deputies and one third in the Senate of the Republic.[34] Other representatives in local institutions – not only regional and municipal councillors but also a few mayors – have been expelled from the party over the years, having been accused of violating its basic rules. Expulsions have generally been announced out of the blue from the blog without being preceded by any internal debate.

Shortly after a new wave of expulsions from the parliamentary groups and dramatic protests at the gates of Grillo's villa in Tuscany by groups of activists advocating for more democracy, supporting dissidents, and asking for formalization of *de facto* hierarchies (*Il Fatto Quotidiano*, 27 November 2014), the M5S leader responded on his blog: 'The M5S needs a representative structure that is broader than the current one. This is a fact. Me, the camper and the blog are no longer enough.... Thus *while staying in the role of the guardian of the M5S*, I've decided to put forward the names of five people...able to operate on a broader scale for the M5S throughout the country and in parliament.'[35] The decision was ratified by an online consultation.

The goal of this organism consists in linking the party in public office more effectively with the party on the ground, national representatives with local ones, and with those constituencies that are considered the core of M5S support such as small entrepreneurs (SMEs), associations and students. These are some of the social groups that mostly contributed to the electoral success of the M5S in the 2013 elections (Pedrazzani and Pinto 2015; Mosca 2015a).

Other important changes to the organizational structure of the M5S took place at the end of 2014.[36] The formalization of the organizational roles as well as the clarification of some rules were included in a new regulation[37] required by law no. 13 of 2014, which abolished direct public funding of political parties, imposing on them the requirements of transparency and democracy in order to access forms of indirect and voluntary contributions. Such regulation is a completion of the 'non-statute' and defines other formal organisms that flank the 'political leader' and the aforementioned 'representative structure'. In particular, it establishes an 'appeal committee' made up of three members, with the function of judging the appeals to expulsion orders. The regulation introduces, among other things, the possibility of an online vote if requested by at least one fifth of the members, and the control of online ballots by a 'technical independent body' named by the 'governing council' for three years.[38]

On closer inspection, however, the organizational evolution described above does not seem to question Grillo's role but simply to formalize it as the 'political leader'. To be noted is that the composition of both the 'representative structure' – which is not even mentioned in the regulation and whose functions have never been clearly codified – and the 'appeal committee'[39] are decided by Grillo and then ratified by members with an online vote. Even the new mechanism supposed to provide the possibility of online consultations proposed from below appears very difficult to implement.[40]

M5S' organizational structure can be summarized as follows (Figure 3.4): the party in central office includes Grillo and (while he was alive) Casaleggio, supported by the work of a staff of techies now coordinated by Casaleggio Jr. The party on the ground is mostly constituted by local autonomous groups organized through the Meetup platform at the municipal level.[41] The party in central office is made up of hundreds of municipal and regional councillors, 18 mayors, 126 MPs, and 18 MEPs.

While supposed to ease the relation between the party in central office and the party in public office, communication groups have often clashed with elected representatives since M5S' entrance into national and European institutions. These conflicts are testified by the frequent changes at the top of the groups[42] and by the negative assessment of some MPs (Vignati 2015, 35). MPs and other elected representatives belonging to local Meetups connect the party in public office with the party on the ground through their participation in periodical open meetings ('agoras'). No connections exist between the grassroots and the

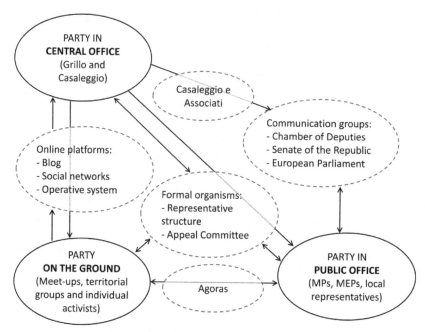

Figure 3.4.   Schematization of the three faces of the M5S and their reciprocal relations

leaders beyond online platforms. The creation of intermediate organisms introduced over time to ease the relations among the different faces of the party represented a response to internal (voice/dissent) or external shocks (adaptation to new laws) that, however, did not solve structural organizational problems.

It should be noted that the rules defining the functioning of the Movement have been incrementally defined over time, in various documents, often due to the need to regulate contingent issues or adapt to specific law requirements. Overall, the rules defining internal functioning appear very fragmented, incomplete, and sometimes unclear or even contradictory. The absence of a detailed constitution defining clear roles and rules certainly represents a relevant limitation for the party.

Digital platforms have been presented as a constitutive element of Grillo's party. As Dal Lago (2014) argued, Casaleggio presents a utopian vision of the internet, conceiving it not simply as a tool capable of improving democracy, but as democracy itself. However, the M5S' organizational structure presents gaps that can hardly be filled by online tools. Online consultations of Movement members via Grillo's blog and their involvement in the discussion on laws sitting in parliament are the main modes of implementation of the party's direct democratic ideals.

Online ballots were introduced with the primary elections of December 2012, intended to select candidates for the national parliament. However, their use has been rather discontinuous: in 2013, only three of them took place; during 2014, members were invited to express themselves twenty-three times; and only four of them took place in 2015. Members' participation in online ballots over three years (December 2012–December 2015) has changed significantly, too. While the first votes benefited from a 'novelty effect' with a turnout of around 60 per cent, from the third ballot onwards, the percentage of participants decreased to a rate that on average fluctuates between 30 and 40 per cent of those eligible. The downward trend has become more pronounced over time, so that the number of participants in the latest ballots declined even further (Mosca 2015b).

The long series of votes on the blog highlighted some critical issues that are still unresolved and make the use of this tool quite problematic: (a) limited transparency of procedures and incomplete displaying of results; (b) the timing of the consultations, often announced by email at short notice, usually lasting one day and available only during working hours; (c) the choice of topics determined exclusively by the leaders; (d) incomplete and asymmetric information – leaders' preference is generally clearly stressed, at the expense of contrasting claims; (e) exclusive control of the voting process by the staff, allowing possible manipulation.

Beyond online ballots, members' involvement in the discussion of laws sitting in representative assemblies (from the European Parliament to regional assemblies) has been made possible since November 2013 with the software 'Lex'. Considering the discussions already closed by the end of 2015, numbers were very similar for the two years: 79 in 2014, and 81 in 2015, slightly below an average of seven discussions per month. Also in this case, participation has significantly decreased over time. The average number of comments per law was 511 in 2014 and 179 in 2015. A regional councillor of the M5S summarized the problematic aspects of this instrument as follows:

> [Y]ou cannot publish on the Internet a text that is already built – and no one knows how or by whom – expecting to amend it with suggestions or changes. A representative does not have the time to sift 6–7,000 comments that for the most part are not even 'adequate' as being too generic, not expressing technical criticisms.... Therefore, a very dispersive, ineffective and inefficient direct democracy has been built, not allowing the legislator to take advantage of collective

intelligence. Right now, I see too many problems and only few benefits. (I4I)

3.4.2. M5S' repertoire of action: Protesting outside and inside institutions

Grillo had been organizing rallies and marches before the official birth of the M5S. As seen, the 'V-days' represented important events in defining the Movement's identity, its contentious nature as well as its shift from latency in the web to visibility through mass protests (Mosca 2014). The party's repertoire comprises forms of unconventional action that have not been discarded since its entry into national parliament: occupations, public protests, sit-ins, and demonstrations have often been used by its MPs. The tactical emulation and imitation of a repertoire of action typical of resource-poor actors (Lipsky 1968) is functional for the M5S to gain media attention and public visibility.

During 2013, 2014, and 2015, demonstrations opposing oil drilling in southern regions, against high-speed trains in Val Susa and in other areas, contesting carbon plants, incinerators and garbage dumps were organized or supported by the M5S with the participation of its elected representatives (Mosca 2015a). Mass events, generally mixing political contents with music, have also been staged by the M5S since 2010 in Cesena, Rome and Imola. The clear goal of these events consists in mobilizing the electoral base of the Movement which, beyond electoral tours and local level events, is not offered other occasions for national meetings as the most important decisions of the M5S are taken on the blog, sometimes involving activists in online ballots. Rituals of national mobilization are not supposed to make any decisions but are essential to providing a recurrent occasion for mutual encounters, strengthening members' sense of belonging, and facilitating the emergence and reactivation of a collective identity (Macaluso 2015, 181). Every event is generally associated with an important issue in the Movement agenda such as signature collection for referenda, proposals of laws, and so on.

In May 2015, elected representatives, grassroots activists, and sympathizers were invited to take part in the Five Star March from Perugia to Assisi. A similar march has traditionally been organized by the Italian peace movement since the 1960s. It represents an important reference for ecopacifist activists and groups and, more generally, for progressive public opinion (della Porta et al. 2003). The March was planned before the 2015 regional elections to press for the approval of a proposal of law on basic income drafted by M5S MPs.

However, the real novelty consists in unconventional forms of action undertaken by M5S elected representatives, not just outside institutions but also internally to them. The interesting aspect is that forms of confrontation disrupting normal parliamentary routine have been brought from the streets into representative institutions by members of those same institutions. The protest actions staged by M5S MPs within the institution *par excellence* (the parliament) often consist of filibustering and symbolic acts with high spectacular content whose 'fundamental communicative elements are public visibility and the "dramatizing" of tones' (Bordignon and Ceccarini 2013, 687). There are only a few and sporadic antecedents of such practice in the Italian parliament's history, mostly associated with the Partito Radicale and the Lega Nord (Biorcio 2003; Tarchi 2003). This phenomenon relates to a process of mediatization and popularization (Mazzoleni and Shulz 1999; Mancini 2011) that has deeply affected politics and institutions in recent decades. Representative institutions, in fact, have shifted from being places for discussion among MPs to loci for public exposition under the media's gaze. Actions staged by M5S MPs within the parliament are often symbolic in nature, 'even though those events are not new in some respects, the 5 star MPs push the exceptionality further, transforming it into a true "style" of parliamentary action' (Bordignon and Ceccarini 2013, 687). This effort to 'de-institutionalize the institutions' is intended to direct public attention to certain issues via means particularly suited to attracting media coverage.

3.5. Conclusions: A comparative assessment of organizational repertoires

In this concluding section we will provide a comparative assessment of the organizational repertoire of the three movement parties, looking in particular at three features: (a) their organizational structure; (b) their method of interest aggregation; and (c) their mixed forms of action.

The three parties significantly differ with regard to the *formalization of their organizational structure* (Table 3.1). While it appears extremely undefined in the case of the M5S, where a short 'non-statute' defines only a few organizational principles, the organizational model is clearly defined in the constitutions of both SYRIZA and Podemos. SYRIZA's structure does not exhibit significant innovations when compared to traditional party types, while Podemos and the M5S present some degrees of innovation concerning funding, membership definition, and participatory tools. All parties display territorial branches that are generally autonomous at the local level. However, although their role tends to be

Table 3.1.   Comparative assessment of the organizational repertoire of the three parties

Organizational characteristics	SYRIZA	Podemos	M5S
Structure	Very traditional	Traditional with innovations	Far from traditional, only weakly formalized
Membership	Traditional – fees	Open – no fees	Closed – no fees
Funding	Traditional model	Innovative model Crowd-funding	Innovative model No reimbursements Micro-donations
Participatory instruments	None	Open primaries Plaza Podemos Appgree Citizens' inquiries	Online primaries Online consultations Lex
Method of interest aggregation	Grassroots democracy (limited since 2013)	Mixing charismatic and grassroots democracy features	Charismatic patrimonialism
Forms of action	Both conventional and unconventional Growing detachment from the protest arena	Responsible behaviour within institutions Unconventional actions outside institutions	Innovative parliamentary 'unconventional' style Recurrent rituals of national mobilization

rather marginal in the overall organizational dynamics, these contribute to the formation of relevant bodies in the cases of SYRIZA and Podemos, while this function is completely absent in the case of the M5S, where such bodies are a direct emanation of the leader. Whereas SYRIZA is based on a more traditional party model, rooted in the territory that gradually developed within a centralized and pyramid-like structure, the M5S lacks bureaucratic structures and substitutes them with digital media. Intermediate bodies between local groups and national leaders are almost missing in Grillo's party, although this function is partially fulfilled by the 'representative structure' and MPs are supposed to act as bridging agents between the two. Podemos is in between the two models, relying both on digital media as participatory tools and on traditional territorial circles. According to interviews, however, the latter have been dispossessed of their influence over time.

From the point of view of the membership, Podemos, and to a lesser extent the M5S, seem closer to the ideal type of movement party, where there is no formal definition of the membership role (Kitschelt 2006). SYRIZA comes closer to more traditional party types relying on a rather formalized membership, even if, according to interviewees, this is also very flexible in practice, especially when compared with the typical organizational model of communist parties. Compared to Podemos, the M5S has, however, opted for a closed membership model limiting participation to blog users who have sent an electronic copy of their ID to the staff that operates as a gatekeeper, checking if conditions for joining are formally met. Podemos' model looks more open as it suffices to fill in an online form with personal details to become a member. SYRIZA is also the only one to officially foresee membership fees, even if these are extremely tiny or even not requested in specific cases (for example, the unemployed, pensioners and those who cannot afford it).

The three parties are rather similar from the point of view of funding mechanisms: the M5S defined explicitly the salary of MPs and used the surplus to fund innovative enterprises, as did Podemos, so as to create links with civil society funding entrepreneurial projects of a social nature. SYRIZA's MPs are asked to provide a significant portion of their salary in support of solidarity structures across the country, too. Still, SYRIZA adopts a traditional model of state financing, while, on the other hand, the M5S sets caps on the salaries of elected representatives, at the same time refusing electoral reimbursement and funding electoral campaigns through micro-donations and institutional activities through ordinary public contributions. Podemos, on the other hand, relies on state subsidies and crowd-funding.

With regard to participatory instruments, digital media have been extensively used by both Podemos and the M5S, but this has certainly not been the case with SYRIZA. However, online consultations have been criticized as poor deliberative democracy tools, as in practice they often tend to ratify the decisions already made in advance by the leaders. While generating occasions for participation, on the other hand, they tend to create a plebiscitarian relationship between the leader and his/her followers. This is even more problematic in the case of the M5S, as the party does not foresee any other participatory process at the national level beyond online consultations.

Coming to *systems of interest aggregation*, movement parties diverge from the institutionalized party model displaying adherence to two different ideal types (Table 3.1). As noted by Kitschelt,

At one extreme, movement parties may be led by a *charismatic leader* with a patrimonial staff and personal following over which s/he exercises unconditional and unquestioned control. At the other extreme, movement parties may attempt to realize a grassroots democratic, participatory coordination among activists. Here all relevant decisions are taken in assemblies of activists and implemented by delegates elected to very short non-renewable tenure in representative political offices, whether they are intra-party or legislative. Both charismatic patrimonialism and grassroots democracy lead to a capricious, volatile and incomplete collective preference schedule. Attention is devoted to a small set of issues, while many others are neglected. The pursuit of these salient objectives may be inconsistent and contradictory. (2006, 280–1)

The three parties seem to approximate to different degrees those ideal types. Each of them combines to a different extent elements of the two models. Nonetheless, while features of the charismatic and patrimonial type seem to prevail in the case of the M5S, Podemos is somewhere in between the two due to the great prominence of Iglesias's charismatic leadership as well as the (decreasing) relevance of assemblarian organisms. While SYRIZA has until recently displayed characteristics of the grassroots and democratic type, since becoming the main opposition and then the ruling party, its institutionalized party status has been significantly reinforced. For both Podemos and the M5S, however, digital media support interest aggregation, allowing periodic consultation of members.

Regarding *political practice*, movement parties present an original mix of institutional and extra-institutional action (Table 3.1). In Kitschelt's words, 'One day, legislators of such parties may debate bills in parliamentary committees, but the next day, they participate in disruptive demonstrations or the non-violent occupation of government sites' (2006, 281). The three parties invest differently in the electoral and protest arena. The blend of conventional and unconventional forms of action clearly characterizes the M5S, which also developed an innovative unconventional parliamentary style. While the M5S relies on periodic rituals of national mobilization (such as 'Italia 5 Stelle' and the march for a basic income) to revitalize a sense of belonging, collective identity, and emotional bonds between followers and the charismatic leader, SYRIZA lacks this need for mobilizing efforts. While the party, through its members and even MPs, has participated in all anti-austerity mobilizations, including unconventional ones, it has, however, drawn mainly from its institutional past and conventional parliamentary resources in order to create the profile of a party capable of running the country. In need of building a public image as a reliable institutional actor able to act properly and replace the old parties, Podemos displays responsible behaviour within institutions and practises unconventional action with

Table 3.2. Comparative assessment of leader's features in three parties

Organizational characteristics	SYRIZA	Podemos	M5S
Power distribution	Until 2013: more balanced (factions) Since 2013: increased verticality	Mix of verticality and horizontality	Unbalanced in favour of the leader
Personalization	Limited but growing	High (winner-takes-all model)	Very high with weak counter-trends

more parsimony, as in the case of the 'March of Change'. The three parties, however, have joined various types of demonstrations, although SYRIZA is becoming considerably detached from the protest arena since taking government.

Beyond organizational characteristics, since they directly or indirectly emanated from the protest field, it is interesting to consider how the three movement parties tackled two issues that all political actors entering the institutional arena have to face, and that may potentially disconnect them from their grassroots origins: power distribution and personalization of leadership (Table 3.2).

In terms of power distribution, until the transformation of SYRIZA into a unified and formalized party, the leadership of what was until then a horizontal coalition of parties was characterized by more limitations compared to the leaders of the other two parties: the composition of the CPC and the PS was proportional to the influence of the factions, which made them powerful actors within the party, balancing and constraining the power of the president (Tsakatika 2014); this was also balanced by the structured system of representation between central and regional and local organs. However, the formal dissolution of its constituent organizations provoked internal strife, as it was seen as bringing along an alleged 'presidential' hegemony. The president is elected by the Congress and thus not accountable to the CPC or any political organ. Still, if the president is not trusted by more than 50 per cent of the CPC, then an exceptional congress could be called (art. 14.4). The autonomization of the party leadership was indeed dramatically demonstrated after July 2015 and the adoption of a third MoU: the entire Youth Section, numerous party and CPC members, along with twenty-five MPs and factions (such as the party's Left Platform and the Internationalist Workers Left faction) resigned, refusing to accept decisions allegedly taken by an impermeable top party team that according to them had cancelled any democratic internal processes since SYRIZA had taken power.

Podemos displays a contradiction between a formal bottom-up participatory structure and a personalized style of decision-making (Font et al. 2015). Despite the presence of factions, votes are generally overruled by the majority of the General Secretariat in a system where the winner takes all.

Differently from SYRIZA and Podemos, the M5S lacks any form of control of the leader, who is not elected. Grillo's party lacks any type of inner dialectic and organized factions. As noted by Vignati, 'The principal strategic choices are made exclusively by the leadership. The attempt at coordination "from below" ... – coordination which, through periodic assemblies, might have led to the formation of a political force that would have greater independence from the centre – was nipped in the bud. By contrast, the organizational strategy implemented by the leadership has been driven by a deliberate will to "fragment" the Movement's base' (2015, 48).

Although *personalization* is clearly at odds with leftist parties' and movements' traditions, it does represent a clear feature of the three parties, though to different extents – more marked in the cases of the M5S and Podemos than in the case of SYRIZA (Table 3.2). To be noted is that in cases where the organizational structure has been created anew, charismatic leadership has served to provide crucial resources for the party.

Podemos' (initial) success and electoral prospects have been closely tied to the charismatic leadership of Pablo Iglesias. Thanks to his convincing public speaking skills and his critical stance against economic-political elites and austerity policies, he became a regular television talk show guest before Podemos' launch. Iglesias and his collaborators designed a strategy oriented to use television as a platform to extend a political discourse and, furthermore, a political project. The personalization around the figure of Iglesias is seen as a strategic device, also as part of the populist hypothesis, where the personal leadership plays (or pretends to play) the particular role of representing the whole idea around the concept of people (*el pueblo*). In this sense, the decision of Podemos to print Iglesias' face on the voting ballots of the 2014 European elections was highly contested by social activists, who ridiculed this decision. But, electorally, it worked due to the higher level of his social recognition compared to the name of the new party. Extreme importance has been given by high ranking members of Podemos to political communication as a strategic mechanism to connect with its constituencies and build up social hegemony in terms of discourse. This is something that has traditionally been absent in the left and alternative social movements in Spain, where the idea that conventional media were 'inaccessible or technologically obsolete' prevailed (Rendueles and Sola 2015).

The M5S' success has been strictly related to Grillo, the well-known Italian comedian who became famous with his television shows at the end of the 1970s. During the 1980s, he was banned from public television because of satire against the governing Socialist Party. He then decided to move his shows to squares and theatres (Vignati 2015). Grillo was a celebrity with groups of fans and followers; he was able to channel and translate this popular support into a political creature, using his blog as a coordinating hub, with the help of Casaleggio (Biorcio and Natale 2013). Although some MPs have gradually acquired recognition in the media and Grillo has declared that at a certain point he will return to his former profession, serious doubts remain regarding the capacity of the party to survive his leader. A first symbolic step in this direction was the decision – ratified online by activists – to modify the party's logo. In Grillo's words, 'It was the first political movement born from a blog. I gave it my face, my name and even my heart, but now that the M5S grown adult and is preparing to govern Italy I think it is correct not to associate it to a single name, but to all the people that are part of it. Thus, I want to change the symbol deleting my name.'[43] However, while the symbol has been depersonalized, Grillo still fully retains its ownership.

Although the legacy of the left seems to provide SYRIZA important resources that are missing in the cases of Podemos and M5S and replaced by leaders' personal resources, personalization seems also to have affected SYRIZA. Especially after becoming the main opposition party and after its founding congress (2013), and despite becoming a 'members' party', there is a considerable concentration of power at the leadership level (I2G, I7G, I13G). Particularly after the signing of the Third MoU in July 2015 and the subsequent split of the party, personalization regarding the figure of Alexis Tsipras has become crucial in SYRIZA's public presence.[44] That is also the case when it comes to the image of the party abroad: the European elections of 2014 marked a turning point as 'the President *as a person* (as opposed to a party organ) dominates party representation' (Font et al. 2015, 10). This might have been accentuated by the fact that the party's leader was the official candidate of the European United Left–Nordic Green Left (GUE/NGL) for the position of President of the European Commission.

It should be noted that experimentation with different organizational models depends on movement parties' peculiar organizational history: while SYRIZA has been limited by the previous organizational choices and the euro-communist tradition of Synaspismos, as well as the legacies of the left in Greece, Podemos and the M5S have had more opportunities for experimentation, developing their organizational repertoires on trials and errors. Thus, while Podemos is closer to SYRIZA in terms of ideological leanings, it more strongly resembles the M5S in some aspects of its organizational model.

First, born as anti-establishment parties stressing the need to reduce the costs of politics, both Podemos and the M5S had to look for alternative sources of funding. Second, because of their fluid membership – differently from SYRIZA – both parties opted for an innovative model not based on fees. Third, the foundation of the two parties was preceded and followed by electoral tests. The official birth of the M5S was preceded by tests of 'five star civic lists' in local elections.[45] Official lists of the M5S were then formed for the 2010 local and regional elections; local tests lasted until the 2013 general elections. In the case of Podemos, the party and the lists for the 2014 European elections were formed only a few weeks before the consultation. The following administrative elections have seen the experimentation with confluence processes (*procesos de confluencia*), which were then replicated in the general elections in the autumn of 2015. The entrance into institutions has represented another relevant turning point for both parties. Fourth, both Podemos and the M5S have developed participatory instruments transcending the typical mechanisms of engagement foreseen by traditional parties. Digital platforms have been provided to create a special linkage with their constituencies, paired with rituals of national mobilization (especially in the case of the M5S) to strengthen members' sense of belonging. Fifth, the three parties present clear evidence of personalization processes, although they also show different trajectories: while personalization was relevant from the start as a way to generate resources in the cases of Podemos and the M5S (with some weak counter-trends in the former case), it tended to increase over time in the case of SYRIZA.

All three movement parties discussed in this book have reintroduced social mobilization within party politics during an era of severe legitimation crisis. Their organizational structures and internal procedures have naturally been quintessential on this aspect, as well as for re-enacting a culture of participation and interaction drawn from the movement field among their members and politics at large. However, as it became evident, the informal practices and ideas running through the three cases have been dissimilar in several aspects, generating different movement party practices while, in the case of SYRIZA, becoming main opposition (2012) and then ruling party (2015) its institutionalized party status has been gradually affirmed.

Summarizing, the 'old' party structure and left-wing legacy of SYRIZA distinguishes it from Podemos and the M5S in terms of membership, funding strategies, and participatory instruments. Regarding systems of interest aggregation and forms of action, SYRIZA adopted (at least until 2012) grassroots democratic elements; the M5S stands closer to the 'charismatic patrimonialism' model, while Podemos combines elements of both ideal types. Concerning power distribution, this is strongly unbalanced in the case of the M5S, while in the case of SYRIZA it was rather balanced until recently; again, Podemos displays a contradictory model where the leader's power is somehow contrasted by factions (completely lacking in the M5S). In terms of personalization, the charismatic leadership is paired with the absence of clear rules in the case of the M5S, and Podemos is also strongly personalized, while SYRIZA displays more limited but growing personalization tendencies.

4

Framing Movement Parties

4.1. Introduction

Research on party families has stressed the role that parties play in structuring social cleavages by providing collective identity and ideological discourses (della Porta 2015a). Parties are indeed supposed to channel those claims emerging in society towards institutions. At the same time, social movement studies have focused on framing as a main cognitive process in political participation. Framing analysis emerged in the social sciences, and more specifically in the field of social movement studies, in the early 1980s as a result of the criticism directed against the established paradigm of resource mobilization theory (McCarthy and Zald 1987). Understanding collective action as a product of rational choices and clear-cut incentives, this theory was challenged for overemphasizing the cost-benefit decision-making through which individuals calculate their participation in mobilizations. Through this structural approach, social movement studies could not account for the very moment protest emerges, in many cases spontaneously and irrationally, and for the dynamics it then acquires. It was consequently unable to explain why people choose to protest for some causes and not for others; issues of contingency, ideology, collective identity, and culture were disregarded.

In the background, the 'new social movements' of the 1970s had brought to the fore such issues as gender rights, the environment, and participatory democracy. As a result, and in parallel with the so-called linguistic turn in social sciences that put forward discourse analysis as a methodological approach, social movement studies shifted their attention towards approaches sensitive to how meaning is constructed through the ways in which people come together. What started to become evident was that in many cases what matters is how people interpret reality, rather than the sum of objective facts taking place around them. Analytical and interpretative approaches focused on collective identities (Melucci 1988) and those cognitive mechanisms that contribute to interpreting grievances, constructing protest goals, and mobilizing people to become collectively active in the protest arena (Snow and Benford 1988).

It was within this context that the term 'frame' emerged, first imported by the sociologist Erving Goffman (1974). In the working definition set out by Snow and Benford, the frame is described as 'an interpretive schema that simplifies and condenses the "world out there" by selectively punctuating and encoding objects, situations, events, experiences, and sequences of action' (1988, 37). 'Framing' refers to the process through which individuals are enabled to locate, perceive, and label occurrences within their life space and world at large in interaction with the wider political culture, public discourse, values and orientations of society, and dynamics of collective action (Steinberg 1998). As Lindekilde observes, this 'is like a picture frame that accentuates certain things, hides others, and borders off reality in a certain way' (2015, 200), giving leverage to the capacity of social actors to interact with contextual opportunities and constraints and use competing frames to organize their experiences and justify their orientations (Snow et al. 2004).

Frame analysis is a particularly fruitful approach when the aim of the study is to uncover the process through which different actors define the issue at stake, propose ways out, and set goals. Snow and Benford described these as three different 'core framing tasks' in mobilization: the 'diagnostic', referring to the identification of the problem and the attribution of blame; the 'prognostic', concerning the proposed solution to the problem, including strategies and goals; and, lastly, the 'motivational', which concerns motives and rationales for action (1988). Identity, agency, and injustice are particularly basic components of what is called a 'collective action frame' (Gamson 1998), while other terms crafted for research are 'master frames', 'frame alignment', or 'frame resonance', which occurs when 'frames successfully "speak to" individuals' existing perceptions and situation, and make them responsive to the content of the message' (Lindekilde 2015, 207). By the mid-1990s, the study of framing processes had been recognized as one of the central pillars of social movement research.

In the background of the rise of framing studies in the early 1980s loomed the protest cycle of the 'long 1960s' that had mobilized people around the globe to protest and understand protest in ways different from those of the labour movements of the past. By introducing an anti-authoritarian frame during Cold War times, these protests challenged both liberalism and communism, calling for a widening of civil rights and forms of political participation; in demanding alternatives linked to 'democracy from below', these movements also led to the formation of Green parties. But tension between political parties and social movements re-emerged within the 2000s global justice movement (GJM), which criticized especially the political parties of the centre-left and traditional unions for having opened the door to neoliberal reforms and disregarded movements' potentials in the policy arena (Andretta and Reiter 2009). The dramatic decline of trust in representative democracy was massively revived in the anti-austerity protests and contentious politics of the 2010s: protests in Puerta del Sol, Madrid, and Zuccotti Park in New York revealed the extent of the legitimacy crisis of late neoliberalism. While putting forward 'politics from below' as a viable alternative to 'party politics' (della Porta et al. 2006), the movements of the early 2000s still believed in their capacity to influence public institutions through conventional channels, and in the possibility of a democratic global governance. The injustice framing of the social movements that emerged during the crisis of neoliberalism was different, though, in totally distrusting any change within the already existing political system. Protesters defined themselves as part of the large majority ('we'), suffering from social and political inequalities caused by 'them', all these political, economic and media elites making up the so-called representative democracy (della Porta et al. 2016).

Against this radicalized anti-party and anti-establishment contentious context and deepening austerity conditions, developments in the countries of Southern Europe came as a surprise: the sudden emergence and stunning electoral salience of movement parties, previously small or even non-existent – like SYRIZA in Greece, Podemos in Spain, and the M5S in Italy – challenged the expected separation of movements from party politics. Thus far, scholars had been studying parties in isolation from grassroots mobilizations, focusing their research on institutional dynamics and party competition. At the same time, social movement studies had increasingly grown indifferent towards parties, believing that politics was taking place beyond institutional developments. Reality, however, proved less rational and predictable, putting political parties centre stage in Southern Europe. We can make sense of this phenomenon by bridging the two subfields to study how these political parties managed to enter the protest arena and align their understanding of the world with the protesters' ideas. Movement parties should be understood not as a static and rational entity, but as a dynamic and contextual process embedded in societal interaction and in historical time: framing has been in any case a key to the genesis of movement parties, which reflect the convergence of two spaces with conflicting interpretations of power and change. This is the case especially during the current critical juncture: amid a contentious culture and a broad delegitimation of representative politics at the periphery of Europe, what has been decisive for the salience of these movement parties is the way they participated in the 'battle for meaning'.

The aim of this chapter is to examine how party actors managed to mobilize feelings of injustice into active support for SYRIZA in Greece, Podemos in Spain, and the M5S in Italy. The framing processes adopted by these parties leading to their becoming 'movement parties' will be examined in four steps: first, we will study the diagnostic dimension that defines who is included in the 'we' and the 'them' in each case; we will then look at the practical strategies and goals set by these parties so as to overcome the diagnosed problem ('prognostic' framing). Departing from this understanding of the crisis and the solutions put forward, we will examine how movement parties chose to mobilize constituencies, focusing particularly on their visions of democracy and of Europe; given the fact that institutional actors, both domestic and European, are considered devoid of any democratic function in the protest arena, how did parties manage to motivate protesters to participate anew in electoral politics? Having examined those three aspects of framing, this chapter moves a step forward by reflecting on the ways parties' framing resonates with the protest context of each case in question, we will first study whether discursive framing strategies have been combined by adoption of movements' claims in the official party programmes and actions (programmatic proximity); we will then conclude by reflecting more broadly about how the framing of SYRIZA, Podemos, and the M5S resonates with how collective action has developed in Greece, Spain, and Italy: to what extent did framing bring these 'movement parties' close to the movements in practice?

4.2. Framing SYRIZA: A 'unity of the left' to take power

Beginning in 2009, tensions were rising and protests were becoming more massive in Greece, as the politicians blaming Greek citizens for corruption absolved themselves of responsibility in cases of grand corruption scandals and extended immunity from prosecution to business and media elites, as well as to neo-Nazi Golden Dawn criminals (Xenakis and Cheliotis 2015). Indicative of mounting public anger is an opinion survey showing that 89 per cent of the respondents agreed in 2010 that the burden of austerity was not distributed fairly, while two out of three respondents thought that people should protest (Rüdig and Karyotis 2014). Notwithstanding the polarization of public life, no compelling alternative narrative from the one projected by the mainstream parties had yet been introduced; persuasion remained the 'key currency of crisis management' (ibid.).

Meanwhile, notwithstanding its presence in social struggles, SYRIZA remained a marginal force. Lacking programmatic depth and ideological coherence, the party was accused of criticizing 'everything that moved as "neoliberal"' (Moschonas 2013), while it resembled mainstream political parties in many aspects. After the eruption of the crisis, however, a remarkable shift was perceived in public discourse: in May 2011, Alexis Tsipras, the 36-year-old leader of SYRIZA, issued a political declaration calling for a 'unity of the left' so as to 'govern the country' (Tsipras 2011). Though doomed to fail, this appeal soon proved apocalyptic, as it surprised the establishment and shook up the rules of the game (Moschonas 2015) by giving voice to what was simmering underground in an informal way, as will be explained below.

4.2.1. Diagnosing the crisis: 'We, the people' against 'them, the elites' responsible for the crisis

SYRIZA introduced an alternative diagnosis of the crisis to the dominant one propagated systematically since 2009 by international and national political elites and mainstream media, which blamed the Greek citizens.[1] Notwithstanding the conflation of global and local realities that generated a crisis far from national and much broader than financial in character, the prevailing interpretation was that of a predictable crisis that had been a long time in coming – one that was to be expected from a country that had never managed to modernize adequately despite the opportunities offered through its membership of the EU (Triandafyllidou et al. 2013). Attached to a backward political culture fed by corruption and clientelism and impeding progress, all Greeks were presented as equally responsible for austerity and not entitled to complain, let alone protest. Implicit in this discourse attributing the roots of the crisis to the idiosyncratic Greek culture was an orientalist (and self-orientalizing) assumption that the Mediterranean countries of the periphery were inferior to the liberal market economies of Northern Europe (Agnantopoulos and Lambiri 2015). This framing soon generated false dilemmas: Do Greek citizens wish to reject Troika policies and exit the euro? Will Greece remain a part of the European Union or become a third-world country? Sticking with austerity was the only route to survival.

According to SYRIZA's discourse, it was not the Greek citizens who were to blame for the crisis, but rather the 'pro-austerity' establishment, including the neoliberal policies dictated by the 'memoranda' and the national governments implementing them, along with their allies, business actors, and media conglomerates. According to the 2012 SYRIZA provisional programme (SYRIZA 2012), the crisis was the result of an 'economic and social system' of 'globalized capitalism' that could survive only through profit and speculation. Greek, European, and international elites made profits through private banks, ships, commercial and industrial enterprises with the aid of the pro-system media. Against this background, pro-austerity politics are unjust, destructive, and lead to a dead end, while people are asked to sacrifice even more with no impact. According to SYRIZA's programme, 'This government cannot make it. Instead of making use of popular discontent so as to put pressure on those abroad, it reproduces the argumentation of the lenders so as to frighten and blackmail its own people' (2012).

Most importantly, in about 2011, in parallel with the Greek Indignados mobilizations, SYRIZA stopped appealing to 'the youth', to 'the movements', or the 'Greek citizens', and launched its campaign with a universal call to 'the people' (Katsampekis 2015). The party aimed at expressing politically 'all those repressed and being exploited' (SYRIZA 2013b) and maintaining that 'the forces of wage labour, the hundreds of thousands of unemployed people, the army of highly qualified young people who cannot find a job, the self-employed, the small and medium-sized farmers, and the small and medium-sized businesses all form a social bloc with fundamentally different interests from the dominant one's' (SYRIZA 2013a). The party discourse became clearly organized around the antagonism between 'us, the people' hit by austerity and 'them, the establishment' – the pro-memorandum elites implementing the Troika's policies while bearing major responsibility for the crisis (Stavrakakis and Katsampekis 2014). This discourse was echoed and recognized the importance of resistance:

> Against this attack of capital there are movements of resistance developing on a global level. In Greece a large popular current of struggles for subversion has been engaged in its battle against memoranda and debt in mass terms, in squares, in the workplace, in neighbourhoods, in towns and in the countryside, reconstituting old social movements and creating new ones. (SYRIZA 2013b)

Aiming at overthrowing a delegitimized political system along with its dependency on international elites, 'the people' in this context became a broader, plural and open community united by 'the common cause of defending popular interests and restoring progressive governance'

(SYRIZA 2012). SYRIZA thus drew a clear dividing line, no longer between the right and the left, but between the 'pro-memorandum' (elites) and the 'anti-memorandum' (popular masses) forces.

4.2.2. Solving the crisis through a (not so) radical left-wing reconstruction plan

While aiming at representing a broad 'anti-memorandum' platform, SYRIZA retained and insisted on its left-wing standpoint. In theory, and according to the preamble of SYRIZA's 2013 Founding Charter:

> Socialism is a form of organization of society based on social ownership and management of the means of production': the way to move forward towards accomplishing this target is 'the overthrow of the domination of the forces of neoliberalism and of the memoranda, the forces of social destruction, and the emergence of a government of the united Left, embedded in a broad social alliance. (2013a)

Departing from this left-wing approach, the party's programme developed in line with the way mobilizations developed around the concepts of renewed democracy, popular sovereignty, and participation (Katsampekis 2015).

> During those times of profound crisis of legitimacy of the political system, political parties and politics...Syriza defends the values of social justice, solidarity, equality and freedom against nationalism, militarism, racism, patriarchy and fascism....This requires democracy in every cell of public life, where collective organizing and solidarity will be proved superior to individualism and competitiveness. (SYRIZA 2013a)

SYRIZA's 2012 and 2014 programme set out the path to achieving this renewed democracy through renegotiating the country's debt, cancelling emergency taxes, restoring salaries and pensions to their former levels, placing the banking sector and strategic enterprises under public control, rebuilding the welfare state by restoring the rule of law, and creating a meritocratic state and taxing the rich (SYRIZA 2012; 2014). Its so-called National Reconstruction Plan included four pillars: confronting the humanitarian crisis, restarting the economy and promoting tax justice, re-creating employment, and transforming the political system to deep democracy (SYRIZA 2014a). This was actually a moderate mixture of neo-Keynesian/social-democratic economic and social policies (Katsampekis 2015): 'Let's be clear, the 2014 programmatic points are very much to the right of what enabled the French

Socialists in 1981 to take power' (I10G). 'You wouldn't call SYRIZA's suggestions leftist...these are social democratic, really, really moderate. But faced with this attack by capital, nowadays, these even seem radical' (I11G).

In 2012 Greece, the demand to restore salaries and pensions and a minimum of rule of law was considered left-wing, but also to be in line with the claims of protest groups (Kousis 2013). As Tsipras declared in 2015, echoing global grievances, the party promised 'to protect the 99% of society that has been looted by the Memorandum, and to find the 1% that systematically evades taxation and make it pay'.

4.2.3. Mobilizing constituencies: 'We' can bring change

(a) A government of the left

What made this framing appealing was the shift that occurred in SYRIZA's public discourse in 2011 concerning its motivational drive, reflected in Tsipras' declaration: 'The time for the left to take charge is coming'. From aiming at a 'left turn' that would build a social and political opposition against neoliberalism and bipartisanship, the emphasis was now put on creating an alliance among left-wing actors that could challenge established power structures and narratives and claim power (Katsampekis 2015).

The alliance proposal for a 'unity of the left' around Tsipras reached out to the non-parliamentary left, the parliamentary left, including KKE, as well as PASOK dissidents. This statement was met with indifference, if not disdain – even by his own electorate and cadres – as unrealistic and utopian; no one believed that the divided political actors of the left could unite, as the divisions among them were perceived as too important to be transcended in the name of an 'anti-austerity' struggle. But SYRIZA gave voice to what was common sense in the streets: those thousands protesting were also rejecting left-wing parties – despite their presence in the protest milieu – as an inherent part of the 'old system', especially when it came to their sectarianism (I9G), defeatism (I3G, I5G), and introvert appeal (I10G).

The unity of the left was an idea circulating at the time in the Indignados' squares: 'everyone was thinking, if the anti-austerity forces join together, they could compete for power, it is absurd they do not!' (I5G). Tsipras, on the contrary, declared that 'the left is meant to unite and not to divide' (2011), as 'We do not call for unification of parties, but for unity in action and in struggles against the memoranda, while we all retain our own autonomy.' This was a great opportunity for the left to catch up with what society was asking for, and through 'paths of unity, struggle and pride' to lead to 'solutions of national dignity that leave no space for divisive choices'. In understanding this, SYRIZA not only recognized the importance of the claims made by the anti-austerity movement, but emphasized its own role in contributing and developing a 'powerful, massive and unifying movement of resistance and disobedience...of pure and effective solidarity with the victims of the crisis...of political reversal' (SYRIZA 2013b). Departing from popular discontent, he managed to challenge audaciously 'his comrades' grey, complacent mediocrity' (Moschonas 2015). The party resonated not only with the material demands of the anti-austerity mobilizations, but also with the diversification and openness that had introduced ordinary citizens as the main agents of protest (Tsipras 2011).

(b) 'Hope is coming, Europe is changing'

In being repeated in the months to come, the call for a unity of the left became 'an inspiring response to the widespread disenchantment of the population with the long-standing bipartisan political system' (Spourdalakis 2014, 359). As an activist and member of the party observed,

> Resistance was not restrained just in denouncing; it was building something else. It was not like KKE saying, 'well, it's pretty bad, but, look, you have no other option than to stay here and die'; no, what SYRIZA was doing was offering some hope. (I6G)

The party understood that citizens were also suffering due to the lack of alternatives at hand. In the words of one interviewee, 'We met each other out there, we found other people, we understood we were many, too many to be ignored; this could not go on like this' (I8G). SYRIZA was the political actor that decided to recognize and address itself to this 'broad alliance of this new social majority' (SYRIZA 2013a). According to Tsipras, 'The widespread peaceful revolt of the "indignados" is trying to sound a bell for the delegitimized government and those abroad...this peaceful and spontaneous revolt of the people is the only hope, the only perspective we have' (Tsipras 2011).

SYRIZA's main slogan for the January 2015 elections that brought the party to power was 'Hope is Coming, Greece is Moving Forward, Europe is Changing'. By shifting the terms of the political debate, the party managed since 2011 'to claim power' (I5G), offering a way out of hopelessness. SYRIZA did not remain trapped in debating 'Grexit', which created the dilemma of either suffering austerity within Europe or exiting Europe and becoming a 'failed state'. The struggle was, according to the left-wing coalition, between the 'unfair austerity implemented by the elites' and the 'anti-austerity demanded by the people' and 'social Europe' versus 'neoliberal Europe'. As interviewed party members declared, 'We were pro-European in terms of strategic planning: we could not deal alone with austerity, Europe was a favourable platform within which to create solidarity' (I1G), while the emphasis on a social Europe and 'the people of Europe' (SYRIZA 2013a) was also a tool against 'nationalistic exceptionalism' (I7G, I12G). This reframing of the crisis raised important issues: until then it had been commonly assumed that, on the one hand, the clientelistic nature of the Greek state had constituted an impediment to (neoliberal) reform (Agnantopoulos and Labiri 2015), and, on the other, that anti-austerity protest was a sign of Euroscepticism and isolationism. The party changed the framing: the participation of Greece in the European institutions was not even questioned, as SYRIZA called for 'another' Europe, built on solidarity and major democratic accountability.[2] The party's pre-electoral campaign departed from the slogan: 'We're voting for Greece, we're voting for another Europe' (SYRIZA 2014b). This discourse revealed that it was the austerity policies inflicted upon Greece that were actually Eurosceptic: in being unjust and non-democratic, they were challenging the ideology of a liberal and progressive Europe.

While ordinary people on the ground felt injustice – as they knew that 'we' were not to blame and 'we' were paying for a crisis caused by 'them' – until 2011 there was no way out. But Tsipras declared in 2011 that 'there is no dead-end in democracy' and 'Syriza was transformed from a protest to a power party' (I5G). Proposing to recognize and represent 'this broad new social majority' (SYRIZA 2013a) and linking protest with taking power, SYRIZA encouraged those in the 'we' to become agents of their own history, according to what Gamson labelled as the 'agency component' (Gamson 1995). The party's main slogan for the May 2012 election campaign is telling: 'They decided without us, we're moving on without them.' Against a political establishment declaring that there was no alternative to austerity, the slogan 'we don't want you to vote as a protest, but so that we can govern' proved successful (Moschonas 2015). Accepting to represent a broad anti-austerity movement was precisely the reason that allowed SYRIZA to jump from being a marginal coalition of the left to a party on the brink of power (Stavrakakis and Katsampekis 2014).

4.2.4. Frame resonance with social movements: Proximity and distance

(a) Programmatic proximity
On the one hand, those 'producing' the framing, SYRIZA members, were ordinary people and not part of the well-known, corrupted political

elites. As a party member notes: 'Everybody can see that he, Dimitris, he has been a unionist for so long, spending days, months, years in the movement, he has lost his personal life and he has earned nothing, no money, no power, no administrative post. People recognize that' (I9G).

On the other hand, this framing was compatible with its 'receivers', as the dramatic fall in party identification had also affected SYRIZA, whose voters after 2012 were not only those who self-defined as left-wing or radical (Teperoglou and Tsatsanis 2014b; Rüdig and Karyotis 2014); at the same time, while anti-austerity mobilizations radicalized citizens in a way that transcended conventional left–right cleavages (Kousis 2013), protests in Greece retained a left-leaning orientation and commitment to left-wing values. A left-wing actor, the party aimed to establish itself as the most viable voice of the anti-memorandum front within the party system, by incorporating protest claims. By recomposing diverse and fragmented anti-austerity claims in a coherent and left-wing program-matic framing, SYRIZA managed to express at the official political level the high point of the anti-austerity struggle: what was common sense in the streets of the country was now heard in the parliament and was transformed into a political and electoral dynamic that challenged the dominant interpretation of the crisis. The Political Resolution of the 1st congress of SYRIZA emphasized the 'great social and political movement of subversion':

> We should refer emblematically to the great strikes and demonstrations of workers, the movement of the 'indignant', the movement in Skouries [against gold mining] and in Keratea [against the opening of a landfill], in Evros [against the building of immigrant detention centres and fences], in the movements against the special property tax and against paying tolls, in the anti-fascist movement and the movement in defence of ERT [the national broadcaster]. (2013b)

Its programmatic discourse also incorporated 'the great movement of solidarity that is developing throughout the country. Under the slogan "no-one's alone in the crisis" and on an equal basis – everyone offers according to their ability and receives according to their needs – multi-form structures and solidarity networks are created' (SYRIZA 2013b). Apart from recognizing the 'anti-austerity campaign' as a central actor in politics, the party also endorsed local and ad hoc social movements' claims, promising to give jobs back to those thousands of public sector workers laid off by the government, systematically exposing racist vio-lence in the parliament, and supporting harassed migrants and refugees; SYRIZA MPs visited the cleaning ladies camped outside the Ministry of Finance and Solidarity4All assisted them. At the same time, Tsipras himself visited the self-run Vio.Me factory in Thessaloniki, declaring that the labour struggle of self-organization could function for SYRIZA as a pilot-project to deal with increasing unemployment.[3] The party leader also visited Skouries in Halkidiki to reassure protesters that 'Syriza is determined to clash with interests...people know that there cannot be a government of the left without the movement.'[4] Telling in this respect was the candidate list for the 2014 European Parliament election, which contained fourteen non-party members including activists in movements against austerity policies, such as the Cleaning Ladies movement, the ERT Open movement, and the movement against water privatization in Thessaloniki. Up to 2015, overlapping membership had become commonplace in terms of both rank-and-file party members of local groups and elected representatives.

(b) Both an internal and an external relationship

Framing strategies adapted to the social movements' claims, as well as the party's programmes. According to our interviewees, it was exactly due to this relationship with grassroots movements that the party came to power in January 2015 to 'abolish the MoUs'. In the ensuing months, the Greek government devoted all its attention to negotiations with its European counterparts and the Troika institutions, which, however, reached a dead-end, leaving no space for the Greek government to draft an alternative strategy within the EU. On 25 June, the prime minister announced a referendum for 5 July to decide whether Greece would accept the bailout conditions proposed jointly by the EC, the IMF, and the ECB. A huge 'pro-Yes' campaign was waged by political and business elites, both domestic and international, and the mainstream media, while capital controls were imposed and opinion polls were pointing towards a 'Yes' victory. However, the 'No' side won an impressive 61.3 per cent following a massive grassroots horizontal campaign. All interviewees consider the referendum as a watershed for the social movements and for Greek politics, as it demonstrated a whole people's resistance against despotism and unfairness. However, three days later, the will of the Greek people proved irrelevant: according to media coverage, on 12 July the Greek delegation bended to severe pressure by signing a new MoU that included sweeping austerity measures demanded by lenders in return for new multi-billion euro-bailout package.

The 2012 and 2014 elections and most importantly the referendum reflect rather decisive moments, during which collective action had a decisive impact on electoral politics through the diffusion of patterns of mobilization and the emergence of alternative frames as socially hegemonic (Serdedakis and Koufidi 2016). Building on the anti-austerity movement framings and repertoires of action, SYRIZA developed a master frame that challenged hegemonic realities. But the relationship between the two developed in less linear ways throughout those years, as a party member explains:

> First, it was the party that was influenced by anti-austerity mobilizations and this encounter granted SYRIZA's perspective and activities with some movement-like elements. The convergence between party members and movements was materialized in various local spaces, in the way local initiatives and interventions mounted. Then, it was some people, not all, but some people who were participating in movements and who collaborated with the party, some of them even became part of it. But those individuals, not many, they became part of already existing structures, they tried to fit in the party, they did not make their own. And, lastly, the third mode of connection was the vote: well, most of the people who were activists or protesters, they expressed themselves politically through the party, they all voted for SYRIZA; that was clear. (I4G)

SYRIZA managed to come close to the protests, and the vast majority of the people engaged in movements indeed supported and voted for SYRIZA; however, *they did not become party members*. Notwithstanding the proximity to protest, there was from the outset a distance, or even a conflictual relationship between a parliamentary and grassroots actors, which is linked to the political culture of the country. The 'movement milieu' in Greece has traditionally been hostile towards political parties and their co-opting strategies towards grassroots struggles (I17G, I24G, I30G). Especially after 2012, this generated an internal division within movements between those who opposed the institutionalization of contention and delegation attitudes that SYRIZA's rise seemed to bring along (I17G, I22G, I23G, I28G, I30G) – 'at the very end, SYRIZA is a political party no different than the others' (I27G) – and those more supportive of a shift in power (I21G, I26G, I29G).

A telling case is the movement in Skouries, scene of a conflict between the mining company Hellas Gold, a subsidiary of the Canadian Eldorado Gold, and local communities that argue that the planned investment will damage the environment and livelihoods. Their ongoing struggle has gathered huge support and solidarity, including from abroad. SYRIZA has supported the local movement: in repeated visits there, Tsipras, MPs, and party members declared that a left-wing government would stop the destructive mining policies. This had an impact at the local level: one activist was elected as MP in SYRIZA's list in 2012, another one supported by SYRIZA became mayor in 2014, and others municipal councillors. None of them previously engaged with the party. As reflected in the interviews conducted there (I29G, I30G), the local movement became divided, especially after 2012, between those favourable to SYRIZA and to solutions of an institutional nature, and those advocating an anti-authoritarian approach objecting to parties' engagement. Since 2015, relations between the party now in government and the movement have become even more complicated and in many cases hostile, as SYRIZA has not delivered its pre-electoral promises. As an activist said: 'here, we are accountable to the people with whom we live; we are first and foremost part of this community that has been on the streets for so long' (I30G).

But this complex relationship has also been played out within the party itself; as a result of the July 2015 agreement, twenty-five MPs, two factions, along with numerous SYRIZA members (mostly with overlapping memberships), as well as the entire Youth Section resigned from the party, protesting against the lack of democratic processes and the shift towards an excessively centralized approach to politics that had begun in 2012 (I5G). The framing that brought the party into power could not be defended anymore: eight out of our fifteen respondents are no longer party members, proving that the 'party' versus 'movement' relationship is not only external, but also internal, taking place within the party: some SYRIZA members have also self-identified as movement activists (I2G, I4G, I7G) and feel accountable to social movements (I1G, I9G), while many adopt a more conventional, hierarchical, and top-down approach to governmental politics (I13G, I15G).

While for a brief period SYRIZA managed to converge with movements and achieved great electoral success, the two are again clearly separated. Interviewees ask themselves whether movement activity decreased after 2012 exactly because SYRIZA was on the rise – whether, in other words, 'people abandoned movement activity, delegating their fate to a political party' (I17G, I28G, I30G). Others testify to the tiredness, exhaustion, and repression of protesters (I3–4G, I20G, I26G, I29G) – 'movements were defeated' (I25G) – while others believe that, on the contrary, they reached a peak: 'Everything we had asked for, took place. Everyone took to the streets, in every city of the country, the whole country was in protest' (I24G). However, there are more pessimistic views believing that 'after 2015, voting but also demonstrating is over' (I3G): the identity crisis experienced by both parties and movements is still in force.

4.3. Framing in Podemos: A leftist populism in Spain?

As has been noted by Martínez and Domingo (2014), one of the main outcomes of the 15M movement, as well as anti-austerity mobilizations in the country in general, has been the construction of counter-hegemonic discourses regarding different issues and public policies. Podemos' strategy since the outset has been oriented towards transforming the political status quo through a radical change in discourse and, as a result, the importance of framing has been quintessential to the party's politics.

4.3.1. Diagnosing the crisis regime: 'We are the people, not politicians'

Some of the party's prominent leaders have studied the idea of hegemony as developed by Antonio Gramsci or explored discourse analysis ideas in the work of Ernesto Laclau or Chantal Mouffe. The elaboration of these theories in practice generated what has been known as the 'populist hypothesis' by Podemos' founding members or, even, the attempt to create a kind of 'leftist populism' in Spain (Errejón 2014).

Regarding the diagnostic frame put forward by Podemos, the point of departure upon which most spokespersons agree is that Spain is currently experiencing a 'crisis regime' which, according to Íñigo Errejón, is:

> ...a breakdown of the social and political consensus and a dismantling of traditional identities. This breakdown makes possible the existence of a populist left, which is not located in the symbolic distribution of positions of the regime, but is seeking to create another dichotomy, articulating a new political will with the possibility of becoming majority. (Errejón 2014)

Thus, this critical conjuncture allowed the transformation of the political and ideological divisions among citizens. As the leader of the party, Pablo Iglesias, observes, 'the Spanish organic crisis was generating the conditions for the articulation of a dichotomizing discourse, capable of building the 15M's new ideological constructs into a popular subject and in opposition to the elites' (Iglesias 2015a). In this way, the political crisis, thus, enabled the creation of a populist left project in Spain by addressing a newly formed majority through a novel discourse: while the emotional and symbolic aspects are extremely important, new cleavages have emerged (Errejón 2014):

> This constructivist approach to political discourse allowed making transversal interpellations to a disappointed social majority which went beyond the left–right axis, upon which the regime shares positions and ensures its stability. We are proposing a dichotomy based on the axis 'democracy/oligarchy' or 'citizenship/caste' or even 'new/old':

a distinct border which aims to isolate the elites and create a new identification in front of them. (Errejón 2014)

The framing 'el pueblo versus la casta' (*the people against the elites*) makes a clear distinction between 'us' and 'them' that resonates with the most recent social movement cycle in the country, which contrasted those below with those above and has actually sought to revive and mobilize those who participated in some ways in the 15M mobilizations (Stobart 2014). The same applies to the non-ideological self-definition of Podemos as 'neither leftist nor rightist', which instead differentiates between ordinary lay people and corrupt politicians, while at the same time introducing Podemos as a guarantee that would defend people's rights: 'we are the people, not politicians', as eloquently stated in the 'Electoral Programme for Regional Elections' (EPRE 2015, 8).

In 'diagnosing' who 'they' and 'we' are, Podemos also presents itself as a movement for political renewal introducing a novel cleavage between the new against the old in the way Podemos performs politics. This different imaginary and unconventional framing of Podemos has also challenged the symbols and identities of the traditional left by adopting a series of discursive strategies that have been considered as 'taboos' for the left (I7S, I10S, I13S). For instance, several party members and particularly its leader, Iglesias, have used the concepts 'patriot' or 'homeland' to connect the idea of the nation with social rights (Bassets 2015). During a television debate between Iglesias and Pérez-Rubalcaba (the former PSOE general secretary) before the party's formal establishment, the former stated: 'I'm not requesting you to be a socialist, but a patriot.'[5] The term 'patriot' has been strategically used to criticize political corruption ('those politicians who have the money in Switzerland are betrayers'),[6] the privatization of public services ('to be a patriot is to defend our public services'),[7] and the lack of sovereignty ('to be a patriot is to defend sovereignty, as they are selling the country and our rights').[8] After the 2014 European elections, Iglesias explained how intertwining the concepts 'patriot', 'democracy' and 'sovereignty' moved beyond the 'left':

> It is pretty obvious that I am leftist, but I think that the fact of being a leftist at this point is irrelevant. I think that we're in an exceptional social situation in which emergency measures are required. Measures that all Spaniards who love their country should defend. They are merely democratic measures: recovery of decency, dignity and sovereignty and a perspective of building a different Europe that protects its citizens, social rights and assumes that popular sovereignty is the basis for building democracy. (Iglesias 2015e)

4.3.2. Solving the crisis through democracy

At the same time, Podemos puts forward ways of dealing with the crisis by presenting itself as a movement for political renewal against corruption and traditional parties. This connects with the idea expressed by the above mentioned cleavage of 'new' vs 'old'. In this sense, there has been a discursive construction oriented towards building a social imagery distinguishing between 'old politics' and 'new politics'. This new politics would be represented by Podemos as a tool to lead participatory mechanisms, increase public and social controls over institutions and political parties, and put an end to the 'privileges' of representatives and thus to politics as usual. At the same time, Iglesias and his colleagues have also driven a moralist conception of politics. In a context in which corruption is the second largest political problem for Spaniards, Podemos' spokespersons have regularly denounced the 'revolving doors' between governments and the advisory and executive boards of corporations (Stobart 2014). In this sense, Podemos' campaign letter used to combine 15M's ordinary citizen discourse with its anti-corruption and democratic regeneration stance (Flesher-Fominaya 2014).

The concept of democracy has been a key issue in the development of Podemos' discourse, in terms of not only diagnostic, but also prognostic framing. Two years before the party's foundation, Iglesias pointed out in a public conference that 'we have to build social majorities around a basic axis: democracy'.[9] The understanding of democracy as a conflicting signifier draws from the idea put forward by the recent mobilizations in the country, namely that Spain is currently experiencing a crisis of democracy, which makes democracy a concept in dispute. As a result, the idea is used for defining the self – 'we, the democrats' – and the country as 'robbed and kidnapped by the oligarchy' (I10S, I12S, I15S), an outcome of the political limits of the Transition and the progressive lack of autonomy of politics due to the prominence of economic powers (I6S, I11S). Podemos, thus, draws a line between democracy ('those who are democrats and defend social rights') and oligarchy ('the country's elites and the power of the markets'). From a theoretically and historically informed approach, Iglesias (particularly during the party's initial phase) has even described democracy as an 'expropriating movement oriented towards taking away the power of a privileged minority and sharing it with the majority'.[10] This understanding of a dichotomized political landscape allows the party to create a collective subject that identifies with the Podemos project as a way to overcome the regime crisis in the country.

In this context, democracy has also been used in a functionalist way to solve the debates concerning territorial problems and diverse national identities in Spain. In an attempt to overcome the 'national cleavage',

Podemos has defended a democratic consultation in Catalonia as a way to make possible 'the right to decide' while stressing the 'social problem' in the region.

4.3.3. Mobilizing constituencies

(a) Change and hope
In order to modify the situation and resolve the social and political problems in Spain, Podemos has developed a strategic mobilizing framing to attract active support and enhance collective engagement through an optimistic rhetoric. This has been articulated around the notions of change, excitement, and hope. Hope has been used as a mechanism to challenge the rhetoric of reaction (Hirschman 1991) and as an alternative to the widespread narrative of fear and crisis (I14S, I15S). At the same time, it is directly linked with the domestic social movements' legacy and the 'Sí se puede' (Yes, it is possible) slogan expressed by movements like the Plataforma de Afectados por la Hipoteca (PAH). This message seeks to spread a feeling of excitement, an abstract notion connected to the emotional dimension of politics that has been so evident in Podemos' framing, and the need to present the party as radically different from the traditional parties (I10S, I13S). An eloquent example is the poster for the 2014 European elections and its slogan, '*When was the last time you voted with excitement?*', which linked Podemos to the idea of excitement as a way to stimulate the passions of joy (I5S).

Change has also been used by Podemos to discursively respond to the social demands of the era. This has been particularly relevant in the party's repertoires of action, such as the 'Marcha del Cambio', while 2015 has been termed 'the year of change', as an electoral victory in the general elections could open the opportunity for a new political era in the country. The idea of change is not, however, clearly defined (I14S), but abstractly associated with building 'a new country', promoting a new constituent process (I11S, I13S), and deepening democracy – as quoted in the electoral programme for regional elections, 'change means to achieve by ourselves the higher levels of democracy' (EPRE 2015, 63).

But it is the concept of democracy that links together diagnostic and prognostic framing as a way to motivate people, providing a rationale for action and change: this coherence in framing is evident in the 'Marcha del Cambio', when Iglesias claimed in front of thousands of people: 'they say change is chaos and an experiment; we say change is democracy'.[11]

(b) Critically pro-European
Traditionally, Spain has been presented as a case of consensual Europeanization (Vázquez 2012), with no 'hard Euroscepticism' cases

(Szerbiak and Taggart 2003; Benedetto and Quaglia 2007). Except for minoritarian right-wing parties, the main political parties converge on the issue of the European integration process (Sánchez-Cuenca 2000). Some of these have adopted a kind of soft Euroscepticism for different reasons: in the case of the PP, this is targeted against a federal EU model or, in the case of centre-left and especially left-wing parties, against the democratic deficit and the lack of social policies in European institutions (Jiménez and Egea de Haro 2011; Vázquez et al. 2014).

Within this context, Podemos' framing of Europe can be understood as a kind of left-wing soft Euroscepticism, similar to the one developed by Izquierda Unida. To begin with, the European framework has been extremely important in the general framing of Podemos, as Iglesias observes: 'the strategy we have followed is to articulate a discourse on the recovery of sovereignty, on social rights, even human rights, in a European framework' (2015b). At the same time, in the initial party Manifesto 'Mover ficha: convertir la indignación en cambio político' (*Making a Move: Turning Indignation into Political Change*), criticism is levelled at the 'crisis of legitimacy of the EU' or references to the 'financial *Coup d'Etat* against Southern European countries'. In addition, the programme for the European elections particularly underlines the lack of democracy in communitarian institutions.[12] This ambiguity is explained by a Podemos activist in Madrid:

> There is a paradox on this because most of Podemos' voters are the more Eurosceptic ones in Spain. However, Podemos' discourse on Europe has been very pro-European but critical. For me this has been very interesting and similar to the one displayed by SYRIZA: we are against the EU as it is constituted but we are in favour of a new type of relations in Europe; we need more Europe to overcome the crisis, we are against a two-speed Europe, the centre and the periphery, etc. It is true that even the discourse was not Eurosceptic. The perception was that Podemos was the party challenging more the neoliberal order in Europe, maybe because Podemos put much emphasis on the issue of sovereignty. That is, to exit the crisis, overcome austerity and restore democracy we need to recover the national sovereignty that has been taken from us within the EU and globalization. And this, I think is an interesting balance. We need to recover the ability and the power to decide, but we do not want to be isolated. (I12S)

This ambivalence towards Europe is reflected in the European election results: Podemos' supporters are more interested in the EU than the average citizen (62.4 per cent versus 42.9 per cent), while being in fact the more Eurosceptic voters: 23.4 per cent are 'quite or very much against' the EU, compared to the average of 13.4 per cent. At the same time, Podemos' voters are more likely than other citizens are to blame the EU rather than the government for the Spanish economic situation (CIS, June 2014).

What is interesting is Podemos' alliance strategy with other European parties in order to overcome austerity policies at the European level: the party joined the GUE/NGL[13] along with the parties of the European Left in what was considered as a clear message of Podemos' ideology and strategy concerning political coalitions. Moreover, Podemos has repeatedly shown support for SYRIZA, including during the September 2015 parliamentary elections, while most recently Iglesias has also stated his support for Jeremy Corbyn in the leadership election in the British Labour Party.

4.3.4. Frame resonance with social movements: From proximity to ambiguous co-existence

The party's framing draws from the movement milieu, exactly because the origins of Podemos cannot be separated from the anti-austerity mobilizations. As Flesher-Fominaya (2014) notes and as already observed above, the very name 'Podemos' reflects the PAH slogan 'Sí se puede!' Iglesias himself usually describes Podemos as the 'principal political expression of the 15M' (Iglesias 2015a): the relationship between Podemos and social movements is to be found in some of the political and cultural outcomes of the 15M movement, which managed to challenge the existing political consensus prevalent in the country since the Transition. Podemos' spokespersons, however, declare that the party's strategy was not built on the appropriation of the movement,[14] but around the recognition of the positive effects and opportunities created by the 15M. Nonetheless, the linkage of the party with social movements goes beyond relations with the 15M, as the ongoing political and organizational evolution of Podemos is itself generating different ways to relate with grassroots movements in terms of framing, both in the programmatic inclusion of social movements' claims and the party's strategy towards civil society.

(a) **Programmatic proximity**
Some authors have underlined the ideological 'ambiguity' of Podemos' programme (Galindo et al. 2015, 8): although Podemos declares itself to be beyond left and right, its political programme has gradually been drafted as a typical social-democratic project, while it has adopted a

Nordic social-democratic approach with respect to its public policy agenda (Iglesias 2015d).[15] Regarding its specific programmatic discourse, there has been a significant evolution from the radical left 2014 European elections programme to the more moderate one for the 2015 regional elections (I13S, I17S) (Rendueles and Sola 2015).[16] While some issues, such as the public debt or basic income, are still debated and under discussion (I10S) through a series of participatory online tools, the following five resolutions were approved by a Constituent Assembly: defending public education – as a right and not a business; anti-corruption; winning the right to housing and putting an end to financial impunity; for the right to health – a public health system for all; audit and debt restructuring – a proposal for Podemos. These resolutions reflect the proximity of Podemos' framing to the main claims expressed by the movements during the anti-austerity wave of protests. While proposals had been elaborated by experts (on economy, culture and the healthcare system),[17] in many cases these guidelines were indeed launched by social movement activists who were also Podemos members. On the other hand, it has been noted that Podemos has been increasingly withdrawing from a series of crucial social movements demands, such as 'degrowth, feminism or migrants' rights' (Arribas Lozano 2015, 161). For instance, regarding the general elections, Podemos presented a programmatic manifesto with five main claims that would form a new agreement for a new country:[18] (1) a new democratic model reinforcing participatory democracy; (2) independence of the judiciary; (3) measures oriented to fighting corruption; (4) the constitutional guarantee of social rights; (5) a territorial model for the country defending the 'unity within diversity'. The development of such an electoral strategy is not a deep reform of the existing Spanish Constitution nor a constituent process, as understood during the initial phase of Podemos.

(b) Continuities and discontinuities

The programmatic inclusion of movements' claims and more generally the framing adopted by Podemos reflect the existing continuities between the party and the 15M, which are also to be found in the use of a consensual approach introduced by the movement with the goal of ideological transversality, as well as the use of ICTs for organizational and participation purposes (Lobera 2015). Moreover, there are manifest biographical continuities between the party and the movements, which allow us to understand Podemos as the result of the 'political incorporation of a sector of the 15M, precisely that sector with more political experience' (Calvo and Álvarez 2015, 118). Some of Podemos' spokespersons, such as Iglesias or Errejón, have been activists in the GJM and the student movement, and many Citizens' State Council members have been social movement activists: according to Martín (2015, 110), thirteen of them actively participated in the 15M, seven in JSF, six in the student movement, and three in the PAH. Moreover, numerous current elected representatives have been active in various grassroots mobilizations – including trade unions, social centres, ecologist or feminist movements and so on – reflecting a co-option strategy oriented to get political legitimacy and electoral support from movements. Iglesias comments on the transfer of activists from the movements to the party as follows:

> Many of those who acquired an experience of leadership came to join Podemos; the party's leading ranks are by and large filled with people from the social movements. It was a natural outcome: the 15M movement politicized civil society, then followed this process of activist formation, and that led to taking the next step, of giving the movement a political and electoral expression. (Iglesias 2015b)

At the same time, in order to establish a permanent linkage with social movements, Podemos has launched the 'Area of Civil Society' led by Rafa Mayoral, an ex-lawyer for the PAH and a close collaborator of Iglesias. On 11 July 2015, the Area secretary organized the 'Forum for Change', with the participation of more than 2,500 activists.[19] This forum followed the April 2015 'Meeting of Activists for Change',[20] which drew 200 activists, who shared problems and suggested alternatives as experienced on the ground, for instance, in workers' movements, internationalist movements, or the defence of public services. The open call for this Forum stated that the meeting was oriented to

> ... include the main demands and citizen proposals that will serve as raw material for the elaboration of the 'People's programme', the electoral programme that will concur to the general elections. Today we face a historic opportunity to transform the institutional, social and economic reality of our country and therefore we consider it essential to create a large space for dialogue where we can first listen to the proposals of social movements and civil society.[21]

This was an attempt to transform Podemos into a mediator between civil society and political institutions.

However, as seen in the previous chapter, even if Podemos' structure has adopted certain organizational structures of the 15M mobilization (Martín 2015), some of its organizational features are in sharp contradiction with the movement. Moreover, the call for a constituent process, as rooted in the movement field, has gradually faded from its programmatic claims. The relationship with grassroots actions has also been controversial on the ground, for instance with the trade unions and especially the two major ones, CCOO and UGT, which it has also challenged along with the political system and bipartisanship (Calle-Collado and Candón-Mena 2013; Espinoza Pino 2013). Within a general tendency of public distrust,[22] Podemos could not show much proximity with those organizations (I7S); but on the other hand, these could prove to be potential allies because of a common social basis, a dilemma that has led to an unclear strategy towards the unions.

At the same time, Iglesias has himself underlined the limits of the 15M and its relations with Podemos:

> The crisis brought to the fore by this upsurge, which surprised the world, was also a crisis of the existing Spanish left. The 15M held up a mirror to the left, revealing its deficiencies. It also put on the table the main component of a new common sense: rejection of the dominant political and economic elites, systematically labelled as corrupt. The 15M also crystallized a new culture of contestation that could not be grasped by the categories of left and right – something that the leaders of the existing left refused to acknowledge from the start. The logic of the 15M movement led to its exhaustion; it didn't achieve the effects desired by its committed activists, who hoped that the social could substitute for the institutional. Aiming to reduce politics to the mere expression of countervailing social powers, built through mobilization and patient activism, was one of the major blunders of the movementist intelligentsia in Spain, which failed to realize that the 'in the meantime' was precisely that: a way of working up until the arrival of the moment for audacity, which would require quite different political techniques. (Iglesias 2015b)

Podemos' conflictual relationship with social movements was reflected when, during the primary elections for the Citizens' Council of Madrid, Podemos spokesperson Carolina Bescansa distinguished between two different projects within the party – one oriented to electoral victory (represented by Iglesias and his team) and the other focused on protest (referring to an alternative list presented by some groups in Madrid).[23] What she revealed had been obvious, but, still, confusing: that Podemos is two-sided. One part is connected to horizontal and grassroots processes and the other focused on the party field, trying to create links with the non-mobilized constituency (Galindo et al. 2015) (I10S, I12S, I14S). As a party member from Madrid notes:

> I think that there is an ongoing tension with social movements. On the one hand, Podemos needs to disassociate itself from the movements in order to appear as a serious and governing political force, but not too much because of its social base that comes directly from the

movements and is still present. On the other hand, it is obvious that Podemos, even with its problems and defects, remains the political expression of the struggle against austerity, but there is an obvious tension with the movements that is expressed in the participation of more activists, for example, in the local candidacies. (I12S)

To conclude, as reflected in the framing strategies of Podemos, the linkage between the party and the 15M and other social movements 'exists, but is partial, is not institutionalized and is causing a certain internal tension' (Martín 2015, 109). In any case, the party does not officially represent the organizational continuity of the anti-austerity and real democracy cycle of protest, and has not established a 'formal, open and stable' relationship with any social movement (Martín 2015, 111). This ambiguity is described by a Madrid social activist as follows:

All these social movements have fed Podemos. Podemos does not have a single cadre who is not from those spaces. Therefore, the critique against activism and activists displayed sometimes by Podemos' leaders is ridiculous because they themselves are activists. What is the future relationship that will give...? I have no idea. What I do know is that where that relationship is proactive it will be successful, and where not there will be failure. (I8S)

4.4. The M5S framing: A catch-all party?

4.4.1. Diagnosing the crisis: A catch-all movement against the 'castes'

Among the most important aspects of the M5S programme, neo-environmentalism and the moralization of politics have been underlined (Passarelli et al. 2013). On the one hand, most of the Movement's proposals were initially developed with reference to the local level concerning environmental issues. On the other hand, the Movement employs a vehement anti-establishment discourse against the 'caste' of politicians that is said to enjoy privileges and that should be suppressed. In Grillo's words, politicians are 'zombies' who plunder public money and must now hand over the floor to honest citizens. According to the comedian, there is no difference between the two main parties of the centre-right and centre-left – Grillo refers to the PD as 'the PDL minus the L'. This idea of indistinction recalls the label 'PPSOE' used by the Spanish Indignados to indicate that no distinctions exist between the People's Party (PP) and the Socialist one (PSOE). Consistently, activists define parties as deviant filters that do not represent the needs of the majority of citizens, but the interests of a few (Macaluso 2015, 171; Biorcio 2015a), and engagement within the M5S is often contrasted with involvement in traditional parties.

Although the M5S participates in elections, Grillo publicly opposes any kind of mediation. Beyond the 'caste' of politicians, other intermediaries such as media professionals and trade unions form part of the M5S targets. Public employees are also attacked as unproductive and costly. The narrative of the M5S outlines a society divided into two antagonistic blocs: on the one side the moral citizens, and on the other the Italian and international political, mediatic and economic elites.

> Class conflict has been replaced by caste conflict, or rather the battle between those who produce wealth and social services and the parasite class, the caste....In fact the castes are everywhere....The political caste, the caste of the newspapers, the caste of the bureaucracy, the caste of the public administration, the caste of the useless entities, the caste of the companies partially owned by the State, the caste of the companies managing concessions, the caste of the golden pensions. Infinite castes that strangle the citizen like a boa constrictor....The power of the caste does not stem from the control of the means of production, but from the control of the media. Without the daily lies, the caste would be nude and visible in their arrogance and uselessness....The battle against the castes is the true political battle.[24]

This interpretative scheme constructed by the M5S can clearly activate a demarcation between 'us' as opposed to 'them', in a context dominated by a political, social, and economic crisis (Biorcio 2015b, 18).

Another important aspect of the M5S framing concerns its political positioning. Since its emergence it has presented itself as beyond left and right, considering traditional ideologies as something archaic and functional to reproducing power.

> The time of ideologies is over. The M5S is not fascist, nor right-wing, nor left-wing. It is above and beyond any attempt to isolate, to oppose, to mystify his words classifying them instrumentally. The M5S does not have prejudices against people. If they are uncensored, not joining another political party or movement, if they identify with the programme, our gates are and will always be open to them.[25]

The post-ideological discourse of Grillo and Casaleggio resonates in the words of grassroots activists, both in refusing ideological cleavages and in considering the encounter of different political traditions as something positive from which better ideas can emerge (I1I). According to them, 'The left–right divide is part of a big theatrical trick. Good ideas are neither right-wing nor left-wing' (Naples activist, cited in Lanzone and Tronconi 2015, 63); and 'Left and right are two sides of the same coin. The words "left" or "right" don't mean anything to us' (Piacenza activist, cited in ibid.). Locating itself beyond left and right translates into a rejection of any kind of compromise, collaboration, or alliance with the traditional parties that are considered responsible for the moral, social, and economic crisis.

In the economic domain, the Manichean discourse of the leaders contrasts small (honest shopkeepers, artisans, and small and medium-sized enterprises or SMEs) versus large players (finance, banks, corporations) as well as 'good, competitive' capitalism versus 'evil, state-assisted' capitalism (Caruso 2016a). The anti-capitalism of Grillo and Casaleggio focuses on the criticism of money, consumerism, and work. As such, it takes the shape of a 'romantic' anti-capitalism, since their analysis does not concern, as in leftist anti-capitalism, the social relations and the exploitation of labour, but is limited to some specific degenerative aspects of contemporary capitalism – particularly the Italian model (Caruso 2016a).

In an attempt to explain the success and the catch-all nature of the M5S beyond the analysis of the official programme presented for the 2013 general elections, Tronconi has noted that Grillo's party programme was an ambiguous and contradictory 'manifesto in the making' that was integrated with relevant and new claims during the electoral campaign – both with an official letter to the Italians ('20 points to come out of the darkness')[26] and with a series of posts on his blog. While leftist voters were attracted by 'the emphasis on the environment, the pledge for a universal basic income, support for the public health and education systems, all issues that have been present in the M5S' political discourse since its very origins' (Tronconi 2015b, 223), conservative voters were charmed by proposals to lower taxes on house property, criticisms of the euro, support for small entrepreneurs and a cautious approach towards any opening on immigration policy, 'all issues added to the original manifesto and particularly emphasized during the 2013 campaign' (ibid., 224).

In line with its incongruous manifesto, M5S voters place themselves in a central position among the main parties, not displaying a clear left or right ideological connotation: 'the high level of inconsistency seen in M5S voters is due to the above-average presence of those voters whom we have called "post-ideological", that is, politically well-informed individuals who nevertheless display contradictoriness with regard to the left–right ideological axis' (Colloca and Corbetta 2015, 205).

4.4.2. Solving the crisis through citizen engagement, online disintermediation, and small businessmen

Grillo sees the solution to the democratic crisis in citizens' direct participation in politics, as this has to be reappropriated in transforming an immoral terrain, where corruption and private interests prevail over honest people and where public goods are left at the margins, into a transparent setting of equal participants. In the words of its leader:

> The M5S wants the entry of the citizen into active politics, an event that has never happened up till now. The democracy of the mass-man is the past. The democracy in which each person counts as one is the future. The transparency of every public action, permitted by the internet, individual responsibility, politics as a time-limited civic duty.[27]

Hence, the Movement asks for a drastic reduction in the cost of politics and a term limit in parliament and in local councils to give all citizens the possibility to engage in politics for a restricted period of time. In this framework, political inexperience is considered as a strength rather than a weakness. According to Grillo, the ability to effectively carry out a profession or manage a family in the private sphere can be easily and unproblematically translated into work within the institutions. As the comedian stated, 'I want to see a mother of a single-income family with four children become mayor of a town. She would most certainly know how to run a town council. A Prime Minister who is an artisan, a teacher or an electrician, not some two-bit corrupter.'[28]

A cyber-utopian discourse is one of the main distinctive features of M5S' rhetoric (Treré and Barassi 2015). In fact, 'cyber-utopianism and the idea of the internet as a force liberating contemporary socio-political systems from all constraints, combined with the M5S' close identification with the web have been crucial in representing the Movement as a disruptive entity not comparable with any other political actor' (Mosca et al. 2015b, 130). The internet is presented as a panacea for contemporary 'corrupted' democracy, as it is supposed to both promote communitarian dynamics – creating the conditions for horizontal and cooperative relations – and favour virtuous competition, helping the emergence, by virtue of its endogenous mechanisms, of the best ideas, practices, and people (Caruso 2016a). Disintermediation – which can be attained via the internet – is understood as demolishing any kind of mediation, any type of filter and organism between the citizens and their spokespersons. The kind of disintermediation advocated by Grillo and Casaleggio is both political and mediatic: from the point of view of the leader, disintermediation translates into structurelessness and direct communication with the base, bypassing traditional gatekeepers (parties and media); while from the citizens' point of view, it equates to direct democracy and continuous control of elected representatives, mainstream media monitoring, and active production of information (Biancalana 2013, 102).

Regarding specific social actors, small businesspeople are seen as heroes fighting for the survival of the Italian industrial system. As such, the M5S declares its unconditional support for them as a possible way out of the economic crisis. SMEs have become central in the speeches and political proposals of the M5S since the 2013 general elections campaign (Corbetta and Gualmini 2013). The values of the dominant players in the most advanced sectors of capitalism (such as the green economy and the ICT sector) as well as the SMEs (including shopkeepers) are identified as virtuous, as opposed to the parasitic elite of the political class, assisted capitalism, big finance, banks, and corporations (Corbetta and Gualmini 2013).

4.4.3. Mobilizing constituencies

Two important aspects of the M5S' mobilizing frame concern democracy and Europe. Regarding democratic conceptions, Grillo has often stressed the need for citizens to take direct responsibility and engage in person on public issues. Direct democracy facilitated by the internet is seen as the solution to the moral, economic, and social crisis. Concerning Europe, Italy is presented as constrained by the Brussels elites' imposition of austerity policies and expropriation of national sovereignty. The M5S' discourse on Europe appears as contradictory, both advocating more integration (for example, the request for Eurobonds) and more national sovereignty (for example, the exit from the common monetary system, seen as an *extrema ratio* to regain control of the domestic economy).

(a) Framing democracy: A (limited) notion of direct democracy in the M5S
The democratic conception of the M5S – stressing direct democracy, alternative ways of organization to party models, and a critique of delegation and leadership – has been equated to the elaboration developed by new social movements and the new left of the 1970s and 1980s (Biorcio and Natale 2013; Gualmini 2013). Democratic ideals in the M5S are based on some core beliefs, such as the idea that traditional forms of organization (that is, political parties) are historically overcome and the need to supplement representative democracy with elements of direct democracy (Caruso 2015).

According to Grillo and Casaleggio, direct democracy is currently made possible by the wide diffusion of internet access, which favours 'disintermediation' processes in every area of human activity. The internet is seen as allowing the overcoming of hierarchies and power concentrations and favouring the emergence of leaderless and structureless movements that will replace traditional mediators (Casaleggio and Grillo 2011, 9). In the long run, the internet will make the existence of the M5S unnecessary, as any decision could be simply made online by citizens without any intermediation.

Four pillars help to describe their democratic conceptions: (a) rules aimed at making representatives more accountable; (b) the defence of the constitution and representative assemblies; (c) the introduction of new instruments of direct/participatory democracy; (d) online voting. Although the Italian constitution prohibits binding mandates, M5S representatives are simply considered as spokespeople and citizens' employees executing their will; as such, they should be constantly monitored (and even revocable) by their constituencies.[29] At one of his speeches during the third V-day, Grillo even said, 'I want to change our Constitution and introduce a recall election, as in the United States, to remove from office elected officials who do not deliver on their promises' (cited in Farinelli and Massetti 2015, 224). The M5S has included in its internal regulations (such as the codes of conduct for elected representatives) rules approximating to the idea of recall. According to an activist from Palermo, '[MPs] are not "honourables", they are our spokespersons...we could even put them in minority and, if any of them fail to achieve the objectives of the movement, we can revoke their mandate' (cited in Macaluso 2015, 174). Moreover, local representatives present themselves every six months before the assembly of activists, to illustrate their achievements and explicitly seek confirmation. In most cases, the assembly generally confirms the elected representatives, but there is some evidence of territorial groups forcing local representatives to resign.[30]

Beyond rules aimed at making representatives more accountable, the democratic conception of the M5S is based on two pillars of representative democracy: (a) the idea of the centrality of the parliament, which must be safeguarded from the intrusiveness of the government and the president of the republic; (b) the constitution, which is often perceived as under threat from risky attempts at reform (Caruso 2015).

The democratic conception of the M5S is not only expressed in negative prohibitions but also substantiated in positive provisions. The M5S claims for an extension of instruments of direct democracy. Some of them, such as referenda without quorum and the obligation to discuss laws of popular initiative, were symbolically introduced in the new statute of the municipality of Parma, governed by the M5S. Moreover, participatory budgeting formed part of the programme of Livorno's M5S mayor, while draft bills are published online on a dedicated platform before their approval, in order to receive comments from registered members. In Pomezia, the mayor and his councillors meet once a week with all interested people, as 'A direct contact of the mayor and the local government with their citizens has been lacking for a long time. In seven months we have met more than 500 people' (I2I).

Lastly, the M5S' democratic narrative is strongly based on the idea of direct democracy, in which voting through the internet is central. Paradigmatic of this approach is the following claim made by Grillo: 'We want instruments of direct democracy in the hands of the citizens. I dream of my son voting yes or no on a computer from his home, deciding whether to go to Afghanistan or not, whether staying in Europe or not, whether to leave the euro or not. This is what I want.'[31] However, 'no regulated or consistent mechanism of web consultation has yet been put in place. Party members are consulted only when the leadership wishes to do so, and on questions framed and phrased by the leadership' (Farinelli and Massetti 2015, 226). Criticisms of online consultations on Grillo's blog are voiced by activists perceiving the different alternatives as presented in a different light (Milan activists, cited in Boffi 2015, 53). Whereas political practices are inspired by a vision of participatory democracy at the local level, a centralized leadership acts at the national level backing a conception of direct democracy that is actually translated into a plebiscitary model, based on the direct and immediate relationship between the leader and the crowd made possible by ICTs (Floridia and Vignati 2014, 70; see also Treré and Barassi 2015).

(b) Framing Europe: against the 'Brussels caste'

Prior to the 2013 national elections, the M5S did not really dedicate much consideration to Europe (Franzosi et al. 2015). The M5S projected in Europe its anti-establishment rhetoric against the 'Brussels caste': 'rather than being elaborated *ad hoc* for the EP elections, the criticism of the EU democratic deficit seems to represent a transposition at the supra-national level of the M5S' electorally successful condemnation of the Italian political system' (Castelli Gattinara and Froio 2014, 23).

The synthetic programme of the M5S for the European elections consisted of seven points that were presented by Grillo on the occasion of the third V-day in Genoa in December 2013. Interestingly, the programme does not include arguments against European integration but opposes specific austerity policies. In presenting the electoral manifesto, the Movement is even defined as 'the only grouping of people that is truly pro-European'.[32] As explained on the blog, however, the M5S advocates a different Europe: 'The M5S is neither pro-Euro nor anti-Euro. The M5S wants a *return to the principles of solidarity and community*.... The M5S wants an inclusive Europe, or no Europe.'[33] During the electoral campaign, several posts were published on Grillo's blog to explain the seven points included in the manifesto. In one of them, the M5S leader went beyond the traditional critique of the EU democratic deficit. He stressed, in fact, the imposition of unelected governments by European institutions, as 'governments are created and dissolved in Brussels and in the halls of the ECB'.[34]

A very relevant point included in the European electoral programme concerns the intention to collect signatures for a consultative referendum on Italy's exit from the euro – something that had already been proclaimed during the 2013 general electoral campaign. The key targets of the electoral manifesto – the abolition of the fiscal compact, investments in innovation excluded from the constraints of the Maastricht Treaty, the abolition of the balanced budget as a constitutional requirement – are austerity policies that need to be contrasted by relaxing fiscal policy. The manifesto also proposed an alliance among the countries of Southern Europe, which have suffered the most dramatic effects of the economic crisis and financial rigour. Another important point concerns the request for Eurobonds adoption, which is a measure implying a further decline of national sovereignty and the strengthening of Communitarian institutions (Caruso 2016b). The M5S' Euroscepticism is not reflected in a cultural aversion to the EU. It has a simply pragmatic aim: 'The goal, albeit distant and utopian, is not the destruction of the Union but rather to change it, in order to make it "democratic, transparent, with shared decisions made by referendum", "liable, and really communitarian"' (Biancalana and Tronconi 2014, 133–4).

After the European elections, the decision to join UKIP in forming a common political group – Europe of Freedom and Direct Democracy (EFDD) – in the European Parliament has been particularly contentious, mobilizing groups of activists against it (Mosca 2015b). Grillo has claimed, however, that the alliance with Farage was constrained by European Parliament rules that impose harsh penalties for MEPs who remain unaffiliated (fewer resources, exclusion from institutional roles, reduced speaking time and so on).[35]

Indeed, when reading the EFDD's statute, the autonomy of M5S' MEPs seems safeguarded. The fourth paragraph of Article 1 – entitled, 'Respect for national differences and interests: Freedom of votes' – claims that 'the Group respects the freedom of its delegations and members to vote as they see fit'. According to Article 2, 'each subgroup or member has complete freedom to act in accordance with his/her own conviction'.[36]

Going beyond the content of formal documents, an interesting study analysed the factual behaviour of M5S' MEPs in the European Parliament in the first six months of their parliamentary activity (from 1 July to 31 December 2014). The authors have noted that the cohesion rate of the EFDD group was the lowest of all parliamentary groups, with its members voting together only 51 per cent of the time against 95 per cent of the EPP, 90 per cent of the S&D, and 76 per cent of the ECR (Franzosi et al. 2015, 119). Another remarkable result regards intragroup cohesion, which shows an exceptionally different loyalty rate between the two main parties belonging to the EFDD: while the M5S voted with its group only 42 per cent of the time, UKIP did so 89 per cent of the time. Differences in voting behaviour between the two parties emerge in policy fields as diverse as the EU budget, foreign and security policy, international trade, immigration, employment and social affairs, environment and public health, civil liberties, justice, and home affairs. In sum, 'there is hardly a single policy field in which the two parties have any degree of cohesion...UKIP is the party with which the M5S voted the least in the first six months of this term (only 21 times out of 97)' (Franzosi et al. 2015, 121). Interestingly, the M5S MEPs most often united their votes with the GUE-NL (66 per cent) and the Greens/EFA (72 per cent), particularly with respect to foreign and security policy and international trade. This seems consistent with the observation made on national MPs by Farinelli and Massetti: 'in spite of Grillo's rhetoric, M5S parliamentarians are not beyond political ideologies. Most of them are ideologically much closer to the left on both socio-economic and socio-cultural issues, and with some important variations they generally think that SEL [Sinistra, Ecologia e Libertà – Left, Ecology and Freedom] is the party with the most affinity with the M5S' (2015, 222).

As such, despite their membership, M5S MEPs appear closer to pro-EU parties than to hard Eurosceptic ones. Their affiliation appears then to be a consequence of tactical positioning and seems mostly motivated by party competition and peculiar incentives provided by the EU institution.

4.4.4. Resonance with social movements: A peculiar (and disputed) relation

In the framing of the M5S, an important role has been played since the outset by references to social movements and grassroots campaigns. For instance, the Occupy Wall Street and Indignados movements are considered as models for their horizontal organization and anti-leaderistic rhetoric (Casaleggio et al. 2013). The very name of the party immediately recalls social movements.

The channel through which emphasis on participatory democracy has become part of the political culture of the M5S is to be found in local networks of civic activism against large-scale infrastructures or giant waste treatment plants, mobilizations on water as a common good, or initiatives inspired by the critical culture of consumption that have bloomed in Italy during the past decade (Floridia and Vignati 2014, 63). An analysis of electoral manifestos drawn up by the M5S for national and local elections clearly shows a sort of appropriation of social movement claims, ranging from environmental struggles to the defence of common goods, from the expansion of civic rights to alternative ways to measure growth, from the protection of vulnerable social groups to direct participation by citizens in policy-making (Mosca 2015a). However, the more recent programmatic evolution really blurred the ideological profile of the M5S: 'in the proposals of the M5S, approaches and traditions in many respects alternative to one another converge: those of social movements, socialist and radical left, with those of large ICTs enterprises, populist right, and employers' associations' (Caruso 2016a).

In any case, despite thematic proximity with social movements, the relationship established with grassroots groups has rarely been characterized by common work and shared purposes. Although it defines itself as a 'Movement' and valorizes collective mobilization, the M5S does not build alliances, common claims, or mobilizations with other organized social forces (movements, associations, committees), even when they are active on issues at the core of its programmatic action (Caruso 2016b). Moreover, protests within institutions have been considered by leftist journalists and *engagé* intellectuals as a mere 'simulation of a civic war', demonstrating 'its lack of interest in taking roots in and mingling with social conflicts confirming its purely spectacular nature' (Santoro 2014, 21; see also the Wu Ming Foundation's blog).[37]

Criticism has also been directed more generally to the M5S' instrumental parliamentary behaviour. For example, after long declaring support for a bill legalizing same-sex civil unions in Italy, the sudden decision to allow party MPs to vote according to their conscience was harshly criticized by LGBT activists for opportunistic electoral reasons (*Guardian*, 19 February 2016). Some of the party's elected representatives – mayors in particular – have been harshly criticized by movement activists for betraying their goals when in power. According to a spokesperson of a local committee in Parma, 'The M5S has created great expectations throughout the electoral campaign, in all its discourses, the proposals for a different, new and special way to interact with the citizens...something that resonates probably also with Grillo, who for a while has proposed a different way to practise democracy. Then after the elections nothing, almost nothing' (I3I). In the words of another local activist in Civitavecchia, 'now these people govern and a number of former activists like me are back again to the streets to demonstrate against the 5 stars... because these people have not respected and do not intend to comply with the agreements'.[38] Meanwhile, some activists also argued that the presence of the M5S prevented social movements from building a common collective identity able to transcend boundaries and to constitute the backbone of a new political entity more similar to those that flourished in other Mediterranean countries (Andretta 2016).

Although not strongly connected with anti-austerity protests – like SYRIZA and Podemos – and despite growing criticism from the social movement arena, the M5S has partially captured and incorporated activists, grievances, claims, and action forms from diverse Italian social movements of the past decade. Despite growing criticism from the social movement milieu, contentious themes and images, squares and symbolic dates have been appropriated over time by local groups, activists, and their leaders.

4.5. Conclusion

A new wave of contention has shaken the world since 2010, taking local forms – in the squares of Madrid, collective kitchens in Athens, local movements in Italy – while being tuned transnationally, protesters include ordinary citizens, not previously engaged in contentious action, who deeply distrust the existing political establishment; mainstream parties (including those of the left); and representative institutions at large. At this critical juncture, when those taken-for-granted pillars of the status quo are being challenged, the parties that proved (partially) successful in electoral terms have been those that either emerged from the movements or developed while maintaining an organic link with them. This has been the case, to a lesser or greater extent, with SYRIZA in Greece, Podemos in Spain, and the M5S in Italy, all of which managed to frame their political discourse in ways compatible with the understanding of politics and democracy voiced by grassroots mobilizations.

SYRIZA, which was founded as an electoral coalition, became for a short period a 'movement party' in between two contradictory processes: on the one hand, it draws from the history of the Greek left and its eurocommunist tradition (with respect to top-down organizational structures and adherence to parliamentary politics and the idea of Europe); on the other, during those crisis-ridden years, it remained connected with the protest field and was fuelled by the popular anti-austerity movement. This grassroots aura has faded since it became the main opposition (2012) and then the ruling party (2015).

In the case of Podemos, some authors have categorized it as an 'anti-establishment party' (Galindo et al. 2015) while others, such as Wallerstein (2015) or de Sousa Santos (2014), have repeatedly defined it as a movement party. The inherent relationship between Podemos and the real democracy movement that developed in Spain during the last years, the so-called 15M, has been indubitable; however, since its recent electoral advances, the party has been oriented towards institutions, gradually withdrawing from its horizontal and constituent drive.

Regarding the M5S, while it started out as a movement criticizing the institutions of representative democracy, it has since transformed into a 'movement party', shifting most of its focus to the electoral arena. Its growing formalization and rapid evolution into a (relatively) stable force of the Italian political system cast doubts on the persistence of a 'movement party' model. Despite efforts to resist the iron law of oligarchy, the next national elections will probably represent a further step towards its full development into a political party. For a period of time, though, SYRIZA, Podemos, and the M5S managed to converge with movements, especially with regard to their framing of reality; according to our interviewees, this was the key to their great electoral success.

In terms of the framing strategies adopted, there has been an important divergence among the parties concerning their points of departure on political positioning. While connected with protests that transcended the traditional 'left versus right' cleavage to attack all political parties, the three movement parties related differently with the left: criticizing the existing political system, SYRIZA chose not only to acknowledge its left-wing tradition and ideology, but insisted on the 'unity of the left' vision and on the slogan 'First Time Left!' (2015). Podemos emphasized the 'neither on the right nor on the left' line as a way to denounce the past and introduce itself as a different actor worthy of (electoral) trust. Its ideological profile, however, remained built around left-wing values. Drawing from the same anti-political stance as Podemos, the M5S defined itself as beyond left and right, although it remained more ambiguous: while in many cases it seems aligned with ecological and left-wing actors in the country, its discourse indeed entails positions that cannot be traditionally related with left-wing ideology.

While different historical traditions and socio-political factors may account for this divergence, the points of convergence supersede contextual particularities. For instance, an innovative aspect common in the framing of the three movement parties concerns references to nation, country, homeland, and similar concepts that have traditionally been considered 'taboo' for left-wing parties and social movements alike, associated mostly with the framing of right-wing actors. This shift seems to resonate with a similar turn in anti-austerity demonstrations already underlined. As noted by della Porta and Mattoni, 'national pride was called for in an inclusive framing of the self by movements that claimed to represent...the largest possible majority....Tunisian, Egyptian and Greek demonstrators referred to national symbols (flags and anthems) within a discourse of defence of national sovereignty against the dominance of powerful states, international organizations and big corporations' (2014, 7). Although with varying gradations and against different understandings within each political culture and protest milieu, Podemos, SYRIZA, and the M5S define their identity with reference to national sovereignty (Font et al. 2015). However, differently from the M5S, SYRIZA and Podemos also put forward a left-wing understanding of democracy and social change.

Diagnostic framing in all three cases is similar: a sharp dividing line is drawn between 'them' – the establishment, including political, business, and media elites, at the national, European, and international levels – and a broad 'we, the people', all those ordinary citizens suffering unjustly from and paying daily for a corrupt status quo, while being unable to have an impact on politics. This interpretation of the crisis and of those involved has been embedded in mass protests that are growing due to high levels of inequality, impoverishment, anger, and distrust towards representative institutions and politicians across Southern Europe. While the distance between mainstream parties and their constituencies is increasing, these parties were the only ones to engage with protesters attempting to voice their anti-austerity demands in defence of democratic and social rights. All three parties recognize and aspire to represent this 'new social majority' along the lines of a 'new populism' influenced by different legacies and political ideas: SYRIZA is a left-wing party with 'movementist' accents and social-democracy claims, while in the case of Podemos this has been the result of an elaborated 'populist hypothesis' reflecting Laclau's and Mouffe's imprint; as for the M5S, its catch-all nature has been rooted in local popular struggles. Even if populism has been considered and officially declared the main enemy of the EU establishment in all three cases – although to different extents – a distinct 'inclusionary populism' has emerged (Stavrakakis and Katsampekis 2014).

Prognostic framing draws from this diagnosis of the problem, which calls for 'inclusionary' solutions: the financial crisis and the crisis of legitimacy will be resolved in Greece, Spain, and Italy when people become engaged in politics and decide their own fates. Movement parties' spokespersons speak in 'common sense' discourse about 'shared conceptions' about democracy, the crisis, and austerity (Subirats 2015b; Errejón 2015), both at a national and at a European level. Their identity is built around a 'we' with the potential to embrace majorities that have been excluded, imagining a new kind of democracy ('renewed' or 'disintermediated'). Gradually, however, differences start to emerge in how parties understand this: Podemos displays most features of an ideal type of 'inclusionary populism', putting forward a series of participatory mechanisms around which a new kind of democracy is built. While the M5S has also capitalized on the inclusionary role of the internet in building a new and unmediated democracy, it has been considered far from this ideal type because of its position on welfare extension (limited to a minimum income scheme) and political inclusiveness (with a very selective idea of participation restricted to those registered online). SYRIZA has been considered in between the two for its stance on universal welfare expansion and its encompassing definition of the people while advocating a widening of participation; however, this has been only in principle, as any specific mention of direct democratic institutional devices is lacking (Font et al. 2015). Solutions put forward by SYRIZA concerned an institutional party different from the others, but not a different kind of democracy.

But what proved decisive in all three cases is how the diagnosis and prognosis of the crisis came together through motivational framing to form a convincing interpretation that mobilized protesters to trust a political party anew. Why and how should people defend the broadly delegitimized concepts, such as democracy and Europe, on which all three parties insisted? SYRIZA managed to convince social movements by linking protest with power: through this small left-wing party, ordinary people in the streets could actually take power and change things. Change was also a core aspect of Podemos' rationale for action, as brought forward by citizens' renewed participation and recreation of democracy. Optimism and hope formed an emotional package suitable for mobilizing constituencies. In the case of M5S, emphasis was put on change through a totally new kind of participatory politics that negated existing political elites and their privileges. By capitalizing on change and hope, and resonating with popular mobilizations, these movement parties managed to mobilize the *agency* of the people, defending the vision of a more just and inclusionary democracy and of 'another', 'social' Europe. In examining how parties mobilized constituencies to support what was considered a delegitimized political party, however, research should also account for the mounting disappointment concerning the impact protests and grassroots grievances were able to have on politics in Southern Europe; austerity policies and economic sanctions imposed by international financial organizations on the periphery of Europe seem irrelevant with the growing popular anger, frustration, and inequality.

A concluding question raised is whether proximity in framing also reflected actual proximity between the parties and social movements:

another point in common concerns the relationships that developed between those parties and social movements, which has been complicated or even, in cases, conflictual. SYRIZA, Podemos, and the M5S incorporated movements' claims in their programmatic manifestos, supported grassroots campaigns, and framed themselves as the main political expression of 'ordinary citizens' in the streets; in all three cases, however, part of the movements criticized the parties for troubling, confusing, or even co-opting grassroots processes, and part of the party became (or remained) focused on formalized party politics. A successful party is not necessarily a movement party and vice versa: even if the picture described is dynamic and rapidly evolving, it seems as if all three parties gradually chose to move along the 'party field' in response to contextual constraints and opportunities.

5

Comparing Movement
Parties' Success
and Failures

The previous three chapters have pointed at some structural and strategic choices that characterize successful attempts at building movement parties during the Great Recession in Greece, Spain, and Italy. In particular, we singled out the neoliberal critical juncture, with ensuing societal and political crisis, as well as the development of strong movements with very critical stances towards the established system as a relevant context. The crisis had particularly nefarious consequences for the party system as the centre-left parties were considered as supportive of austerity measures, and thus as betraying the ideals of social justice. As parties emerged whose framing and claiming, action repertoires and organizational models were resonant with the anti-austerity movements, initial electoral victories acted as empowering mechanisms, attracting attention in public opinion and bringing in not only social movement activists but often party activists from the left. The hysterical reactions from a delegitimized establishment further attracted sympathy and support for those parties.

The aim of this chapter is to test and specify this explanation, by comparing positive with negative cases at those two levels: the context and the strategy.

- *Party strategies and success.* A first comparative perspective looks at the party level, comparing cases of movement parties (or, at least, movement-near parties) in Italy, Greece, and Spain that did not succeed in turning social discontent into electoral support. We shall in particular analyse here the literature on parties of the radical left, looking at cases such as Sinistra, Ecologia e Libertà (Left, Ecology and Freedom, SEL) in Italy, the Greek communist party versus SYRIZA, and Izquierda Unida (United Left, IU) in Spain, in order to understand how specific choices related to organizational strategies affected party electoral results. These parties, we will argue, have tried unsuccessfully to build structures and strategies that resonate with those present in the movement field.

- *Contextual conditions within party systems for the emergence of successful movement parties.* A second comparative perspective addresses the contextual dimensions. In particular, some of the countries in which the crisis has been more severe did not experience the emergence of movement parties: Ireland and Portugal are two relevant examples of 'dogs that didn't bark' we shall address. We will discuss here the relevant responses provided by the political parties of the respective country, particularly those on the left. Moreover, we will address some expressions of the crisis of representativeness and responsibility in European countries that were less hit by the financial crisis, but still affected by the neoliberal policies with ensuing increases in social inequalities and insecurity.

- *Expanding beyond Europe.* In the last part, we shall control the extent to which the model we used to explain both the emergence and the strategies of movement parties in Europe could travel to other continents. In doing this, we shall focus on social science research that addressed movements and parties in Latin America during the neoliberal critical juncture.

5.1. Party strategies and electoral success: Movement parties that failed?

In Spain, Italy and Greece, the emergence of Podemos and the M5S as well as the development of SYRIZA contrasted with the difficulties of other radical left-wing parties to exploit the strong socio-economic grievances that were triggered by austerity policies and the ensuing earthquakes in the respective party systems. While at the level of their policy proposals these parties seemed ready to represent such grievances, their failures to develop into movement parties could be explained by their lack of capacity to develop linkages with groups both inside and outside their party organizations.

Some knowledge about parties that tried to build linkages to social movements – but failed to obtain electoral success – can be found in recent research on the radical left. In the definition proposed by March and Mudde (2005, 25), the radical left is *radical* 'first in that it rejects the underlying socio-economic structure of contemporary capitalism and its values and practices (ranging from rejection of consumerism and neoliberalism to outright opposition to private property and capitalistic profit incentives). Second, such radicals continue to advocate alternative economic and power structures involving a major redistribution of resources from the existing political elites.' Moreover, it is *left* as at the core of its agenda it places economic inequalities and advocates collective social and economic rights; and its anti-capitalist and internationalist identity pursuing cross-national networking and solidarity and stressing global structural causes (such as 'imperialism' or 'globalization') (ibid.).

Radical left-wing parties in Western Europe have been objects of limited research, which indicated, by and large, a decline in the (far) left-wing party family (Katz 2015, 509). While their crisis was explained by changes in class structure as well as the growing stigmatization of the Soviet regime, the parties of the anti-capitalist left also underwent transformations in critical moments, like 1968, 1989, and the 2000s (Botella and Ramiro 2003). While they have attempted to forge strong ties with various progressive movements, they have generally remained peripheral parties. After 1989, while electorally weak (at around 10 per cent of the electorate), some of them have given up revolutionary claims and even entered governmental coalitions albeit with modest policy results (De Waele and Seiler 2012).

A process of recovery of radical left parties in Europe has been noted, however, during the 2000s (Olsen et al. 2010; March 2011; Bale and Dunphy 2011). It has also been observed that these parties have sometimes kept some electoral appeal as well as coalition power. Moreover, they have challenged the cartel party organizational model, as they remained loyal to their social basis, even introducing some changes in their organizational structure in order to improve those linkages (Tsakatika and Lisi 2013). United by a rejection of neoliberal capitalism coupled with a defence of welfare and employment, they have become, however, quite pragmatic, often accepting offers to enter governments, even if the trade-off could be negative in terms of electoral support (Bale and Dunphy 2011). Participation in government (or even just an office-seeking strategy), together with general mistrust in institutional politics, are said in fact to have reduced the mobilization potential of these radical left parties.

Research indicated, however, the presence of different (sub)families in the radical left, with a main distinction between orthodox post-Soviet communist parties and variously reformed ones. The former openly oppose individual liberalism, support the Soviet and Stalinist past and tend to organize around the iron principle of 'democratic centralism' in the Marxist-Leninist tradition. However, a new, somehow 'populist' radical left was also singled out as detached from orthodox Marxism and for its anti-establishment stance juxtaposing 'the moral people' to 'the corrupt elite' (March and Mudde 2005).

These various types recently faced further challenges and opportunities. In the mid-2000s, the situation was summarized as characterized by both decline and mutation: the former especially visible in the marginalization of pro-Soviet left-wing parties in the post-Soviet world; the latter with the rise of a new type of radical left, bridging social rhetoric with appeals to the people and the development of transnational ties within European institutions – particularly in the EU with the United European Left-Nordic Green Left (ibid.).

In research on radical left parties, particular attention has been paid to the differential strategies in the maintenance of participatory linkages (oriented to the mobilization of members) and the environmental linkages oriented towards civil society (Lawson 1980; Schwartz 2005), with some variance expected in relation to achievement of their primary goals, as well as the survival of historical links (Allern 2010). As policy-seeking and ideological, radical left parties are expected in general to aim at establishing linkages with civic society organizations that share values of social justice and participatory democracy (Tsakatika and Lisi 2013). Radical left parties have been differentiated, in fact, based on their linkages, internal and external. As Tsakatika and Lisi (2013) noted, as far as the internal participatory linkage is concerned, one group of parties – including the Cypriot *Anorthotiko Komma Ergazomenou Laou* (AKEL, Progressive Party of Working People), the Greek KKE (Communist Party of Greece), and the Partido Comunista Português (PCP, Portuguese Communist Party) – has maintained a hierarchical conception of the relations with society, with party leadership in command of ancillary organizations. On the other hand, IU in Spain, Bloco de Esquerda (Left Bloc, BE) in Portugal, SYN/SYRIZA in Greece, and Federazione della Sinistra (FdS, Federation of the Left)[1] as well as SEL[2] in Italy, have been more innovative in allowing for more influence from rank-and-file members but also from sympathizers in their attempt to increase participation and support. As for the external, environmental linkages, it has been noted that while AKEL, the PCP, and the KKE attempt a top-down steering of civil society through ancillary organizations, SYN, FdS, SEL, BE, and IU have tried to develop more horizontal and open ties, particularly through their participation in the national Social Forums that emerged from the global justice movement (della Porta et al. 2006). This opening has been limited, however, as it aimed especially at increasing the participation of non-members and institutionalizing relations with civil society organizations. However, 'Rarely have social movements formally participated in the manifesto-making of these parties, although they have certainly influenced their programmatic offer, given that parties' way of befriending the movements is by prioritising "new politics" issues in their platforms' (Tsakatika and Lisi 2013, 13).

Strategic shifts in radical left parties have been explained by looking at relevant turning points – both the challenge that emerged in 1989 with the fall of real socialism in Eastern Europe, and the opportunities developing with the global justice movement a decade later. However, these changes proved too limited to address the movements that developed as more and more sceptical of party politics. With the one exception of SYRIZA, in fact, in none of the mentioned cases have radical left-wing parties been able to provide representation for emerging discontent with austerity policies.

This is, first of all, the case in *Italy* with regard to the FdS, but also to SEL. The former achieved only 3.4 per cent at the European elections of 2009 and, with the Rivoluzione Civile (Civil Revolution) electoral coalition, in the 2013 elections a very modest 3.2 per cent. After increased hopes following some success in the administrative elections as well as the good visibility of Nichi Vendola, his participation in the primary elections of the centre-left coalition tamed the party's campaign in 2013. While the party almost doubled its percentage among the young (under thirty years old), students, and unemployed, it did not capture the electorate on the radical left (Lello and Pazzaglia 2013).

Grown from the two declining splinter parties that had tried to keep the Communist orthodoxy alive at the time of the transformation of the Italian Communist Party into the Party of the Democratic Left (Calossi 2007, 220), the FdS' organizational structure and related internal linkages were based on traditional democratic centralism. Before converging in the FdS, Rifondazione Comunista had attempted some modest organizational transformation. Notwithstanding some limited openings towards the rank-and-file as well as sympathizers – for example, some autonomy given to the local Circles as well as the youth federation, or support for the associations of the alternative left, the critical and anti-capitalist movements, and the class unions – the party structure remained mainly vertical (Bertolino 2014; Calossi 2007). The opening up of the party towards the global justice movement in the early 2000s (Andretta and Reiter 2009) was soon reversed.

As for the FdS, at the central level, a large political council was elected by a national convention; a smaller coordinating body and a spokesperson were both elected by the political council (Bordandini 2013). Only limited environmental linkages were created through the opening of grassroots structures to non-members. Below the federations, at the provincial and regional levels, 'houses of the left' and workers' circles were organized at the local level. These were open to (single or associational) supporters, although they had no voting rights.

Based on the charismatic leadership of its president, Nichi Vendola, the organization of SEL also remained quite traditional, even if formally advocating participatory democracy. According to democratic centralism, a national convention elects a national assembly which, in turn, elects the national presidency and the national coordinating body. The territorial structure is also designed in a quite traditional way, including circles at the local level as well as federations at the provincial and regional levels (ibid.). Also at the local level, 'Nichi's factories' organized support for the leader.

Regarding their external linkages, both parties have praised relations with social movements, national party delegates participating in various forms of protest including the occupation of public buildings or boycotts. About 70 per cent of the delegates at party congresses had their first political engagement in social movements (Bordandini 2013). While both parties aimed at increasing support in both unions and new social movements, the FdS was more interested in the former while SEL, although also concerned with labour issues, had better connections in the latter, seeking a closer and more defined link to labour unions. More in general, 'SEL presents itself as a pluralist party, open to ground-level labour union committees (*comitati di base* [COBAS]) and to the manifold associations present in civil society, but without the intention of establishing privileged relationships with them' (Bordandini 2013, 75). In both cases, however, the parties' presence in social movement events remained weak and was often unwelcome by movement activists who, even if often voting for the radical left, were hostile to what they saw as parties' attempts at steering the movement (della Porta 2009).

Similarly, in *Spain*, notwithstanding some transformations in their linkage strategies, neither the Partido Comunista de España (Communist Party of Spain, PCE) nor IU were capable of gaining much consensus within the very dynamic social movements. In particular, while better located than the PCE, the United Left's attempts at strengthening relations with social movements met with little success (Ramiro and Vergé 2013).

Already in the mid-1980s, reacting to electoral defeat and internal crisis, the PCE decided to innovate its strategies by creating in 1986 a new organization, IU, with the PCE in a central role. In fact, hoping to improve their image as an internally democratic organization, the leaders underlined participatory linkages, giving more power to rank-and-file members. At the same time, they tried to improve environmental linkages through a closer relationship with civil society, beyond the traditional range of the left (ibid.). The party remained, however, very divided on issues such as the relations with the Partido Socialista Obrero Español (Spanish Socialist Workers' Party, PSOE) and the unions, as well as broader organizational and ideological matters. Early attempts at innovation were reversed later on, with ideological radicalization against the PSOE in power.

While IU was successful until the mid-1990s, reaching a peak in electoral support with 10.5 per cent of the votes in 1996 and attracting disaffected PSOE voters, it then began a steady decline as PSOE joined the opposition. It dropped to 5.4 per cent in the general elections of 2000, keeping just one seat in the Deputies' Chamber and none at all in six out of the seventeen regional parliaments (Ramiro and Vergé 2013). It was after dramatic losses in the 1999 local and European elections, and in the legislative elections the year after, that the party tried to re-profile itself as a post-communist and eco-socialist party – although with no success (ibid.).

The transformation in the organizational model was indeed limited, and membership remained low (Ramiro 2003). Paying lip service to the ideas of grassroots participation, IU party conferences in 1989 and 1990 had proclaimed its participatory nature in promoting involvement in the party and opening local organizations to members and sympathizers. Opposing the 'old politics' to the 'new politics', IU presented itself as 'a new type of participatory organization open to the involvement of members, non-members and civil society groups' (Ramiro and Vergé 2013, 47), also through open structures. The party practices were, however, assessed as falling far from the original purposes concerning the selection of candidates and leader, as well as policy-making. Regarding the selection of the party leader, this remained centralized, with a national party conference electing party delegates who, in turn, chose half of the members of the Federal Political Committee, that then selected the party leaders, respecting the weight of the different lists in the elections of the delegates (ibid.). As for policy issues, since the 1990s, party members and social movement activists were invited to participate in the elaboration of the party's electoral manifestos, also establishing working groups on various policy areas, which, however, were scarcely developed in practice. The attempt to open the party to the civil society – with the very self-definition of IU as a 'political and social movement' and participation in protest campaigns and platforms – was also unsuccessful, limited, and incoherently implemented:

> Besides not having created social organizations of its own, IU has also lost influence over those groups the PCE had long controlled through overlapping memberships, partly due to decreasing membership levels

and partly due to increasing autonomy demands from civil society organizations. (Ramiro and Vergé 2013, 53)

The electoral decline then continued in the national legislative elections of 2004 (4.9 per cent) and 2008 (3.7 per cent). Not involved in the organization of the 2011 protest, IU made some electoral gains in the local, regional, and national elections that year (6.9 per cent), declining again to 4.7 per cent in the 2015 general elections (even if votes increased to 9.9 per cent in the European election in 2014). In sum, IU's contribution to protest has been defined as indecisive, irrelevant, and even negative for its divisive effects. Additionally, the participatory linkages were not really implemented, with ensuing failures to either empower the grassroots or extend the membership, which in fact remained small (Méndez, Morales, and Ramiro 2004; Ramiro-Fernández 2005; Ramiro and Vergé 2013; Rendueles and Sola 2015).

IU's difficulty in establishing stable linkages with social movements can be related with the very type of transition (based on a pact among the elites), which gave a central role to large parties and unions but within a limited conception of citizen participation (Flesher-Fominaya 2007), as well as to the late emergence of new social movements (Pastor 1998; Jiménez 2007). While the main parties have presented lower levels of party membership and party identification in the last decades (Mair and Van Biezen 2001), their strategies towards civil society have been oriented to the creation of social organizations by the parties and, on the other hand, the co-optation of leaders of civil society in order to achieve political legitimacy (Vergé 2012). This traditional weakness of parties and movements in Spain can also be observed in the marginal presence of left-libertarian or Green parties at the national, regional, and local levels. Social movements in Spain have therefore tended to maintain their autonomy, trying to appear as actors totally independent from (usually, leftist) parties, as was particularly visible during the anti-globalization cycle and also during the 15M movement (della Porta 2007). While IU received the most votes among the participants in the Indignados movement (Martín 2012), its electoral limits were related to its difficulty in penetrating the PSOE's electorate and presenting itself as a new alternative in a new political context in which the old political consensus could be overcome. One of the activists involved in the launching of Podemos addresses this cleavage between the 'old' and the 'new' as an explanation for IU's incapacity to transform the party system dynamics:

I think the problem is that the mobilization cycle that created the 15M is also a challenge to the traditional Left and to the entire regime of '78. It is also challenging every institutive part of the Regime, and IU is part of it. The PCE signed the Moncloa Pacts, the PCE said yes to the Constitution, the PCE and IU co-governed Andalusia with PSOE. Then obviously they did not appear as a party of the establishment, but they did not appear as a party that was out of the establishment either. Then, the old-new axis that was developing showed that we needed to build our own tool, because the previous ones were not useful to defeat bipartisanship. And in the end IU is conditioned by that. (I12S)

While the political opportunity to challenge bipartisanship in Spain in the age of austerity was also open to IU, its strategy remained conservative, and the party made neither organizational changes nor policy proposals capable of aggregating new voters (especially those disaffected with PSOE) in the framework of a critical political juncture. It remains to be seen to what extent the choice of building a common list with Podemos at the national elections of June 2016 after the failure of the elections held in December 2015 to produce a parliamentary majority might change the perspective for IU.

Besides IU, however, the Partido X – which had built upon the organizational model and concerns promoted by the 15M movement – also failed to achieve electoral success. In the post-15M context and according to a logic of the 'assault on institutions', some sectors of social movements in Spain launched the idea of articulating a political project (which they named Party X) based on the democratic possibilities available with the use of techno-political tools. As some authors have pointed out (Subirats 2015b; Calvo and Álvarez 2015), the Red Ciudadana Partido X (Citizen Network X Party) was a political actor more akin to the 15M movement, both in performance and in aspirations. Party X was presented as a working method and a non-ideological minimum cross pact between citizens; a proposal focusing on democratic innovation through new technologies (wiki-government, wiki-law, etc.). It has also pursued a logic of overcoming the representation and the model of parties following a pattern of a kind of 'anti-party party' (Feenstra and Keane 2014) focused on the supposedly greater efficiency and effectiveness of citizenship, which resonates with the criticism developed by the M5S.[3] However, their election results were extremely modest (0.64 per cent of the vote), showing the limits of a techno-euphoric and technocratic-based model in challenging the two-party system in Spain.

In *Greece*, as well, the radical left was divided and, for a long time, weak. In fact, the Communist Party of Greece (KKE) as well as Synaspismos (Coalition of the Left and Progress) addressed their 1990s electoral decline with some opening towards social movements (Tsakatika and Eleftheriou 2013). SYRIZA emerged during the evolution of the KKE-Interior (KKE Esoterikou), a euro-communist split from the pro-Soviet KKE: the two conflicting factions collaborated in 1988 in order to contest elections and PASOK's hegemony over the left's mobilization in the country. They even entered government, in an unholy alliance with the centre-right party New Democracy (ND) and, after that, in a national unity government along with both PASOK and ND under a non-elected Green banker. This move was a watershed for the Greek radical left: on the one hand, it proved divisive, as the KKE pulled out of the coalition in 1991 and the 'renewing faction' formed Sinaspismos (SYN) as a unified party; on the other, and against the background of fatal transformations in the communist bloc, it broadly delegitimized the left in the country, causing continuous electoral hardship over the next fifteen years (Panagyiotakis 2015). This crisis had severe organizational consequences, pushing in fact towards an attempt to 'rewire themselves in order to fulfil a protest role vis-à-vis the established party "cartel", re-emphasise their ideology, distinct policies and principles and rearticulate their appeal to their traditional constituency' (Tsakatika and Eleftheriou 2013, 6). This strategy became visible after the end of the 1990s as a shift towards civil society in what concerned their appeal, internal organization and establishing links with the movement field and trade unions (ibid.).

Whereas changes in the Soviet Union paved the way for organizational and programmatic innovations even within the KKE (ibid.), still, the party's relations with civil society remained top-down. KKE remained as one of the strictest orthodox communist parties, representing itself as the Soviet political and ideological legacy in Europe. So, even if it is indeed a working-class party in terms of membership and strength, it has adopted a totally isolationist and purist approach since 1991 (Panagyiotakis 2015), developing hierarchical and institutionalized links with socio-political actors. In the late 1990s, KKE established the All Workers' Militant Front (PAME), a centralized trade union, broadly controlled by the party, but recruiting also outside the party. Despite efforts to differentiate itself from the union, political positions and slogans were practically indistinguishable and PAME members attended KKE's marches and protests (Tsakatika and Eleftheriou 2013). Similarly, top-down strategies – which had some success in light of dissatisfaction with the official unions – were implemented with other ancillary organizations.

The strategy towards social movement development in what became SYRIZA was totally different, as it emerged from the failures of Synaspismos. Founded from a merging of activists of the new left, environmentalists but also old KKE and euro-communist party cadres, SYN presented itself as a pluralist party within the tradition of democratic socialism, promoting a mixed economic model but also opening up to new social movement concerns such as the environment or women's rights (Tsakatika and Eleftheriou 2013). The foundation document appealed to 'the men and women of work and culture, the young and the excluded', reflecting a trans-class approach (ibid., 9) coupled with an appeal to internal democracy: SYN stressed party pluralism and thus the importance of rank-and-file members, calling them to form factions, vote in internal referenda, and participate in policy-making as well as candidate selection, while opening the meetings of the party's Central Political Committee and granting autonomy to local and regional branches (Tsakatika and Eleftheriou 2013).

In practice, however, the party remained small, constantly struggling to pass the three per cent threshold in election results (Panagyiotakis 2015). It was also considered reformist and elitist, 'with no relations whatsoever with what was happening on the ground, men dressed in ties; who really cared about them?' (I21G). Significantly, the majority of the interviewees who belonged to the SYN Youth throughout the 1990s and until the early 2000s admitted that when at university they were not openly declaring their political allegiance, as 'the party had moved too much to the right, it was an institutional party...almost hostile to movement-like activities...taking sides with the mainstream parties against which the whole student movement was protesting' (I3G). A SYRIZA Youth member commented that, even in 2005, she still had to apologize for her political identity, as the party was 'still dominated by the Synaspismos' "reforms" mentality' (I7G): the party's managerial discourse and technocratic approach to the Europeanization of the country (Lyrintzis 2005) was to be criticized by the left in the years to come for introducing neoliberal policies in the disguise of 'reforms'. Throughout the 1990s, the traditional left as a whole, and SYN in particular, were delegitimized in the eyes of leftist voters (Tsakatika and Eleftheriou 2013) and broadly irrelevant for the movements.

It was in this context that SYN decided in 2001 to take part in the Space for Dialogue for the Unity and Common Action of the Left, a loose, horizontal platform for the encounter of leftist and radical leftist groups, organizations, and movement networks. Synaspismos' participation was 'a strategic choice, a choice of survival...a vital space had to be created between the centre-left PASOK and the communist KKE', so as to attract electoral support (I3G). Social movements started to become of quintessential reference in the self-definition of the party, enabling SYN 'to move beyond the traditional poles of the left – the communist orthodox as against the reformist – that did not pay attention to movements, did not care about what people thought; they just instrumentalized the movements to their interests...No, that was something totally different', as a party member observed (I1G).

Stressing discontinuities, in 2003 the party re-named itself Coalition of the Left of Movements and Ecology (I13G). In view of the 2004 parliamentary elections, SYRIZA was formally established as the electoral alliance 'Coalition of the Radical Left'. SYN thus aimed at appealing to the younger cohorts and the social and political activists by actually creating this category in the Greek political discourse. Eloquent in this respect is the 2005 CPC Resolution 'Left and Youths: a Dynamic Relationship, a Relationship of Subversion'[4] or the constant references of the party leader, Alekos Alavanos (2004–08), to the 'youth' and its struggles in the field of education and precarious employment (SYN 2005). This was presented as a response to the 'reform-oriented' politics and the 'centrist neoliberal consensus' that the two major mainstream parties had managed to create by converging on the decision to implement neoliberalism in the country. Thus the 'dividing lines might surface' (SYN 2005) among those who could no longer benefit from the economic system: the lower salaried strata, the pensioners and, of course, the unemployed young people.

After internal debates, in its Fourth Congress (2004) the party was transformed from a 'renewal' to a 'radical' left-wing party (Balafas 2012), abandoning its organic links with euro-communism with regard to its exclusionary reference to parliamentary institutions, purporting instead to give voice to the grassroots movements against neoliberalism (Katsampekis 2015). The candidacy of the then very young Alexis Tsipras as Mayor of Athens in 2006 and as leader of the party in 2008 also came as a surprise for the party cadres. SYN was understood as part of a delegitimized system and as a product of the defeat of the left in the 1990s, both in Greece and in Europe; SYRIZA and its different movement-like attitude was an attempt to enact new values that would grant the radical left a different parliamentary role.

While pluralism had the negative effect of increasing factional strife, it instead proved useful when the Greek party system collapsed in 2012. In fact, both SYN and the KKE had been involved in the protests of the last decade, stressing their proximity to trade unions and social movement organizations. Committed critics of neoliberalism since the very beginning, both parties were hit less severely by the ensuing crisis in popular trust in parties since 2010. It was, however, SYN/SYRIZA that benefited electorally, attracting votes from disappointed PASOK supporters and unemployed youth, while KKE even reduced its electoral share.[5] In fact, as examined above, loose organizational structure, coalition-based functioning and internal pluralism stopped being a weakness for SYN and SYRIZA after 2010 turning them into a clear advantage attracting new groups and movements as well as individual supporters. 'SYRIZA's participatory linkage made it easier for the party to adapt to rapid electoral change', while, on the contrary, 'KKE's participatory linkage strategy seemed to be relatively successful while voter preferences were relatively stable but proved ineffective at times of deep social change' (Tsakatika and Eleftheriou 2013, 14), as the party's centralized structure, rigid membership and sectarianism made it difficult to adapt to a volatile environment.

As discussed above, SYRIZA's advantage proved particularly important in relations with the broad anti-austerity movement and the 2011 mobilizations in the squares, with the party youth, intellectuals, and union components particularly visible at demonstrations and ad hoc protests, while KKE remained rather isolated.

In sum, while in each of the three countries the radical left was split between a more traditional communist party and a more innovative one, the latter's attempts at developing participatory and environmental links were generally of limited success – with the one exception of SYRIZA.

5.2. Broadening the scope of the analysis: Critical junctures without (yet) new movement parties in the European periphery

In Italy, Greece and Spain, unpopular austerity measures, imposed from abroad but with bipartisan implementation, produced a deep political crisis, with electoral breakdown of the major parties. However, in other European countries, like Ireland and Portugal, that suffered greatly from the crisis, the neoliberal critical juncture did not (yet) bring about the emergence of new parties near to social movements. Although the crisis is one and the same, it had different timing and characteristics in different countries, influenced as it was by previous structural conditions as well as contingent developments. Variables that are usually mentioned when assessing the economic conditions that influenced the evolution of the world crisis are related to public debt, public deficit, private debt versus savings, financing of debt through domestic versus foreign financial institutions, payment balance, levels of competitiveness. Some of these factors played a role in buffering the effects of the crisis in Ireland and Portugal. The timing and speed of the manifestation of the crisis is also relevant in explaining why the most disruptive developments in terms of party systems happened in Greece, Spain, and Italy, while this was not (or much less) the case in Portugal and Ireland. Moreover, the austerity measures were adopted in different political contexts, with important effects on the legitimacy crisis that unfolded. As we will show, while in Ireland and Portugal austerity measures hit the citizens hard, with consequences at the electoral level, for various reasons the party system was able to absorb the shock, with high volatility but no significant new party emerging. Most importantly, in these two countries, anti-austerity protests developed differently in size, time, and forms than in Spain, Greece, and even Italy.

5.2.1. Ireland

As in other cases in the European periphery, the crisis in Ireland was fuelled by the weakness of the financial system as an increase in public debt (from 40 per cent of GDP to about 120 per cent in 2013) resulted from the government decision, in 2008, to save heavily indebted banks. In fact, while the state's guarantee for the debts of six of the most important financial institutions was initially presented as a short-term intervention on a temporary liquidity crisis, in reality it was quickly clear that risky lending had produced a crisis of insolvency (Hardiman and Regan 2013). Ireland reacted to the crisis by bailing out the banks, as well as implementing an austerity policy strongly based on cuts in public spending that affected an already critical economy.

A structural weakness in Ireland, already in the buoyant years, had been its low tax basis. As the crisis in construction activities and financial market cooled down, the deficit in public expenditure grew from 7.3 per cent of GDP in 2008 to 14 per cent in 2009, while government expenditure increased from 37 to 47 per cent of GNP, given an increase in unemployment. The dynamic export-oriented sector is moreover powered by foreign-based investments, which repatriate the profits. In total, between 2008 and 2015, the Irish economy experienced cuts of about 20 per cent of GDP (Hardiman and Regan 2013). The construction bubble was financed by a rapid growth in loans from the international banking sector (in particular, Germany, Britain, and France) to consumers on the European periphery, particularly in the real estate and financial sectors – with house building covering as much as 15 per cent of national income before the bubble exploded. Thanks to very low taxes and massive deregulation, Ireland attracted export-oriented industries.

After the emergence of the global financial crisis in 2007, and the end of financial flows, the government intervened to bail out the banks, thus transforming private debt into sovereign debt (Mair 2011, 4). Since 2008, austerity budgets followed one after the other, although without avoiding the intervention in November 2010 of the EU and IMF, which lent money at high cost and with high conditionality. Austerity measures included tax increases, which disproportionally penalized the lower and middle classes, as well as cuts to an already small public sector employment, particularly in health and education. Poverty, unemployment, and emigration ensued.

Relevant in assessing the dynamics of the crisis and the social movement reaction to it is the broad agreement among political actors and unions to continue to attract capital investments through low taxation, as well as the economic dualism, with an export-oriented sector that remained less affected. Politically, the austerity policies were based on a compromise to maintain a low-tax regime, especially for the business sector, keeping a very small 12.5 per cent corporate tax rate as well as low social insurance contributions for employers, with fiscal adjustment based instead upon cuts in pay and services in the public sector. While in 2011 the Fine Gael-Labour government passed new tax breaks for the financial sector, in the two previous years the government had cut public sector pay cheques, as well as the minimum wage, by about 15 per cent; of similar proportion were cuts in social welfare, also increasing eligibility controls and means testing. Moreover, together with cuts in public sector salaries and social security payments, there was a downsizing of an already small public sector (especially in health, education, security, and civil service), incentivizing voluntary redundancies (Hardiman and Regan 2013). Trade unions were involved in the deal through the Croke Park agreement that included a promise of renouncing further pay cuts in exchange for an industrial peace with increase in productivity. Earlier retirements were used to reduce employment in the (already small) public sector, especially in health and education (Hardiman and Regan 2013, 12). Meanwhile, unemployment increased from 6.4 per cent in 2008 to about 15 per cent in 2012 (Hardiman and Regan 2013).

These policies accompanied a loss of sovereignty brought about by the signing of an agreement with the EC, IMF, and ECB (the so-called Troika) for a loan programme in December 2010, which introduced severe constraints on budgetary discretion as budget decisions had to be cleared with the Troika, with fiscal performance subject to a quarterly review process and personnel from the troika assigned to the most important administrative positions (Hardiman and Regan 2013). In fact, while the responsibility of the ECB in allowing for risky lending deals remained covered, the Irish government and its citizens were held responsible for the crisis, with ensuing resentment among the population (O'Connor 2016).

Incumbent parties were then heavily punished in Ireland. The 2011 elections have been defined as some of the most dramatic in terms of net electoral volatility in Europe's entire post-war history, with substantial effects on the traditional party system (Marsh and Mikhaylov 2012). In 2011, after the failure of the coalition government between Fianna Fáil and the Green Party, new elections brought into power the opposition, which had campaigned for a renegotiation of the Memorandum but in practice ensured continuity. So, the main party in government, Fianna Fáil (FF), fell from the first to the third party while the other centrist party, Fine Gael (FG), became the first party for the first time, forming a governmental coalition with the Labour Party, which had also gained in the elections, almost doubling its support. In general, the parties on the left gained a very high 31 per cent of the votes (Marsh and Mikhaylov 2012). It was noted, however, that electoral results represented rather a conservative revolution, as the main players remained the same, with just a switch in power between two centre-right parties (ibid.).

Politically, in fact, the consequences of the crisis have been buffered by the local orientation of Irish national politics and its inherent clientelism, as well as the weakness of the parliament. The important role of personal ties seems to have mitigated the intensity of the change, as did the traditional ideological proximity among the main parties (Marsh and Mikhaylov 2012). Indeed, vertical cross-class kinship as well as patronage networks proved more resilient than did potential horizontal solidarities (O'Connor 2016). An already weak parliament was moreover sidelined by the Economic Management Council, composed of economic ministers and various unelected consultants, which had been established to liaise with the Troika and which *de facto* legislated on economic issues independent of the remains of the cabinet or by the parliament (ibid.).

The survival of the old system has also been explained by the traditional weakness of the left: since independence, the Irish republic has been governed by two centrist parties, in occasional coalitions with a moderate Labour Party. In addition,

> Traditionally Ireland's political culture has been characterised by a consensus-oriented centralism which has not facilitated mobilization at the ends of the ideological spectrum. The nature of Ireland's prolonged struggle for Independence and the need for a broadly defined unity in opposition to colonial occupation undermined any class-based mobilization. (O'Connor 2016)

The two radical left parties in the parliament, the Socialist Party and the People before Profit Alliance, are very small, even if active in the social movement scene. While Sinn Fein also supported protests and indeed reached quite significant electoral success (recently close to 20 per cent of votes in electoral polls), being greeted by SYRIZA's leader as part of the new radical left wave, its imbrication with nationalism remains a source of tension for the left (ibid.).

Signs of change are, however, also visible in the peculiar Irish politics. First of all, as mentioned, elections in 2011 – the most volatile in

Irish history – saw the dramatic defeat of Fianna Fáil, which had been in power for as many as sixty-one of the previous seventy-nine years. It now became only the third party in parliament, dropping from fifty-seven to twenty MPs, while its partners in the governmental coalition remained outside of parliament. In addition, the new parliament had the highest proportion of left-leaning MPs than ever before in Irish history (32 per cent), a level for the first time comparable to other European countries (O'Connor 2016). Meanwhile, Labour renounced the possibility of building a left-wing opposition to pressure a Fine Gael minority government, instead joining Fine Gael and giving up any attempt at renegotiating the MoU. As mentioned, Sinn Fein increased its electoral support, as did, at the local level, the People before Profit Alliance; the Socialist Party also continued to expand in the local elections, although they remain strong almost exclusively in urban areas and there is a plethora of leftist independents (ibid.).

These contextual conditions affected the strength and timing of the anti-austerity mobilizations, which were, however, overall weaker than in other European peripheries. Protests, initially in the form of union activities, were limited during the peak of the crisis but grew afterwards. In fact, the co-optation of civil society, especially unions, and their de-politicization during the period of the Celtic Tigers – as well as the traditional lack of left-wing party traditions and clientelistic ties with the electorate – delayed the crisis of the party system. As O'Connor (2016) aptly noticed, various reasons explain why Irish society was seen as totally inactive against austerity:

> [First,] Successive governments have actively projected an image of a stoic Irish people assuming collective responsibility for the financial recklessness of the Celtic Tiger period. This presumed guilt is rooted in the recognition that the political architects of the crisis were repeatedly validated by resounding electoral victories, even as late as 2007....A second reason why the level of political dissent is lesser acknowledged is because it had been until 2014 overwhelmingly peaceful and relatively small, thus less newsworthy for international audiences....Thirdly, when there was extensive mobilization in the early stages of the crisis – a series of national strikes in late 2009 – it did not attract attention as it preceded much of the mass protest which subsequently occurred across the PIIGS countries. (ibid.)

As the long wave of the crisis was felt at the political level, protests emerged, after the crisis peaked, from a critique of neoliberal logic. Indeed, relevant eventful protests included the 2014 mass mobilization in the Right2Water campaign, deeply rooted at the local level against policies of privatization, liberalization and, more broadly, the dismissal of the public sector and conceptions of public services as well as common goods (ibid.). To a certain extent this delayed contentious response to austerity politics and its consequences have been reflected in the electoral results of the 2016 general election, with Sinn Fein (often taking positions against austerity policies) recording its best results under Gerry Adams' leadership, resulting in being the third most-voted party and more than doubling its seats, with percentage of voters increasing from 9.9 per cent to 13.8 per cent, while the Labour Party (compromised with austerity policies) instead went down from 19.4 to a tiny 6.6 per cent of votes.

5.2.2. Portugal

In *Portugal*, as was also the case in Spain, the crisis originated as a financial crisis, linked to the speculative reactions to the information spread about the sovereign debt crisis in Greece. Moreover, as in Spain and in most of the European periphery, its dynamics were fuelled in part by the external debt and the negative balance of payments. Low competitiveness, which had been a structural problem of the Portuguese economy, showed its most dramatic effects when the country joined the euro. In fact, while before the trade deficit, related net external debt could be controlled through devaluation, this was no longer possible under the euro as the automatic stabilizers keeping under control the levels of net external debt and balance of income deficits were abolished (Cabral 2013).

The dynamics of the recession were also aggravated by the fact that, after Portugal had to sign a memorandum with the ECB and EC, these institutions imposed a reading of the crisis as derived from 'fiscal laxity' and related failure to comply with the Stability and Growth Pact (SGP) (Cabral 2013). Aiming at reducing the payment balance, the MoU imposed very specific measures, triggering a social crisis as well as a democratic one. In fact, with its 222 main action recommendations, the first MoU has been presented as a plan oriented to re-engineer the entire country, as 'It foresees measures for a very wide swathe of private and public economic activity. It seems much more like a plan drawn up by central planners in a command economy than an adjustment pro-gramme for a market economy' (ibid., 29). Among other requirements, the MoU imposed a new bank re-capitalization programme, leaving decisional power in private hands; increases in VAT and property taxes as well as in personal income taxes; higher fees to access public services (including hospitals); and the freezing of hiring and promotion in the public sector. Cuts to the public sector affected all services, particularly education – while all the sacrifices demanded by lending institutions proved ineffective, as the general government debt rose from 93.5 per cent of GDP in 2010 to 120.5 per cent in 2012 (Cabral 2013). Measures adopted included cuts in public budgets through wage cuts; limits on unemployment benefits, pensions, and social protection; cancellation of public investments; privatizations in the transport sector. A third austerity plan was announced, which included measures that cut pensions, raised taxes, and reduced health and welfare services. After a general strike and various protests, the parliament rejected the last plan that had not been discussed with the unions and employers organizations, and the government resigned.

While the crisis certainly affected dramatically the quality of life of a large majority of Portuguese citizens, there were, however, some buffering effects offered by a quite inclusive welfare state that had emerged from the 'carnation revolution' in 1974. As Tiago Fernandes (2016) noted,

> the impact of the crisis on the welfare of the population was less severe than in most Southern European countries (e.g. risk of poverty). This was the effect of two institutional legacies: a state-civil society partnership for policy delivery to the poor, which had been established since the 1980s, unique in Southern Europe, and which the pro-austerity government did not dismantle and even expanded; and an active constitutional court which rolled back many of the more severe austerity measures.

In particular, a main social legacy of the eventful transition in Portugal had been a broad institutional focus on social inequality as well as a recognition of the positive role of civil society actors (Fishman 2011; della Porta 2017). Thus, since the beginning of the crisis a Social Emergency Plan based on a greater role for the partly state-funded social welfare organizations (the IPSSs, *Instituições Privadas de Solidariedade Social*) was adopted by the government (Fernandes 2016).

In addition, the political situation was in part different from the ones in Spain and Greece, especially as far as the centre-left party was concerned. The political effects of the crisis were also visible in Portugal, but in a less dramatic fashion than in Greece or Spain. As in Greece, the centre-left Socialist Party that was in power when the MoU was signed got its worst electoral results. What is more, even if it campaigned for less austerity, its diversity in social and economic policies was not recognized by the electorate. As in Ireland, EC plus IMF intervention suspended not only democratic accountability in terms of decision-making, but also the democratic dialectics between the government and the opposition, as the austerity memorandum was required to be signed by all main parties: the government's Socialist Party (Partido Socialista Português, PSP), as well as the centre-right opposition Social-Democratic Party

(Partido Social Democrata, PSD) and the Social and Democratic Centre-Popular Party (Cento Democrático Social-Partido Popular, CDS-PP, right) (Magalhães 2014). In fact, 'the basic tenets of the policy endorsed by the PSD, which the Socialists harshly criticized during the campaign, were, after all, the same that all major parties, including the PSP itself, had committed to implement with the EU and the IMF after the election took place' (Magalhães 2014, 193). Immediately moving into the opposition was, however, a blessing for the PSP, which could from there express critiques of austerity policies.

The first austerity programme was approved in the spring of 2010 by a Socialist minority government, with the support of the centre-right PSD in the opposition. A second programme followed in the autumn, and a third in the spring of 2011. In April, international financial support was requested from the EC, ECB, and IMF, and a Memorandum was signed in May by the PSP, the PSD, and even the right-wing CDS-PP. However, the PSP quickly changed its position. After the resignation of the PSP government the PSD' electoral campaign was focused on a neoliberal agenda claiming to adopt even more liberal reforms than those requested by the Troika and blaming the socialists for the bailout. While acquiescent towards the Memorandum, socialists warned that greater cuts to welfare and public education had to be expected in case the right succeeded in the elections (Fernandes 2016). The electoral results punished the PSP, falling to 28.1 per cent against 38.7 per cent for the PSD, 11.7 per cent for CDS, 7.4 per cent for the PCP and only 5.2 per cent for the BE. As the new centre-right government embraced a plan of privatization in electricity, gas, railways, telecommunication, and postal sectors as well as deregulation of the labour market, further cuts in pension and unemployment benefits, higher fees for healthcare and reduction of expenses in education, and increased VAT taxes, the PSP opposed all these measures. With changes in leadership and strategies, the PSP regained the support it had lost according to the results of local elections in October 2013 and European elections in May 2014, while in parallel PSD lost about 10 per cent.

The two Portuguese radical left parties, the Partido Comunista Português (Portuguese Communist Party, PCP) and the Bloco de Esquerda (Left Bloc, BE), were also, initially at least, unable to capitalize on the crisis in electoral terms. Both had a quite relevant presence, with BE increasing electoral support from 2.4 per cent in 1999 to 9.9 per cent in 2009, and the PCP declining instead from 18.1 per cent in 1983 to 8.8 per cent in 1991 (Tsakatika and Lisi 2013) and 7 per cent in 2002. Founded before the dictatorship, the PCP had played an important role during the carnation revolution, keeping a mass party structure within a model of democratic centralism, with a rather top-down decision-making process in the internal organizational structure. No pluralism is allowed, as factions are prohibited and members have to obey congress decisions (Tsakatika and Lisi 2013). Relations with civil society, mainly with unions and cooperatives, as well as with the ancillary youth, student, and women's organizations, are also characterized by attempts at domination by the party. Orthodoxy limited potential innovation, bringing about fossilization instead (Cuñha 2003).

In contrast, the BE – formed by two small leftist radical parties and by dissidents from the PCP – is more open to social movements. In fact, in its constitution, BE was defined as a 'political movement of citizens', praising a culture of participation in order to find alternatives to capitalism (Tsakatika and Lisi 2013). At the organizational level, the BE promotes an organizational model based on horizontal links between members and leaders, with a participatory and decentralized involvement in decision-making. In an explicit critique of the vertical model adopted by the PCP, BE has chosen a loose type of membership and a low structuration around network organization, with no clear leadership and a pluralist model (Tsakatika and Lisi 2013). Some centralization followed success in the 2005 legislative elections, while the party remained weakly rooted in the society and had a quite volatile electorate. While the PCP aims at unanimity, the BE has been quite factionalized, with the effect that the old factions reduce the influence of the new members. So, 'The overall picture of the organizational model adopted by Portuguese radical left parties reveals two distinct genetic models. While social movements and left libertarian parties clearly influenced the BE's organizational identity, the PCP has preserved the traditional communist organization' (Lisi 2012, 26).

Even though in the early months of 2010 both the BE and PCP supported several protests, the influence of civil society on the radical leftist parties remained limited in terms of both frames and organizational characteristics (Tsakatika and Lisi 2012). In general, social movements have been quite dependent on established political parties but also strongly divided by partisan conflicts resulting in reduced autonomy and independence from parties as well as growing fragmentation and internal splits (Lisi 2012).

The BE had overlapping memberships with various civil society organizations, from associations for the defence of women, migrants, or human rights, to students' associations and environmental groups. Particularly close was the relationship with the global justice movement, in which both parties took part – although BE maintained more open relations while the PCP kept closer relationships with the union CGTP. In fact, both the PCP and the BE supported the labour movements, although they differed in their attitudes towards anti-austerity protests and mobilizations by precarious workers. Here, the BE supported new movements' protests, while the PCP remained sceptical (Tsakatika and Lisi 2012). Given the heterogeneity of the movements, while the BE offered much organizational support, relations remained loose, given that many social movement activists share a mistrust towards parties and praise instead their autonomy.

Overall, with regard to participatory linkages, notwithstanding pushes for change the PCP has implemented a Leninist model based on firm vertical links, strong members' control and great institutionalization. In contrast, in the BE, opening to members' participation has been coupled with low institutionalization. Despite this, in practice centralization increased over time and members' mobilization became increasingly problematic. As for the environmental linkages, while the PCP built top-down relations with its ancillary organizations, the BE opened up to more horizontal and informal types of relations with social movement organizations. The rise of the global justice movement in particular boosted overlapping memberships and broadened interactions with the movement field (Lisi 2012).

Finally, protests, while sustained, took more traditional forms than in Greece or Spain, relying on a tradition of inclusiveness towards contentious politics (Fishman 2011). Protests indeed were very intense since the inception of the economic and financial crisis but led by the 'usual suspects' such as the main trade union confederation and radical left parties (Fernandes 2016; see also Accornero and Ramos Pinto 2015). In fact, during the crisis, those signing a petition grew from 21 to 32 per cent; participation in demonstrations, from 12 to 24 per cent; participating in legal strikes, from 11 to 25 per cent; occupying buildings, from 1 to 3 per cent; and blocking roads and railways, from 1 to 2 per cent (Amador 2013, 34). Between 8 and 15 per cent of the population participated in huge anti-austerity marches with up to 1.5 million participants. The number of demonstrations also grew: in Lisbon, from 244 in 2010, to 298 in 2011, and to 579 in 2012 (ibid.).

While using a wider range of disruptive forms of protests, the mobilizations, however, remained peaceful, with de-escalation also promoted by a soft style of protest policing. Moreover, in a practice that had been legitimized by the eventful transition, protesters interacting with institutions, brought their claims inside the very parliament. The carnation revolution was indeed often evoked, in times of crisis, to strengthen the call for justice and democracy. This was evident, for instance, in the *Grandoladas* – that is, protest events in which, mainly during contestation of public authorities, the 1974 revolutionary song *Grândola* was sung (ibid.).

The elections in October 2015 have, however, started to change this scenario, with BE in particular achieving its best results ever, with more than 10 per cent of the votes and more than doubling its parliamentary seats. Given also the partial success of the Unitary Democratic Coalition (formed by the Communist and the Green parties), which achieved almost 8 per cent of the votes, and of the PSP (with 32.7%), the minority government chaired by António Costa is now dependent on the support of the left, opening up new opportunities for movements' claims.

In conclusion, while in both Ireland and Portugal the austerity policies had spurred suffering and discontent – which in turn fuelled protest – some characteristics of the socio-economic crisis as well as the capacity of the political system were able to buffer the effects of the Great Recession at the social level, and also to better absorb, through clientelistic or neo-corporatist ties, the disruptive potential of the anti-austerity mobilizations.

5.3. Broadening the scope of the comparison: The left, movements and parties in Latin America

Further broadening and testing our reflection and explanations for the emergence and the strategic choices of movement parties – defined as characterized by intense organizational links with social movements – in this part we shall address the Latin American experience with late neoliberalism and anti-austerity protests, which started at least ten years earlier than in Europe. In this case, as well, neoliberalism increased socio-economic inequalities and discontent that affected the party system in various ways. As we will see, some contextual characteristics in Latin America were similar to those in the European cases we analysed, as the neoliberal critical juncture hit semi-peripheral economies with lower productivity than core capitalist countries. Here as well, austerity policies, introduced under strong international pressures, increased poverty and inequality, triggered a strong delegitimation of political elites that had claimed to be capable of providing not only for freedom but also for economic growth. As in our cases, strong movements de-structured the party system, especially where the centre-left parties were perceived as supportive of austerity against their own constituencies. Not only votes, but also ideas and human resources then moved towards new emerging parties that resonated with the claims and frames of the anti-austerity protests. Having a longer history than in the European countries we studied, the emerging radical left in Latin America shows how different types of relations with movements were developed in different countries, and with which tensions and trade-offs.

5.3.1. The debate on movement parties in Latin America: An introduction

In Latin America, a wave of left-wing electoral victories started with Hugo Chávez in Venezuela in 1998, continuing with socialist Ricardo Lagos in 2000 in Chile; Partido dos Trabalhadores' (Worters' Party, PT) Lula da Silva in 2002 in Brazil; left Peronist Néstor Kirchner in 2003 in Argentina; Tabaré Vasquez of The Frente Amplio (Broad Front, FA) in 2004 in Uruguay; Evo Morales in 2005 in Bolivia; and Rafael Correa in 2006 in Ecuador (Levitsky and Roberts 2011a). Long-term causes for these victories included persisting inequality and severe poverty, notwithstanding growth, with particularly de-structuring effects from the economic crisis of 1998–2002. The wave of left-wing electoral victories spread thanks to the export boom. During this process, movement parties were formed and alliances between movements and parties intensified.

While all of these leaders and their parties had in common the promise to reduce inequality – extremely high in Latin America – there were notable differences between the institutionalized left-wing parties in countries such as Brazil, Chile, and Uruguay and the so-called populist left of Chávez in Venezuela, with Argentina, Bolivia, and Ecuador in between.[6] Levitsky and Roberts (ibid.) have distinguished the left-wing parties in these countries on two dimensions: a generational one (established versus new parties), and an organizational one (dispersed versus concentrated authority). The results are summarized in Table 5.1.

The societal resistance to neoliberalism in fact found different forms of expression in the various Latin American countries: from social movement protests – using forms such as strikes and demonstrations, but also riots, road blocks, and occupations of land or public buildings – to electoral ones, either through support for the left-wing opposition or through the emergence of new parties on the left. The different forms of resistance were influenced by the political alignments as well as the institutional outcomes of neoliberalism. In fact, as Roberts (2015, 61–2) noted, the countries that saw the most explosive patterns of social protest

Table 5.1. *Left-wing parties in Latin America (adapted from Levitsky and Roberts 2011a)*

	Established party organization	*New political movement*
Dispersed authority	Institutionalized partisan (Chile, Brazil, Uruguay)	Movement left (Bolivia)
Concentrated authority	Populist machine (Argentina)	Populist left (Venezuela, Ecuador)

(especially Venezuela, Argentina, Bolivia, and Ecuador) were character-ized by bait-and-switch market reform that had the effect of de-aligning the party systems, triggering reactive sequences, which went from partial decomposition of the party system to the rise of new parties. As he noted, 'The political expression of societal resistance was quite different where conservatives imposed market reforms over staunch leftist oppo-sition and critical junctures left in place party systems that were both institutionalized and programmatically aligned – the outcome of con-tested liberalism. Under contested liberalism, societal resistance could be channelled towards established parties of the left, thus weakening anti-systemic forms of social or electoral protest. This outcome moderated the reactive sequences of the aftermath period, which largely consisted of the progressive electoral strengthening of these institutionalized leftist or center-left parties' (ibid.).

While in Brazil, Chile, and Uruguay it was the centre-right that pushed for neoliberalism, with centre-left parties remaining in opposition (with Peronist groups switching power in Argentina), in Venezuela, Bolivia, and Ecuador there was instead a mass protest against the neoliberal process seen as embraced by all established parties. So,

> Where this resistance cleaved party systems – that is, where clearly-differentiated partisan alternatives existed in support and opposition to the neoliberal model – electoral competition was more stable and institutionalized in the post-adjustment era, moderating the eventual turn to the left. Where this resistance was left largely outside party systems, and partisan competition was not clearly structured by pro-grammatic distinctions, post-adjustment reactive sequences destabi-lized party systems and outflanked them with new and more radical leftist alternatives. (Roberts 2015, 40)

Massive protests triggered the emergence of new parties when they destabilized the existing party system.

The interactions between movements and left-wing parties then influ-enced their paths to power and the policy orientations of the latter when in government. While Venezuela moved towards the most statist policy, Argentina, Bolivia, and Ecuador adopted heterodox policies and Uruguay, Chile, and Brazil tended towards neoliberalism even if in a rather social-democratic form, with adoption of some social policies towards redistribution (Pribble and Huber 2011). In parallel, promo-tion of participation (radical democracy) and plebiscitarian appeals to direct popular majority have been especially present in Bolivia, Ecuador, and Venezuela, with only Chávez pushing for more radical democracy, while Brazil and Uruguay moved towards corporatism. Once in power, left-wing parties became in general more and more divided on the role of participatory democracy, with overall a fading of initial radical democratic principles, substituted by 'revamped versions of societal corporativism' (Goldfrank 2011, 163) as well as by difficulty in addressing the new challenges in terms of citizenship rights (in particular, concerning security and identity issues) (Yashar 2011).

Scholars have related some of these differences to socio-economic conditions, observing that there has been more capacity to act on the left where the global commodities boom had reduced the needs for external financing and related conditionality, increasing in parallel the freedom to perform redistributive policies (Murillo, Oliveros, and Vaishnav 2011). While a political economy explanation has pointed to the specificities of rentier states, alternative explanations have stressed the constraining effect of a more institutionalized party system. In general, while the older left parties had tended to abandon state interventionist policies, the emerging left-wing movements grew at a time of widespread discontent with neoliberal policies (Madrid 2009). In Brazil, Chile, and Uruguay, Marxist parties – which had been strongly repressed under dictatorship, were founded before the democratization but had institutionalized afterwards, having control of various societal organizations, and access to government through routine alternation – tended to maintain a liberal democratic orientation and programmatic moderation. Differently, an outsider path characterizes parties that emerged after democratization, did not consider the democratic regime as an effect of their struggles, and mobilized against the entire party system. Quickly achieving power in the collapse of the party system, they aimed at a plebiscitarian refoundation (Levitsky and Roberts 2011b).

5.3.2. On the genesis of movement parties

As in the case of European countries, a sort of movement parties also emerged in Latin America, in opposition to a general trend by traditional left-wing parties to de-emphasize activities targeted at a specific constituency, given the decline of unions but also the increase in new forms and actors of contentious politics. New popular organizations grew, in fact, with fewer ties with parties, in particular in terms of shared member linkages (Handlin and Berins Collier 2011) during intense waves of protest. As in Europe, anti-austerity movements developed in the continent from the late 1980s and early 1990s, their characteristics and outcomes being strongly influenced by political opportunities and constraints provided by the party system. The specific form of these relations depended in fact on the political alignment around neoliberalist policies, with more intense and radical protest where the party system seemed unable to represent emerging claims against austerity. In particular, in countries in which the conservative parties promoted neoliberal reforms, the existing left-wing parties could capitalize on the discontent by providing institutional channels, which led to left-wing presidents in Chile, Brazil, and Uruguay. Here, protests remained limited and populist leaders weak. On the other hand, in countries such as Bolivia, Ecuador, and Venezuela, where the centre-left or the labour-oriented populist parties had first campaigned against but then promoted neoliberal policies, dissent, with no institutional channels, was expressed through massive protests as well as populist outsiders or left-wing movement parties, with total or partial breakdown of the party system (ibid.).

Looking at the left in power, these two paths seemed to lead to different outcomes, with a distinction between a 'liberal left', which adopted moderate market-oriented economic policies, and an 'interventionist left', which instead embraced more interventionist policies and increased public spending. As Madrid (2009) noted, the two types of the left differ in their political strategies and organizational structure, with the interventionist left being more critical of the United States, more radical on intervention on social inequalities, more determined to overhaul or work outside of the existing political institutions, and more innovative in terms of internal structuration. Once again, the role of the left-wing parties during the neoliberal critical juncture explains these differences as interventionist left movements arose in those Latin American countries, where the traditional left after taking power had moved to the centre by introducing neoliberal policies during the 1990s. This shift thus created political space for new, radical left-wing movements and actors while frustration with market-oriented reforms started to grow – this was not the case with the countries where left-wing parties did not become governing ones.

> In these countries, traditional left parties were able to head off the rise of new, more-radical left movements by criticizing neoliberal policies and the parties that implemented them, even while they reached out to more centrist voters by abandoning certain radical features of their platforms and embracing the more popular aspects of the market model, such as free trade. (ibid., 588)

Similarly to its European counterpart, the interventionist path was often analysed under the label of populism, with populist organizations characterized by low institutionalization, strong attachment to the leader, movement-like structures, and use of disruptive tactics. Comparative analysis has shown that populism represented a reaction to systematic corruption, especially if combined with economic crisis (Hawkins 2010, 160). Legitimacy declined, in fact, as established parties prevented access to new groups, systematically breaking the rule of law through corruption, for selfish purposes (ibid., 95). Presented as a reaction to the elitism of delegative democracies with their weak accountability (Peruzzotti 2013), populist leaders have promoted a notion of democracy as quasi-liturgical incorporation of the common people, with appeals to authentic democracy and promotion of the poor through social, economic, and ethnic inclusion (Arnson and De la Torre 2013). Activating non-participants around an agenda of incorporation (Roberts 2013) and implementing expansionary social policies with strong pro-poor orientation (Weyland 2013), they have constructed antagonism through relations of differences and equivalence among people whose demands were not channelled (Panizza 2013).

Populism has also been defined as a characteristic of emerging indigenous parties. As during the crisis trust in other parties fell, given their failure to reduce poverty and respect the rule of law, under certain circumstances indigenous parties also emerged as successful due to their critique of both neoliberalism and corruption. Avoiding exclusionary nationalist rhetoric, new ethnic parties developed instead populist appeals, attracting disenchanted voters by bridging a denunciation of the traditional parties with a state interventionist agenda: their charismatic leaders rejected US-led market-oriented policies while putting forward the redistribution of wealth and the nationalization of national resources.

> These strategies have enabled the ethnopopulist parties to fuse traditional populist constituencies – politically disenchanted urban mestizos with nationalist and statist views – to their rural, largely indigenous base. (Madrid 2008, 14)

It was noted, however, that, while appealing to the people, these parties also tend to follow a conception of radical democracy in which the public and the private appear as intertwined, resembling Mansbridge's (1983, 3–5) conception of unitary democracy: preference for consensual decision-making, direct face-to-face participation, assumption of commonality, and ethics of respect, which resonate with indigenous people's long tradition of self-governance.

In short, in Latin America as in Europe, party politics interacted with social protests, which became all the more disruptive where the party system did not provide for institutional channels to challenge neoliberal reforms. Relations between parties and movements also varied within this path, however, with different relations between social movements and parties close to them in Bolivia, Venezuela, and Ecuador. Looking at this variance allows us to specify the analysis of the contextual dimensions for the development of movement parties by also pointing at movements' characteristics as well as strategic choices by movements and parties in their relational evolution.

When looking at recent developments in Latin America, *Bolivia* emerges as the case in which a proper movement party developed. At the origins of the MAS, 'there was little difference between the coca growers'/campesinos movement and the party – the latter was merely the political instrument of the former' (Van Cott 2008, 103). Not only did MAS, as a new party, emerge from within social movements, but social movements also remained influential even after the party achieved power. In fact, Morales' leadership was rooted in social movements that had promoted participatory organizational models.

A strong social movement on indigenous rights as well as a large potential community have been considered as important preconditions for MAS' rise. With Bolivia having the highest proportion of indigenous people in Latin America (62 per cent), the emergence of the MAS was triggered by social movements that were able to overcome the traditional conflicts between the more politicized Aymara in the highlands and the Quechua in the lowlands. Since the mid-1980s, the weakening of the left-wing parties that had traditionally defended indigenous rights, faced austerity, provided the indigenous movements with experienced leaders as well as inclusive frames. Beginning in the mid-1990s, networking was strengthened in the organization of massive Marches for Sovereignty and dignity, while in the same period the constitutional process catalysed the attention of the indigenous organization.

In particular, the formation of MAS is one of the outcomes of the very strong movement of coca growers (*cocaleros*), which mobilized against the eradication policies required by the United States, and the capacity of its leaders – especially Morales – to bridge anti-neoliberal and ethnic calls. Coca growers were in fact particularly successful in Bolivia, in both organizing and developing a dynamic formation of collective identity that addressed the specific challenge of defending a questionable good. This was facilitated by deep-rooted acceptance of coca use in Bolivia, where its criminalization, under pressure from the United States, happened later than in other countries. As the economic crisis, especially after the collapse of mining, made Bolivia more and more dependent on coca – also spreading corruption – miners relocated as coca growers, bringing new resources of militancy to their already rooted union. Low state repression in the 1980s as well as the tradition of structured relations between the peasants and the state under the left-wing military regime also facilitated mobilization, as the coca growers bridged their identity as peasants producing coca with a syndicalist identity, pushing for a politicization of ethnic identities (Ochoa 2014). In a 2002 MAS document, entitled 'Our ideological principle', reference is in fact made to the failure of internal colonialism and of the left, championing the potential of indigenous culture (ibid.).

As in the anti-austerity movements in Greece and especially in Spain, in Bolivia the movement also stressed participatory and deliberative democracy. Indigenous traditions were especially valued in the search for alternative forms of democracy. At its 5th congress in 2003, MAS postulated

> a true participatory democracy of consensus, respect and recognition of the diverse social organizations, where the communities and the people find their liberation from all forms of poverty, misery and discrimination.... The Movement towards socialism expresses its profound commitment to the development of a Communitarian democracy, of consensus and participation, of social and economic content. (Van Cott 2008, 3)

Indigenous traditions were also bridged with a focus against neoliberalism. MAS' success was related to growing opposition to the policies of trade liberalization and privatization that had been supported by all of the other parties, and with calls for redistributive policies against growing poverty. Having emerged within the peasant movement, MAS then extended its appeal to a broad alliance of groups of teachers, street vendors, and factory workers as well as associations of neighbours, with inclusive forms of support for indigenous culture. The MAS is in fact presented as 'a hybrid organization whose electoral success has been contingent on the construction of a strong rural-urban coalition, built on the basis of different linkages between the MAS and organized popular constituencies in rural and urban areas'; the rural background provided the party with non-populist traits, such as direct links with movements, grassroots control over leadership and practices of bottom up mobilization, while its urban features including top down and cooptive strategies resonated with populism (Anria 2013, 38). In fact, movement organizations, particularly the *cocaleros*, continued to constitute its core constituencies in a bottom-up genetic process, with blurred boundaries to separate the party and the movement (Roberts 2015).

The MAS was also able to attract resources coming from disappointed supporters of more traditional left-wing parties. Emerging from the Assembly for the Sovereignty of the People (ASP) – a social movement organization of peasants and coca growers – in the second half of the 1990s, MAS received support from a declining left-wing party, the United Left (IU), to which coca growers gave electoral support. The ASP gave birth to an electoral platform, the Political Instrument for the Sovereignty of the Peoples (IPSP) and then MAS, based on the principle of self-representation. Within a 'supraclass strategy', the MAS tended to attract left-leaning and nationalist intellectuals, as well as the urban middle classes, both indigenous and non-indigenous.

Here as well, relations developed within massive waves of protest from the very need for alliance and coordination. Together with electoral mobilization, contentious campaigns, especially within the Water War, allowed the formation of a heterogeneous coalition against neoliberalism. With twenty-seven MPs in 2002, MAS increased its influence, allowing for further networking: whereas some of them came from the Chapare region and were appointed through participatory mechanisms, others were co-opted by the party leadership, without previous experiences of militancy in the MAS (Anria 2013). While expanding its contacts with social movements in urban areas, such as La Paz and El Alto, MAS built alliances with various groups that included artisans, pensioners, workers in microenterprises, and miners' cooperatives, for which MAS offered a channel of representation for their claims within institutions (ibid.). This penetration within civil society reduced the autonomy of these organizations. As a *masista* noted, 'We can't deny we do that. We aim for our people to become leaders in these organizations. It is an effort to control the social organizations from the top' (cited in Anria 2013, 34). Another agreed: 'The project we have had as MAS is to be able to take control of the social organizations. In order to do that, you need to start working at the district level and from there you can start climbing. The MAS became a national-level force only insofar as it played an articulatory role among the experiences, demands, and internal structures of various base organizations in urban settings' (quoted in Anria 2013, 21).

Relations with social movements were indeed intense, but also varied. In general, MAS has kept strong ties with its core constituency of coca growers, who were able to have some influence on agrarian policy, expanding its network of informal alliances with civil society groups, although with some tensions between social movement organizations and the party. This informality – with the one exception of the Pacto de Unidad, active during the constitutional reform – has been seen as an effect of resistance to institutionalization, as party leaders feared that a formalization of linkages might transform MAS into a conventional party, thus jeopardizing the assembly-like decision-making style of rank-and-file organizations (Anria 2013).

Movement parties did not emerge in the other two cases, Venezuela and Ecuador, in which anti-austerity protests did produce deep changes in the party systems. While the electoral victories of Chávez in Venezuela and Correa in Ecuador had followed waves of protest,

> ...both leaders founded parties from the top-down that were electoral vehicles for their personal leadership, rather than extensions of movement organizations like the MAS in Bolivia. In neither Venezuela nor Ecuador, then, did social movements generate the political leadership of populist figures or the partisan vehicles that carried them to power; popular subjects undermined the *ancien régime* through social protest, but they did not play a constitutive role in the creation of populist alternatives. Their role, in short, was one of plebiscitary acclamation in the voting booth rather than active participation. (Roberts 2015)

This does not mean, however, that the new parties did not have (sometimes close) relations with specific social movements.

Social movements and moments of protest have been important in the history of *Venezuela*. The origins of the Bolivarian revolution are located in the 1970s, in the crisis of import substitution industrialization, within a mono-export petroleum economy. The petro-state provided the political class with resources to share within elite conciliation and mass poverty. In sum: 'Since the 1980s, organizations in Venezuela based in the middle and popular classes have demanded participatory democracy without the mediation of political parties' (De la Torre 2013b, 156). In fact, since the 1990s the two main political parties, Democratic Action (AD) and COPEI, were perceived as closed and colluded parties that had brought about impoverishment through market reforms and a downsizing of the state in both social services and economic policies. Massive protests, like the Caracazo in 1989, had been met with brutal repression, and heavy law and order policies were implemented. This widespread dissatisfaction eventually brought to power Chávez, who had campaigned on social justice, participation, and equality, to be achieved through an alternative model of participatory democracy (ibid.).

While no organized social movement was involved in the party's origins, an important role in its creation was played by the Movimiento Bolivariano Revolucionario 200 (Revolutionary Bolivariano Movement, MBR 200), formed by military rank-and-filers who were at the core of the Bolivarian project. These were individuals from the poorer strata, to whom the military gave the possibility of education. The MBR 200 increased contacts with civilians, in particular with left-wing parties that had been defeated in their armed attempts in the 1960s, but also to those who had rejected violence. When MBR 200 organized a failed coup in 2002, Chávez was appreciated for his courage and responsibility in making a television appearance, which was contrasted with the irresponsibility of corrupt politicians. Pardoned by President Rafael Caldera in 1994, he founded the Fifth Republic Movement as a parallel party to the MBR 200, and won elections in 1998.

While, in contrast to MBR 200, the party was vertically organized and rather personalized, the Bolivarian movement also mobilized broadly among autonomous organizations, although remaining weaker than in Bolivia. The party achieved power in a critical conjuncture characterized by acute social crisis, poverty, unemployment, insecurity, and corruption, fuelled by low oil prices, and driven by the brutal repression of the Caracazo in 2000 that eventually produced a collapse of the established parties – already visible in the victory of the independent candidate Caldoro. Chávez's victory did reflect a party system breakdown of the partitocracy, the so-called Punto Fijo system that had been privileged by the managing of oil revenues (ibid.).

Lack of unity in the indigenous movement has been cited in the case of Ecuador to explain its failure to express an alternative party. Less successful than the MAS, Pachakutik in *Ecuador* emerged from the autonomization of indigenous organizations from the tutelage of the left and the Catholic Church, also eventually filling the space opened by a weakened left. Claiming rights on land, bilingual education, and protection against discrimination, in 1998 these indigenous groups succeeded in winning the most progressive constitutional rights for the indigenous population. The collapse of the economy and the party system were at the basis of the success of Correa in 2006 after a decade of corruption, economic difficulties, and massive protests, like *pueblazo* in Quito against the corruption of president Abdalá Bucaram in 2005, and the failure of the new president, Lucio Gutiérrez, supported by the indigenous Pachakutik and Conaie, to break with neoliberalism. A heterodox economist, Correa had briefly been the minister of economy in Palacio's government, expressing a strong critique of the Washington consensus and *partidocracia*. While the idea of developing a broad left-wing and indigenous front (which nevertheless supported him in the second round election) failed, he was said to have built a techno-populist project.

5.3.3. Changing relations: Movement parties in power

In Latin America, as in the European cases, the analysis of the relations between movement parties and social movements points to transformations in time – and this not only in the direction of Michels' iron law of oligarchy. Rather, especially when the radical left parties were in government, relations with social movements changed, with moments of tension and moments of adaptation. These relations showed dynamics somewhat similar to those we noted in Europe, with new parties introducing elements of participation, even when in tension with social movement demands.

Relations between movements and parties have often been read in Latin America through the ambiguous category of populism. Participation in Bolivia, Venezuela and Ecuador has often been dubbed as populist, characterized by plebiscitarian linkages between the leaders and the masses. Barr (2009) suggested that, in a context of high discontent, it is advantageous to use anti-establishment rhetorical appeals, as is indeed often done by leaders located outside the political system who use plebiscitarian instruments as well as mass demonstrations promoted from above. While citizens feel like direct participants, they 'are reduced to following the lines of a drama that has assigned them a central though subordinate role. They are expected to delegate power to a politician who claims to be the embodiment of their redemption' (De la Torre 2000, 19). In this sense, plebiscitarianism is associated with 'a form of "direct democracy", albeit a highly majoritarian, Rousseauian version, where any intermediation or distribution of the responsibility of representation leads to inefficiency and ineffectiveness' (Barr 2009, 36).

According to some analysis, populism tends to push weak democracies into forms of competitive authoritarianism. This happens as populist leaders are outsiders, with little experience in negotiation and coalition-building, as well as no stake in the survival of representative institutions. Considering the elites as corrupted, populist leaders instead promote big changes, with frequent conflicts with other institutions such as courts or the parliament (Levitsky and Loxton 2013). Left-wing populism has been singled out as even more dangerous for democracy than the right-wing version, as it increases state power (which can then increase political loyalty); anti-poverty intervention provides it with the support of the poor; and economic nationalism insulates it from pressure by international organizations (Weyland 2013).

A more complex picture has been drawn of the degrees and conceptions of democracy developing in the three countries, however, pointing at the same time at limiting but also empowering elements for the citizens. In general, leaders in all three countries have increased participation by 'the inclusion of marginalized groups in society, but limits (the possibilities for) contestation' (Mudde and Rovira Kaltwasser 2012, 20). For Bolivia, Venezuela and Ecuador, it was in fact noted that power in these three cases is concentrated in the executive limiting opposing, or even alternative views and thus undermining civil liberties and pluralism in the name of the electoral act, which is understood as the ultimate expression of democratic legitimacy. At the same time, though, these governments act for the inclusion of those disempowered and marginalized groups of people through reducing poverty, redistribution of wealth, or referendums.

> Chávez, Morales, and Correa empower the subaltern by using a populist rhetoric that pits the virtuous people against elites. (De la Torre 2013a, 28)

Differences have also been identified in the ways in which the three countries 'undermine contestation and promote the material inclusion of the poor'. In fact, as De la Torre (2013a, 29) summarized, contentious politics differed as the three parties entered government. First, in Bolivia, very strong social movements have contrasted Morales' temptation to present itself as 'the voice of the unitary people, forcing him to negotiate and even to reverse policies. Participation is mostly bottom up, and the government relies on the mobilization of social movements in conflicts with the opposition'. While, however, Morales ascended into government at the peak of a protest cycle, in Ecuador Correa was elected as the indigenous movement was losing mobilizing capacity. Therefore, the opposition did not have the resources necessary to oppose Correa, while at the same time his technocratic leadership strategy was coupled with the lack of participatory democracy mechanisms.

Finally, Chávez reached power in a situation of relative weakness of social movements which allowed him 'to create organizations of the subaltern from the top down'. Moreover, the opposition used its available organizational resources to activate collective action so as to oppose Chávez, which was met with further attempts at popular organization by the government. 'Even though organizations of the subaltern were created from the top down, citizens use these organizations to try to push for their autonomous agendas' (ibid.).

In *Bolivia*, relations between the MAS and the social movements became strained when the MAS took power. Once in power, the Morales administration was rhetorically very radical, even if it had more ruptures in foreign than in economic policies, where various constraints pushed for continuity allowing for heterodox policies, but with high fiscal discipline. The partial nationalization of the natural gas industry granted the state resources to invest in welfare, even though unemployment and poverty were still high and land reform still limited. While initially power was dispersed, it was later concentrated in the hands of Morales, although with still some opening for representatives of the various social movements. In a plebiscitarian trend, Morales used repeated electoral events and social mobilization to push for its political agenda. The new constitution strengthened the power of the president who, in 2009, was re-elected with 64 per cent of the vote. Tensions between the party – as well as the government and parliamentary party faction – and social movement organizations were clearly felt, with the party growing more and more detached from civil society (Anria 2013). Not by chance, the presence of leaders of social organizations in the cabinet has tended to decrease over time (Zegada et al. 2008), and participation of social movement organizations in the legislature and executive has been reduced, even though it remains significant (Anria 2013).

However, participatory tendencies remained alive. Several of its political leaders even rejected the 'party' label, as they tended to consider parties as divisive and feared institutionalization. Moreover, based on principles of self-representation of the masses, leaders tended not to speak for their constituencies, but rather as spokespeople, while also maintaining an interest in non-institutional political mobilization (Anria 2013). The very fluid organizational structure of the party left space for internal opposition, as 'It is precisely the MAS's fluidity, or its informal features and absence of routinization, that leaves wide manoeuvring room for the social organizations allied with it. In many cases, these organizations maintain considerable autonomy from the MAS, and they mobilize both for and against the government, placing limits on Morales's authority by mobilizing resources even if Morales does not approve' (ibid., 37). As mentioned, while social protest was channelled into electoral forms, the expansion of MAS from the countryside to the cities implied the addition of more negotiated alliances with already existing organizations to the organic relations with coca growers, who saw their autonomy reduced even if not totally constrained, as its social movement networks remained important for the party (Roberts 2015). There continued to be consultation with social movement organizations and activists (Madrid 2011), with a national coordinating body in which leaders of social movement organizations met with institutional leaders. Moreover, social movements – such as independent mining cooperatives and lowlands indigenous communities mobilized against the construction of a highway through indigenous territories, or protests against a government decree to cancel fuel price subsidies – kept putting pressure on the party or even managed to cancel MAS' policies by taking to the streets:

> The ongoing capacity for autonomous collective action thus helped to hold the government accountable to its social bases and at least partially counteract the tendencies towards top-down control associated with party bureaucratization and concentrated, charismatic executive authority. (Roberts 2015, 690)

In particular, the party kept strong relations with communitarian movements. Several ministers came from humble backgrounds, and the party often appealed to the *pueblo* against its enemies (Crabtree 2013). In 2009, the constitution defined the nation state as 'plurinational and communitarian', granting indigenous people autonomy, self-governance, and the right to culture and using their own language. It also defined the moral and ethical basis of Bolivia's society based on indigenous cosmological principles, promoting a ' "democratic participatory, representative and communitarian" mode of government inspired by indigenous communities' (Albro 2010, 79). This reflected the communitarian traditions of the social movements that had supported the MAS. In fact, Morales departs from the traditions and practices of communal democracy in engaging in decision-making social movement organizations, as seen in the long-lasting meetings with various social movement organizations (De la Torre 2013a). The empowering capacity of these participatory channels varies, however.

As for Ecuador and Venezuela, a turn towards citizens' participation accompanied the evolution of the left in power. Coming suddenly into power, Chávez had no developed plan, but social movement groups had elaborated various proposals that were incorporated in the new constitution, approved in 1999. In particular, participatory democracy was enshrined in the 1999 Constitution, whose Article 62 states that 'all citizens have the right to participate in public affairs'. In fact, 'the deepening of democracy to make it "participative and protagonistic" was of central importance, and it counted on a broad consensus' (Lopez Maya 2011, 220). There was also a recognition of social rights and civil rights, indigenous and environmental rights. The statist project Chávez implemented represented a departure, but was also built upon the heterodox model that had characterized Venezuela, with the 1961 constitution already expressing commitment to redistribution of wealth. Since 2002, the project was strengthened by a commitment to developing a twenty-first-century socialism, in particular through the idea of Endogenous Development Nuclei (NUDEs), conceived as 'production units designed to offer solutions consonant with the principle of participatory democracy for pressing social problems' (ibid., 223).

Chávez has divided scholars into those who consider him an enemy of democracy, and therefore an expression of Venezuela's problems, and those who see him as a solution to them. Several commentators have stigmatized the populism of Chávez' discourses, characterized by a Manichean, teleological element, with a cosmic struggle between good, as the will of the people, and bad, as a conspiracy of a minority, with a stress on the need for systemic changes revolution, all presented with aggressive and polarizing rhetoric (Hawkins 2010; Lopez Maya and Panzarelli 2013). It is, however, also recognized that he promoted the participation of previously excluded groups. Since 1995, after the attempted coup, circles were created and then strengthened in the early 2000s. They tended to be involved in social activities for the community, with a stress on horizontalism, informality, and a dislike for formal organization (including MBR). Democratic in their internal organization, they valued participation more than freedom, promoting participatory democracy and following a populist logic (privileging members), but not a clientelistic one. After peaking at 2.2 million members, they declined in 2004, as their tasks were accomplished by public institutions.

Various participatory projects, including the so-called 'missions', developed in 2003. Re-elected in 2006 with 63 per cent of the vote, thanks also to sustained economic growth since 2004, Chávez radicalized his project in a statist and plebiscitarian direction, with the re-nationalization of strategic firms. A constitutional reform aiming at increasing presidential power was defeated in a national referendum in 2007, which stimulated a critical debate within the movement, also targeting the repressive turn of the regime. While winning a referendum that removed obstacles to the re-election of the president in 2009, fiscal crisis and social unrest developed as a result of inflation and global economic difficulties.

In sum, starting out with participatory attempts, after the 2006 victory the regime turned more statist. However, Chávez used plebiscitary tools in order to dismantle the existing regime and promote a new constitutional order. The 'protagonistic democracy' mentioned in the constitution established spaces for participation from the grassroots in multiple institutional arenas. Since the beginning of the 2000s, the Bolivarian circles developed in local communities, while social missions encouraged community participation. In parallel with municipal institutions, communal councils allowed for participation in social programmes.

Chávez's relations with social movements were certainly important. After coming to power, he did not rely upon a strong organizational basis, making the organization of the poor all the more important. His administration then supported the creation in 1999 of Technical Water Roundtables in order to manage the distribution of water between communities that shared the same water sources; and, in 2001, it backed the formation of Bolivarian Circles – small groups devoted to studying Bolivarianism as well as participating in local policy-making in order to make, as Chávez stated, participatory and protagonist democracy more effective. With more than two million members, the Bolivarian Circles organized mass demonstrations in support of the president. The next year, Urban Land Committees were created in order to ensure that squatter settlements had the collective entitlement to the land on which the self-built dwellings are located. Since 2005, a programme of Twenty-First Century Socialism was launched with the aim of developing democracy beyond the representative liberal model as, according to

Chávez, 'popular power is the soul, nerve, flesh and bone, and essence of Bolivarian democracy, of a true democracy' (in De la Torre 2013a, 31). These institutions were recognized as having a capacity to empower the excluded groups of the population: 'For those who actively participate in the different Bolivarian institutions, it has meant a new sense of dignity and inclusion. It also questions views of participation in these institutions as entirely top-down. The state and popular organizations negotiate how representative, participatory, and bottom up these experiments are' (ibid., 33). Additionally, left-wing activists used these opportunities to put pressure upon the regime (ibid.). While Chavez' death certainly affected these relationships, the core constituency of the Bolivarian revolution proved difficult to mobilize against the party (Masullo 2017).

The relations between the party and social movements were tense also in Ecuador, where the strong indigenous movement had had difficulty entering the electoral arena. As Conaghan stated (2011, 274), 'Correa regarded Ecuador's turbulent and intrusive civil society as an obstacle, not a building block, for his revolution', and he dismissed organized interests as 'privileged interlocutors representing special interests, while his elected government was deemed the only legitimate guardian of the "national" interest'. Movement organizations – from students to public employees, from indigenous rights' activists to environmentalists – thus kept mobilizing, fighting what they saw as a pervasive control by the interventionist state (Roberts 2015). Social control developed through tripartite corporatist social pacts (Petras and Veltmeyer 2009).

Correa even engaged in open conflicts with pre-existing social movements. Defined as humanistic, utopian, and mestizo, Correa incorporated popular demands, but not social movements. Aiming at re-founding society, he was, however, afraid to transfer power to the people (Montufar 2013). Notwithstanding the government's proclamations concerning participation, this was restricted under Correa's rule merely to the act of electoral voting (De la Torre 2013a). Within a technocratic vision, experts from academia and NGOs formed a National Secretary of Planning and Development (SENPLADES), with the task of developing new policy alternatives to neoliberalism. As De la Torre noted (ibid., 36), 'Differently from neoliberal experts who believed in econometric models, they are interdisciplinary and eclectic, quoting post-colonial theorists, radical democrats, unorthodox economists, and political ecologists in their documents.' Oriented towards rationalization and modernization of the state, Correa accused organizations from civil society – from public employees to indigenous communities or trade unions – of defending privileges.

Related to these differences in the relations between movements and parties was also variation in the conceptions of democracy, which were different in the three cases, even if in all of them there was a search for alternatives to traditional democracy. In all three countries, the leaders promoted some participation, through direct democracy and constitutional politics, also politicizing and mobilizing even the most marginalized social groups (De la Torre 2013a). The way in which they pursued these aims varied, however. Socialized into politics as the leader of the coca growers' union, Morales stressed the power of the streets, as rallies put pressure on negotiation with mobilization as a fundamental democratic act of a 'democracy of the streets'. In fact, 'The MAS conceives "the people" to be inherently democratic and virtuous. Social movements that speak on behalf of the people could challenge Morales' claim to embody the unitary will of all, and at times have forced him to reverse policies because they went against the interests of "the people"' (De la Torre 2013a, 42). In Venezuela, given the pressure coming from his constituency as well as his search for a 'real democracy', Chávez's governments created various mechanisms of participatory democracy. Even if created from above, participatory institutions were then often appropriated from below, especially from the poor, even going beyond the established directions. In Chávez's vision of a 'moral and spiritual' revolution, the individualist and selfish values of capitalism had to be reversed. In this endeavour, the leader had to 'represent, plainly, the voice and the heart of millions' (Zúquete 2008, 104). As for Ecuador, Correa's vision has been defined instead as technocratic populism, with 'post-neoliberal' experts in key administrative positions. Pursuing social justice, Correa and his groups of experts perceived themselves as entitled to speak on behalf of the people as a whole, the leader himself embodying the will of the people. That was the case as the leader along with technocrats depart from an understanding of the status quo as totally corrupt – including dissent which was understood as treason – which thus needs to be entirely rebuilt through new arrangements both in terms of institutions and practices (De la Torre 2013a).

These differences in the relations between movements and parties in the three countries have been linked to the strength of subaltern organizations when the radical left party leaders obtained power; the conflicts between the government and the opposition, as well as their conception of democracy, influenced these developments. While Morales' political success came in a moment of massive indigenous-led protests, Correa emerged as the mobilizing capacity of the indigenous movement declined and the movement remained weak in Venezuela, where Chávez succeeded in mobilizing the poor top-down. Moreover, while there was very strong opposition to Chávez and strong opposition to Morales, Correa encountered less opposition.

5.4. Conclusion

At the party level, the analysis of parties that failed in Spain, Greece, or Italy has shown that even those radical parties that had undergone some organizational reforms in the direction of more participatory structures – as well as opening up their programme in order to appeal to emerging movements – were unsuccessful when those changes remained tame. Limited organizational innovation, ideological opening, and participation in contentious politics were not sufficient to regain the trust of social movements that were calling for radical transformations.

At the country level, the presence of economic strains, political discontent as well as protest were not sufficient for the emergence of new radical left parties in particular circumstances: where the social effects of the Great Recession were mitigated by an inclusive welfare state, as in Portugal; or where clientelistic ties, as in Ireland, buffered the political effects of the crisis on the party system. In particular, anti-austerity protests had less disruptive consequences when they remained more rooted in the traditional forms of expression of social conflicts.

The Latin American cases also confirm that socio-economic shocks, the position of centre-left parties, repercussions at the level of the party system, mass movements, and institutional conduciveness are important preconditions for the emergence of new (and innovative) parties. They also state, however, that relations between governments and movements are certainly not easy, as 'bottom-up participation is difficult to sustain as parties institutionalize, and it becomes particularly difficult when they govern at the national level' (Levitsky and Roberts 2011b, 421). Risks include, indeed, the co-optation of the grassroots, as well as the need to scale up participatory institutions.

6

Movement Parties: Some Conclusions

Movement parties develop in waves, as does the social science literature addressing them. Before the cases analysed in this volume, attention had focused on one specific type of movement party: the Greens. More recently, however, especially in area studies on Latin America, there has been a resurgence of attention to the emergent parties on the left, rooted within the anti-austerity protests.

At the empirical level, our research shows both continuities and discontinuities in the repertoires and framing of both types of party in relation to those rooted in the most recent wave of protests in Southern Europe. In fact, the new wave of movement parties seems (somewhat paradoxically) stronger exactly where the Green parties had traditionally been weaker.

At the theoretical level, bridging research on social movements and parties, we have located the genesis and evolution of these parties within a relational, constructed and dynamic approach. First of all, movement parties inhabit a complex field of interactions with other parties as well as social movement actors. Competition with other parties defines their electoral space and chances; and, in different forms in the different steps of protest cycles, social movements provide for important material and cognitive exchange of resources. Movement parties' action is, to a certain extent, strategic, driven as it is by assessments of opportunities and constraints, advantages and disadvantages, risks and benefits. At the same time, however, those assessments are strongly constructed through cognitive and affective processes that define visions and norms, but also emotions. Additionally, while structured by external conditions, movement parties provide for shocks that unsettle existing structures through open-ended, conjunctural events. Many developments emerge from trial and error, with movement and party actors experimenting with various solutions. Rather than deriving directly from contextual conditions or pure agency, movement parties are the complex outcome of sequences of events through which emerging actors test their own limits, in part producing the opportunities and resources they need in the electoral competition.

In this concluding chapter, we summarize the empirical results as well as highlighting their theoretical relevance for thinking about political parties as well as social movements. We will first reflect on the *conditions for the genesis of movement parties* contrasting them with the conditions in countries where such movement parties have not developed. Additionally, we will reflect on the *organizational characteristics* of these emerging parties, with particular attention to their relations with social movements. More generally, we will single out some *implications of our results for reflections on capitalism and democracy* by very tentatively posing some questions about further developments.

6.1. The party genesis: A multi-layered, sequential approach

Literature on political parties noted that organizational choices are influenced by environmental transformations (as external stimuli), which are filtered through internal factors that empower the coalition that wants to realize change. Organizational sociology pitted theories stressing the selective capacity of the environments against those emphasizing the strategic choices of organizational action (della Porta 2009). Our research has shown that the rise of successful movement parties is linked to choices made within a multi-layered set of conditions, both endogenous and exogenous, and to their sequencing.

The contextual factors that affected the genesis of Green parties have been located within both the electoral and the social movement arenas. In fact, 'some country-specific factors, including both institutional features such as electoral systems and particular national experiences such as a strong conflict over nuclear energy, make it more or less likely for strong Green parties to emerge and develop in specific countries' (Rihoux and Rüdig 2006, 59). In addition, research into other types of movement parties (such as indigenous parties) has stressed the presence of preconditions for their emergence and success – for example, unrepresented issues/grievances/interests/identities, related social movement developments, lack of representation in the party system. However, these are at best necessary, but certainly not sufficient conditions, as party emergence and success also require strategic capacity to exploit those conditions through a sequence of actions endowed with confirming effects.

More specifically in recent times, at the socio-economic level, the emergence and success of left-wing parties in Latin America has been linked to the neoliberal critical juncture (Roberts 2015). In fact, failure by domestic and international institutions to produce growth fuels protest against immiseration (even notwithstanding economic growth), delegitimizing the states. Moreover, austerity modifies parties' and movements' repertoires, as collective actors can no longer rely on clientelistic or corporatist states (Shefner, Pasdirtz, and Blad 2006). At the cultural level, neoliberalism has been seen as accompanied by populism, which 'is now so mainstream in Western democracies that we can talk of a populist Zeitgeist' (March and Mudde 2005, 34–5). Populism has in fact been linked with neoliberalism, given their shared anti-organizational as well as anti-status-quo tendency; moreover, 'the undifferentiated mass of "the people" following the leader is akin to the unstructured market', and 'neopopulists and neoliberals also coincide considerably in their relationship to major socio-political actors. They maintain distance from trade unions, professional associations, and even many organized business groups, which personalistic plebiscitarian leaders see as fetters on their autonomy and power and which neoliberal experts condemn as rent-seeking "special interests" who seek to interfere with the market' (Weyland 2003, 1098). Our research revealed that, in Southern Europe as in Latin America, the neoliberal critical juncture set in motion a twofold process that proved most important for the transformation of the party system: on the one hand, new movement energies were mobilized, and on the other, competitors (especially on the left) weakened.

Movement energies. The findings of the present study indicate that new parties in Greece and Spain, but also in Italy, developed as inheritors of collective resources that have grown during the most recent wave of protest, but which have also been frustrated by the lack of success of intense and long mobilizing processes in the past. In all three countries, there were *important traditions of social movement activity*. While literature traditionally tends to consider civil society as weakly organized in the South of Europe (Gunther, Diamandouros, and Puhle 1995), it proved instead very contentious, with high levels of unconventional mobilization.

Party resources were nurtured within social movements in different ways and in different moments of the *protest cycle against the austerity measures in late neoliberalism* that developed in each country. In Spain and Greece, massive anti-austerity protests acted as critical junctures themselves, in response to the neoliberal crisis. The cycle of protest developed in these countries – which started with more conventional forms and within institutions, continued in massive and innovative forms, and then declined (or was perceived as declining) in terms of mobilization capacity – acquiring, however, long-term effects. Especially in Spain and Greece, the 2011 protests generated a contentious political culture that spread throughout both countries. In Italy as well, 2011 had seen a culmination of anti-austerity protests that brought about the overwhelming victory in the movement-sponsored referendum against water privatization (della Porta, O'Connor, Portos, and Subirats 2017).

The movements had strong *empowering effects*. While deeply critical of representative institutions, movement activists and sympathizers challenged especially the convergence of parties of the right and the left into a stigmatized bipartisanism, with a corrupting impact on democracy. However, the protest cycle offered channels to articulate grievances and organize discontent. Rather than apathy, the strong critique of the political class brought about intense politicization. For instance, in Greece there was a concurrent collapse of citizens' trust in parliament (with the lowest point occurring in 2011) while confidence in parties also declined. Meanwhile, trust in the people and social movements grew. Similar data have been presented for Spain and Italy.

The electoral alternatives developed especially in the *declining phases of the movements*. As protesting for months and years in the streets proved unsuccessful, various alternatives were explored. Podemos emerged from a double condition: the empowering effects of the protest, but also its decline in response to the lack of institutional response. The party manifesto 'Mover ficha: convertir la indignación en cambio político' (Making a Move: Turning Indignation into Political Change) indicates exactly this perceived need for efficacy. In Greece, the failure of protesters to annul austerity policies after 2012 through collective action led to the shrinking of mobilizations and to investment in the electoral party (Serdedakis and Koufidi 2016) – as reflected in the motto 'what else could we do?'. At the same time, concrete experiences with solidarity initiatives multiplied, generating a 'politicization of everyday life'. In Italy, the frustration related to the lack of response to popular law initiatives and abrogative referenda promoted during protest events such as the 'V-days' – as well as the delegitimation of the whole party system related to corruption scandals (Mosca 2013) – facilitated the emergence of the M5S and its continuous support by the Italian electorate.

Declining competition. The movement parties we studied grew from the weakness of the other parties in the party systems. In all three cases, in fact, they developed from a mix of institutional closure to movements' demands, but also from electoral opportunities provided by electoral de-alignment, while organizational resources grew within the protests.

First of all, there existed a *general organizational weakness of parties*, even if coupled with traditional clientelist rooting. In the new democracies of Southern Europe, parties leapfrogged the stage of mass organizations, growing, especially in Spain but also in Greece, as state-based rather than civil society-based structures (Gunther, Diamandouros and Puhle 1995). While in Italy parties had been much more deeply rooted in the so-called first republic working as 'democratic anchors' (Morlino 2005), they underwent rapid decline as political corruption, which had spread as an internal cancer within parties, became public, also producing an external shock in terms of loss of members, votes, and trust (della Porta 1992; della Porta and Vannucci 1997).

Second, protests spiralled with a *crisis of legitimacy*, as the increase in contentious politics was produced by and then fuelled a profound drop in institutional trust. In all three countries involved, the *critical juncture of the neoliberal crisis* in fact triggered the breakdown of the bipolar party systems around which democracy had been built in Spain and Greece, and had developed into in Italy (Chiaramonte and Emanuele 2014). In Italy, the crisis of neoliberalism brought about opportunities in terms of electoral volatility, which in 2013 increased fourfold as compared to the 2008 elections, reaching 40 per cent. This level of volatility was second only to the Greek case, where it touched almost 48.7 per cent; it has been extremely high in Spain as well reaching 34.6 per cent in December 2015, the most volatile national elections since 1982 (Yécora 2015).

This drop in legitimacy (or, at least, support) was all the more visible for the centre-left parties, with their long experiences in government. In all three countries, a general delegitimation of these political actors was coupled with a declining trend in the left-wing parties, which had indeed capitalized on the resistance against fascism, but had then lost their reputation and appeal, in some cases also due to corruption scandals. In Europe, like in Latin America, the movement parties emerged in particular from the *failure of centre-left* parties to address new (but also satisfy old) concerns for social rights and social justice (Roberts 2015). In Spain, austerity has been depicted as a 'cancer' for the political consensus stemming from the 1978 pacts among different socio-political actors. With the centre-left party/ies embracing neoliberalism, the 'political space of social-democracy was empty and we have occupied it', as the leader of Podemos Iglesias declared (2015d). As one can read in the Political Principles of Podemos, with 'its incorporation into the neoliberal social pact', PSOE 'is the one who closes the political space of the "left" and its current political crisis is what opens the opportunities for a new majority' (PPP, 8). This was also the case for SYRIZA, which indeed strengthened its profile as an anti-austerity party by differentiating itself from the way PASOK dominated the centre-left by co-opting left-wing and movement energies. Adopting a partially different discourse, the M5S has also stigmatized cuts and promoted a '*reddito di cittadinaza*', a state subsidy to be supplied to all citizens. In Italy, electoral losses of the Democratic party in the 2013 elections were huge (four million votes) and Berlusconi's party lost almost six million votes (Chiaramonte and Emanuele 2014). The M5S post-ideological profile was then appealing to both left-wing and right-wing voters.

In all three cases, the declining differences between the two major rival parties – especially on socio-economic issues – opened a space for the emergence of a new party. The *unholy alliance of the centre-left with the right-wing parties* was all the more stigmatizing given the long histories of polarized bipartisanism. Thus, grand coalitions (often sponsored by Troika lenders institutions, including the European Commission) had also been responsible for bringing about a crisis, especially, but not only, on the (centre-) left. This was most extreme in the case of Greece, with PASOK dropping from 44 per cent in 2009 to 4.7 per cent in 2015. In Italy, too, the electoral success of M5S started when Berlusconi was replaced in government, in November 2011, by former European Commissioner Mario Monti. Evidence of corruption then spiralled, with a delegitimation of institutional politics. Given these conditions, some causal mechanisms worked towards the development of successful movement parties.

Organizational occupation. Movement activists, besides founding new parties, also occupied existing parties or created special links with existing ones. A telling case is SYRIZA, which is the only parliamentary party in Greece to have been involved in the global justice movement and the European social forums since the early 2000s. This had a generational effect by triggering processes of learning and training of a younger generation of members into activism, generating 'a radical youth, a transformative youth, a youth that learnt to challenge conventional modes of politics' (I1G). Similarly, party members participated in the student mobilizations in 2006–7 and even later on, in 2008, in support of the youth protests and against police brutal repression. As numerous young members took over ruling positions, this generation trained in movements had dragged (part of) the party close to or even inside the protest movements, which, however, kept their autonomy. As SYRIZA's discourse became more radical, it also became more tolerated, or even supported among movement activists who were at the same time growing increasingly more hostile to party politics. In fact, 'It was mostly SYRIZA who was influenced by the movement, rather than SYRIZA influencing the movement itself' (I3G). Similarly, Podemos grew from within a movement that had successfully mobilized a younger generation, strongly hit by unemployment and precarity, by (young) activists' attempt to test the electoral way after others had been perceived as failing. Although the relation with anti-austerity protests has been less relevant for the emergence of the M5S, at least in its genetic phase a significant portion of its activists and elected representatives came from social movements active in the past. According to an activist, 'in the M5S there are people bridging twenty years of environmental struggles, many have fought against nuclear power and water privatization, many others like me come from NGOs, others from volunteer experience in fair trade, others have worked with disability cooperatives or cultural associations…and entered the Movement as a natural evolution to be able to do something within institutions, not only from the outside' (I4I).

Overlapping membership. All three parties see overlapping memberships with movement activists that indeed bring their experiences, skills and preferences within the party. When the protest cycle emerged, some SYRIZA members, especially the younger ones, were already naturally part of it, 'doing what they had already learned to do', as the idea that had started to grow when SYRIZA was formed in 2004 was that 'being members of the party does not mean we are different from other movement collectives' (I2G). As a result, some felt even more part of the movement than of the party, and resigned when they believed that SYRIZA had betrayed the movement – this is especially the case since the party came to power in 2015. In all three cases, participation in protests had a deeply transformative effect on party activists – as a member of SYRIZA declared, 'it is the slogan we shout during the marches, the local movement in which we spend time, the banner we raise and the leaflets we distribute, for some of us these define our way of being, not what the party line says, it is our everyday experience' (I3G). In this way, they also acquired personal trust, or at least acceptance, by the social movement activists. While overlapping membership is also a feature of M5S' activists (Mosca 2015a), the relation with social movements has become much more precarious over time.[1]

Galvanization. Through a mechanism of galvanization, defined as aroused awareness, initial electoral victories acted as turning points. Strategically, the successful movement parties proved capable of creating turning points by exploiting some electoral windows of opportunity. This was for instance the case as Podemos participated in the European elections which, given their proportional electoral system without electoral thresholds, were more favourable than national ones for achieving an initial electoral success. Electoral successes then tended to be, to a certain extent, self-sustained, as they themselves have transformative effects. The 8 per cent Podemos achieved then activated a virtuous circle, followed by a jump in resonance, followed not only by increasing recruitments but also by a different type of membership. Similarly, the M5S contested first local elections, where they could capitalize on their experiences with environmental struggles. Also in Italy, there was then a mechanism of galvanization after the first electoral success, as the electoral fortune of the M5S started with the municipal elections held in May 2012, doubling its support. This unexpected result galvanized the party and the public up to the general political elections in February 2013, with M5S becoming the most voted for party in the low Chamber (excluding votes from Italians living abroad), a result confirmed by a 21 per cent gain in the EP elections. Success then fed upon itself. The electoral campaigns themselves worked in fact as a catalyst of collective energies – thus, 400 circles of Podemos opened shortly before the EU elections.

Initial victories then had cumulative effects in terms of party transformations. In particular, the basis of supporters broadened beyond the movement activists, in two directions: to the marginalized groups, traditionally not represented in the political system; but also to those who were previously members of centre-left and left-wing parties (such as PSOE and IU in Spain; PD in Italy; PASOK in Greece). It thus expanded from informed activists to excluded people, and from middle classes to lower classes. In Italy, as in Spain, the profile of the electorate changed, with electoral success extending beyond the most educated and middle classes, but also among the youngest cohorts, involving a larger proportion of electors previously on the right.

Reverse effects of blame. In all three cases, first electoral victories had a polarizing effect, as the main parties and mass media joined in depicting movement parties as populist, or even violent and anti-systemic. These efforts, however, had perverse effects, as the blame by stigmatized actors increased support and sympathy for the emerging parties. The delegitimation of the elites therefore reduced their capacity to challenge the new party rhetoric. Even virulent media attacks characterizing the new parties as anti-political and/or extremely radical tended to increase sympathy for them. In fact, there was a sort of reverse reputational effect, as the critiques by those who were perceived as responsible for suffering gave credit to their enemies. So, constantly accused by already delegitimate actors, such as mainstream parties and media, of fuelling or even coordinating violent protests, SYRIZA gained rather than lost support. Also in Spain, bipartisan attacks on Podemos backfired; the same happened in Italy with the M5S. The elites' critiques of these new parties as being Eurosceptic, anti-modern, or culturally under-developed had the unintended effect of legitimizing them. Organizational framing singled out the presence of a broad cartel of colluding political and economic elites defending their narrow interests against the common good.

As dissent was stigmatized and protest repressed, the protesters gained increasing support (of up to two thirds of the population in Greece, but also in Spain). Austerity produced polarization as well, bringing about opportunities for *solidarization* between parties and movement activists. As an activist not supporting SYRIZA mentioned, 'all of us taking part in resistance, we were labelled *"sirizaioi"* (SYRIZA supporters)...it was them (*the elites and media*) that led people to ally with SYRIZA, not SYRIZA!' (I20G); or else, 'the attack by the media was so fierce, that you couldn't do otherwise!' (I10G).

6.1.1. The party evolution: Between fields

While it is too early to assess the general evolution of these movement parties' politics, we can see the extent to which actual choices in framing and organizational strategies reflect attention to the movements. Research on the movements/parties relations tend to point at a sort of unavoidable separation between the two. Following Michels' iron law, movement parties – from the Socialists to the Greens – have been described as oriented towards institutionalization and moderation, with the action in the electoral arena taking precedence over the action in the protest arena. Research on social movements has, however, denied, in particular for resource poor and identity strong actors, the existence of an unavoidable trend towards bureaucratization (Zald and Ash 1966). In addition, research on political parties has singled out the permanent advantage of linkages with society and, even more, the need to strengthen these linkages under particular circumstances (della Porta 2015a). Our research revealed how trade-offs, contingent sequences, and unforeseen events influence the development of relations between movements and parties.

Some theories and research in party studies predict a tendency towards increasing separation between parties and movements. According to Herbert Kitschelt (1993), the emergence of social movements is related to structural differentiation as, while complex problems are better dealt with by parties, and interest groups focus on a narrow range of policy issues, social movements address intermittent and discrete decision problems with limited investment in organizational structure. Movement parties are seen as a transitory phenomenon: they are expected to transform themselves as elected politicians act out of opportunistic aims, or to learn from the electoral arena about the relevance of other issues or in response to changing voter preferences. In this view, 'perversely, the more a movement party achieves in terms of procedural gains and/or substantive policy change, the more it might change its voters' preferences or salient interest such that the party experiences growing pressure to abandon its existing profile of organization and policy appeal' (Kitschelt 2006, 284).

Studies on the Greens have indeed empirically noted the progressive moderation of claims, generalization of programmatic profile and bureaucratization of organizational forms. The Green parties were in fact initially radical, with ecologism as an anti-capitalist ideology, *Basisdemokratie* or grassroots democracy, with rejection of bureaucratic power structures as an organizational principle, and broad attention to extra-parliamentary actions (March and Mudde 2005). In the 1980s, they presented themselves as an alternative to traditional parties, expressing 'solidarity with all those who have become active in the new democratic movement: the life and nature groups, the environmental protection groups, the citizen initiative organizations, the workers' movement, the Christian initiative organizations, the movements for peace, human rights, women's rights, and Third World rights' (Talshir 2003, 158). However, the Greens very soon experienced tensions between their social movement versus electoral party natures. As March and Mudde (2005, 33) summarized,

> The Fundis, or fundamentalists, wanted to remain loyal to their radical roots and rejected any compromise or coalition. The Realos, or realists, on the other hand, were lured into moderation and coalition by increasingly warm overtures, most notably from the social democratic parties, who saw a more moderate Green party as a way to increase their coalition options and political power.

In many cases, victory of the Realos then transformed the Greens, pushing them away from their movement origins – so, 'capitalism and (liberal) democracy were broadly accepted, party organizations were hierarchized, and electoral strategies became dominant' (March and Mudde 2005, 33), as the Greens moved towards classical political liberalism, with emphasis on individual rather than collective rights. The party programmes of the German Greens shifted, in fact, from 'a multilevel discourse of diverse sub-ideologies sharing overriding principles: respect for others, social justice, ecological politics, multi-culturalism and participatory democracy', to one that 'unmistakably bears the features of monolithic, classical political liberalism' (Talshir 2003, 158). In parallel, organizational reforms pushed the parties 'away from the grassroots democratic model and ever closer to a more conventional, professional-electoral logic' (Rihoux and Rüdig 2006, 15). At the same time, Green parties have struggled to detach themselves from the image of single-issue parties by acquiring competence in other policy fields (Poguntke 2002b). However, this evolution also brought about increasing strains culminating in an estrangement of their relations with a variety of movements, from anti-nuclear to global justice ones (Rihoux and Rüdig 2006).

According to other theories and empirical evidence, however, these trends in movement parties do not seem unavoidable. While Michels' law of oligarchy has been presented within an evolutionary perspective as necessary development as parties move from one stage to the next, some scholars have noted the role of agency in such processes (Panebianco 1988). Party changes in innovative directions can be facilitated by transformations in the dominant coalition and shock in achieving core goals (Harmel and Janda 1994; Wolinetz 1988, 304), as well as a change in leadership or in the dominant coalition (Harmel and Janda 1994). Past experiences are also reflected upon in a learning process. As Strøm noted, while models of party behaviour are generally static, 'surely party leaders are neither amnesiac nor myopic. Their strategies in elections and coalitional bargaining are typically conditioned by past events, as well as by the anticipation of future benefits' (1990, 569).

In party studies, a mix of exogenous and endogenous challenges have thus been seen as the basis of changes in parties' strategies. For instance, opening towards candidate selection by the rank-and-file has been noted especially in parties in the opposition, in the aftermath of an electoral shock, or in new parties, then spreading by contagion. Especially, a 'disappointing electoral result produces a perceived need to revitalize the party at the grassroots level and tends to weaken opposition to the reform from the parliamentary party' (Cross and Blais 2012, 145). In addition, 'New parties, wishing to appear more "democratic" and less hierarchical than their old-line opponents, make the change earlier on' (ibid.).

As mentioned, movement parties can be expected to pay particular attention to their linking strategy. Linkages can come in different forms, however. Looking at the Latin American cases, Kenneth Roberts (2015, 685) distinguished participatory from plebiscitary linkages as follows:

Participatory linkages or patterns of subjectivity provide citizens with a direct role in contesting established elites or in deliberative and policy making processes. As such, they tend to rely on autonomous and self-constituted forms of collective action at the grass-roots, inside or out of (and sometimes against) formal institutional channels. By contrast, under plebiscitary linkages or patterns of subjectivity, mass constituencies – often unorganized – are mobilized from above to acclaim an authority figure or ratify their leader's political initiatives. Such plebiscitary acclamation often resides in the voting booth or popular referendums, and is not predicated on autonomous forms of collective action at the grassroots. Indeed, plebiscitary appeals often rest on a direct, unmediated relationship between a populist figure and highly fragmented mass constituencies.

Movement parties are supposed to lean towards participatory linkages, this also reflecting the predispositions of their grassroots. Research on Latin America has pointed at the increasing values that linkages with social movements might have for leaders in their struggles for policy change (Roberts 2015).

Our research revealed that throughout the evolution of movement parties, as was the case during their genesis, linkages with movements are pursued at three levels: framing, organizational structures, and repertoires of action.

The *framing* is particularly relevant in linking parties and movements. In all our cases, party frames resonated with movement frames with regard to motivation, prognosis, and diagnosis.

All movement parties we analysed had strong *motivational* frames presenting themselves as instruments for the implementation of movement claims. In Podemos, this is expressed in slogans such as, 'We have come to win', the 'challenge is to become an alternative', or 'It's now'. The movement parties are, in this respect, able to offer a highly emotional discourse, stressing hope for change. Similar to Podemos, SYRIZA came into power in 2015 through the slogan 'Hope is Coming, Greece Moves Forward, Europe Changes', while already since 2011 the party had been calling for a unity of the left so as to govern challenging the political establishment, including the defeatism of the left. Massive participation in protest was understood as a signal that protesters are 'too many to be ignored', but ready to participate in a 'broad alliance of this new social majority' (SYRIZA 2013b). Similarly, the M5S presents a narrative of imminent victory of the citizens over the corrupt elites.

Motivational frames are then triggered into action. Indeed, electoral victories fuel an emphasis on hope and excitement for possible change. This creates a sense of empowerment, as synthetized in the slogans 'Si, se puede' – 'Yes we can' – or 'Claro que podemos' – 'Sure, we can'.

The *diagnostic frames* are also aligned with the movements' ones in singling out the one per cent that oppresses the 99 per cent, within a state of democratic emergency. The diagnostic frames of Podemos and SYRIZA depict a regime crisis that should be addressed by the mobilization of the people against the corrupt politicians and the political establishment. The emergency situation would impose transcendence of the categories of left and right, with some patriotic appeals for citizenship rights and a moral discourse against corruption. The appeal for the building of a new country is accompanied by calls for democracy against the market and the oligarchy, as also embodied in mainstream media. Besides environmentalism, the M5S has proposed a very strong anti-establishment frame against the 'caste' of politicians with a clear opposition between 'us' (the citizens) and 'them' (the caste), formed by Italian and international political, mediatic, and economic elites – with stigmatization of an indistinct convergence of the right and the left. For all, there was indeed a polarization between the 'unfair austerity implemented by the elites' versus the 'anti-austerity demanded by the people', as well as between 'social Europe' versus 'neoliberal Europe'.

The *prognostic frames* also resonate with movements' frames. Podemos presents itself as the 'principal political expression of 15M', a mirror held up to the left, revealing its deficiencies. In parliaments, activities focus around movement issues such as human rights, anti-austerity, anti-corruption, and political renewal. Similarly, for SYRIZA, against a bipolar system that depended on outside actors contributed to delegitimize, 'the people' is constructed as a broad, plural, and open community moving towards a progressive government. From an explicitly left-wing standpoint, though, SYRIZA defends in official texts 'the values of social justice, solidarity, equality and freedom against nationalism, militarism, racism, patriarchy and fascism' (SYRIZA 2013b), while also claiming citizens' rights, sovereignty and democracy. The aim is therefore the creation of a 'powerful, massive and unifying movement of resistance and disobedience…of political reversal' (SYRIZA 2013b). As for the M5S – despite declaring that it is beyond left and right, as ideologies tend only to reproduce existing power relations – it emphasizes direct participation of citizens as a political commitment against corruption and private interests. Not single-issue, it rather works towards environmental protection, welfare expansion, market regulation, and elimination of political corruption. At the EU level, it calls for solidarity against the Brussels caste: its electoral manifesto included the abolition of the Fiscal Compact; exemption from the constraints of the Maastricht Treaty for investments in innovation; abolition of the balanced budget as a constitutional requirement; and alliance among the countries of Southern Europe, which have suffered the most dramatic effects of the austerity policies. Moreover, movements parties call for struggle for a renewed democracy, popular sovereignty, and participation against the 'economic and social system' of 'globalized capitalism', as well as (with the exception of SYRIZA) an extension of instruments of direct democracy – such as the M5S' suggestion for referenda without a quorum and obligation for MPs to discuss laws of popular initiative.

While active in parliaments, and even in government, the movement parties under question also developed a *non-conventional repertoire of action*. When in parliament it attempts to create an image of reliability,

Podemos also uses protest repertoires, as, for example, in the Marcha del cambio, mobilizing hundreds of thousands on 31 January 2015, but also in protests against the Transatlantic Trade and Investment Partnership, for solidarity with refugees, for LGTB rights. It also takes part in trans-national protest events such as Blockupy and the WSF. The M5S acquired visibility through mass protests in 2007 and 2008 with the two 'V-days' – the first against the caste of politicians, the second against the caste of journalists – but also through Grillo's campaigns in the squares. Its repertoire of action includes unconventional forms such as occupations, sit-ins, and demonstrations (including in Val di Susa), as well as civil disobedience and direct actions within the parliaments. The M5S also supports social movement claims, in particular on the environment. Not only do four of the five 'stars' focus on these topics (public water, mobility, development, energy), but the party also supports many local and national struggles, including the most conflictual ones on the building of big infrastructures such as the TAV, the Bridge on the Streets, the Mobile User Objective System (MUOS), and so on. Even if not initiating any campaign itself, SYRIZA has been a parliamentary party fuelled by the contentious culture to become, as observed above, the 'de facto and by default' political expression of protests; at least until its rise to power in 2015, the party had combined its institutional role with participation in non-conventional repertoires of action.

From the *organizational* point of view, as well, the movement parties we have studied propose a participatory model that resonates with movement visions even if – in all three cases – in a moving equilibrium with what is perceived as efficient for achieving power. The movements have been, at least in part, a stimulus for organizational innovation. So, Podemos declared its desire 'to be a 15M of the politics'. The organizational structure is in fact a mix of conventional hierarchy, with personalized leadership and participatory aims. Membership is open: it suffices to fill in a form, without paying membership fees. The effect is fluidity; as a Spanish activist declared, 'I do not really know if I'm a member' (E11). The circles, as basic party units, have to promote participation, through a self-organized, liquid network. The citizens' assembly, which is committed to giving voice to members on important decisions, elects the general secretary, who chooses a coordination council. There is also a Democratic Guarantees Committee and tools of participation such as open plenaries, the digital square Plaza Podemos, and Appgree, which measures answers to various political questions. Other digital platforms are also used as tools for debate, creation, and dissemination. Symbolically and practically relevant is the financing model, characterized by the refusal of credits from banks and the reliance instead on micro-credits, reimbursed after election, as well as crowd-funding. Contributions from the salaries of members elected to representative institutions (who keep only three times the minimum salary, about 1,880 euros) are collected and invested into the project Impulsa, which then uses them to finance initiatives in the civil society. Areas of civil society and fora for change are organized in order to keep alive the linkage between civil society and the protesters.

Even if SYRIZA remained structured as a conventional and hierarchical party, it called itself a members' party and allowed for autonomy with regard to its local and youth sections. Some of its characteristics have permitted appropriation by the movement. Its plural identity (initially formed as a coalition) and, in particular, its loose organizational structure (or the lack of a clear structure) made the party seem like a 'work in progress' and enabled loose militancy. It has therefore been crucial for SYRIZA to develop a network strategy that proved successful in creating, as observed above, what an interviewee called 'a SYRIZA beyond SYRIZA, a broader SYRIZA...and this network had a much bigger impact on the development of the party than the actual work of its organized members' (I10G).

In the M5S as well, the organizational structure presents a mix of direct democracy, including rotation of spokespersons within representative institutions, refusal of some parliamentary benefits, encounters between party members and candidates as well as party members and elected representatives. Participation is stimulated especially online, through various types of consultation, blogs, meet-up platforms, and later on Facebook and Twitter. There are, however, also face-to-face rank-and-file activities at the local level, especially through so-called meet-ups. Such level is recognized broad decision-making power. In addition, 'citizens' Agorà' take place in outdoor public places during the weekends, as MPs meet voters and supporters as well as ordinary citizens. The self-proclaimed 'non-party' (and 'non-association') adopted a 'non-statute', according to which the M5S is 'a vehicle for discussion and consultation'. Membership is relatively inclusive, as compared with traditional parties: subscription to the blog requires a digital identity card and a declaration of compliance with the 'non-statute' (excluding members of other parties or associations that oppose the M5S aims). While no fees are required from members, elected representatives have to devolve part of their salary to a 'solidarity fund', used to provide micro-credits to enterprises.

Movement parties are full of internal tensions, which can be seen as (or evolve into) factionalism, or just pluralism. One such division occurs between conventional versus innovative strategies. In Podemos, for instance, there is a certain hegemony of those who see the party as a machinery for an electoral war. In SYRIZA, a Fordist type pyramidal organization, the lack of horizontal transformations and thus democratic processes, as well as factionalism keep movement activists away, and the party indeed remained very small in terms of membership. The lack of intermediary structure between the leader and his followers clearly characterizes the M5S organizational model. The personalized power of the leaders is criticized in the three parties as well.

The tension between adaptation and innovation is, however, kept open by the parties' need for both types of supporters: those who are convinced by more conventional strategies, and those who aspire to innovative ones. Although to different extents, the three movement parties indeed recruit from the traditional left, and beyond (especially in the case of the M5S) but also mobilize those who had not voted.

Looking at our three cases, the 'movement party' label better applies to some phases in their evolution. In the case of Podemos, which was founded in January 2014, the first Citizens' Assembly (October 2014) represented an important turning point towards the definition of formal organisms and procedures. The linkages of the party with social movements (in terms of demands, discourse, previous militancies of relevant members of the party and some repertoires) is, however, still relevant with a combination of traditional elements of the parties (i.e. structure, organizational form) and others of the movements (i.e. membership, funding). The movement party form has been long lasting and resilient in the case of the M5S. While founded in October 2009, the massive entrance of its activists into the national parliament in 2013 represented a first turning point in the structuration of the party while a second important change happened with the creation of a Directorate (the so-called 'representative structure'). Despite this and compared with Podemos and SYRIZA, the party maintains a fluid and relatively informal organizational structure. An electoral coalition of left-wing groups and parties founded in 2004, SYRIZA experienced a relatively fluid phase until its first congress held in July 2013 that promoted the dissolution of parties of the coalition into a unitary party. Still, at least in relative terms, during the period between the emergence of the anti-austerity protest cycle in 2010 and the creation of a unitary party in 2013 SYRIZA can be considered as close to the movement party ideal type. Departing from its institutional status and euro-communist tradition, the party managed through a combination of external factors, contingencies and strategies to maintain a dynamic and porous interconnection with the movement field, which as a result had a decisive impact upon SYRIZA in what concerns framing and repertoires of action. In the end, the three parties examined in this study can be considered as fully matching the definition of a movement party for some part of their life. In all cases, relations with social movements changed after their entrance into national institutions. This is more visible in the case of SYRIZA since Tsipras became prime minister. As for Podemos and the M5S, while the balance between institutional and extra-institutional activities has clearly shifted in favour of parliamentary politics, they still maintain relations with protest politics although often criticized from social movements.

Despite a weakening in their relations with the social movement arena, recent elections have proved that the three parties under question have become rather stable actors in national party systems. Even after signing the third bailout agreement, the ensuing resignations by party members and leaders and an internal split, SYRIZA proved resilient: the September 2015 snap elections resulted in an unexpectedly large victory for the party, reaffirming its predominance in domestic party politics. This was the case in the 2016 Italian administrative elections where the M5S won mayors in important Italian cities such as Rome and Turin. Although Podemos scored worse than expected in the June 2016 elections, it still confirmed its role as third force breaking the bipolar party system with over 20 per cent of the votes.

Concluding, while it is too early to assess the evolution of the three parties we have studied in detail in this volume, by bringing together studies on social movements and party politics, we have suggested that these parties are not to be viewed simply as given, but rather as processes and works-in-progress embedded in both power relations and grassroots concerns. Our research has revealed that movement parties have gradually produced practices, discourses, and relations that exceeded the words, deeds, and strategies of the activists and politicians engaged in them, forming sums greater than their separate parts. A broad set of factors, contextual constraints and political opportunities, contingency and planning at various levels have contributed to this process, which cannot easily be disentangled but which deserves to be studied in due course in order to shed light upon ongoing transformations during a critical juncture.

Further research will be needed in order to assess the additional transformations that neoliberalism and its crisis bring about in institutional politics: from the extraordinary and unexpected participation from below in forms of direct democracy (such as the referenda on independence in Scotland and the consultation on independence in Catalonia [della Porta, O'Connor, Portos, and Subirats 2017]) to the (also extraordinary and unexpected) successes of candidates that appeal to social justice within 'old parties' such as Labour in the United Kingdom or the Democratic party in the United States. Within this context and following the referenda in Greece (July 2015) and the UK (June 2016) that could signal the beginning of a crumbling process, attention should definitely be focused on how the European Union project is interpreted, supported or rejected by both grassroots movements and political parties. Comparative research on right-wing populism will also be needed to expose the linkages between the changing social cleavages under neoliberal critical junctures and the rise of new parties.

For sure, at the crossing of a trend of party transformations through (more or less) adaptive moves and of the challenges triggered by a critical juncture, the movement parties we have analysed deserve much attention, in the present but also in the future. While it is too early to say where they are going or even how much they will last, they do not seem meteoric phenomena. As we saw, the strategic dilemmas between adaptation and innovation, inside and outside orientation, moderation or radicalism present themselves with force for parties that are achieving more and more governing power, in a situation of strong international constraints. As the revival of the left is losing impetus in Latin America, it would certainly be an excess of Gramscian optimism of the will to believe that the new parties are the winning response to the huge problems of existing parties in terms of organizational linkages and broader societal support. Nevertheless, the emerging scenario is not likely to disappear quickly. In a context of growing volatility and uncertainties, the movement parties have mobilized energies, galvanized electors, empowered formerly excluded social groups. In the space of a few years, they have been able to reach a large proportion of the electorate – much more than the Green parties ever succeeded in doing. While not achieving any satisfying solution to organizational structures' adaptation to current challenges, they offered interesting experiments with alternative models to the logorated hegemonic ones. They certainly do not look like flash parties or only protest parties, rather mobilizing resources for a reorganization or even radical reformation of institutional politics, both in terms of electoral and protest politics, by broadening its capacities and possibly exposing its limitations. As political parties – even if weakened or changed – are still fundamental actors in party democracies, the appearance of movement parties that seem able to represent the concerns of citizens who felt excluded by the mainstream party systems is certainly positive news.

Appendix:
List of Interviews

1. Greece

SYRIZA

(I1G) A., 52 yr, female, Central Political Committee, Coordination Committee, overlapping membership, Thessaloniki (resigned)

(I2G) D., 28 yr, female, Youth Section, overlapping membership, Athens (resigned)

(I3G) A., 41 yr, male, Political Secretariat, Central Committee, Athens (resigned)

(I4G) S., 44 yr, male, Rights' Committee, overlapping membership, Athens (resigned)

(I5G) H., 46 yr, male, Solidarity for All, overlapping membership, Athens (resigned)

(I6G) P., 26 yr, male, Youth Section, Athens (resigned)

(I7G) G., 31 yr, male, Youth Section, Thessaloniki (resigned)

(I8G) M., 58 yr, female, Party member, Halkida

(I9G) A., 64 yr, male, Party member/unionist, Athens

(I10G) M., 43 yr, male, Social Media Committee, Athens

(I11G) S., 40 yr, male, Party member, Athens

(I12G) P., 62 yr, male, Party member, Halkida

(I13G) B., 65 yr, male, MP, Central Committee, Athens

(I14G) V., 50 yr, female, Party member, overlapping membership, Athens

(I15G) T., 40 yr, male, Party member, Thessaloniki

Movements

(I16G) A., 55 yr, male, Vio.Me. Self-organized factory, Thessaloniki
(I17G) A., 36 yr, male, workers' collective, Athens
(I18G) N., 33 yr, female, neighbourhood assembly, Athens
(I19G) M., 36 yr, male, Base Unionist, Athens
(I20G) K., 39 yr, female, Unionist, Athens
(I21G) K., 52 yr, female, Cleaning Ladies movement, Athens
(I22G) C., 34 yr, male, workers' collective, Thessaloniki
(I23G) T., 43 yr, male, Water Movement, Thessaloniki
(I24G) S., 42 yr, male, anti-authoritarian social centre, Athens
(I25G) T., 55 yr, male, Electricity movement, Athens
(I26G) O., 36 yr, female, anti-fascist movement, Athens
(I27G) M., 32 yr, female, solidarity network, Halkida
(I28G) M., 53 yr, female, ERT open movement, Athens
(I29G) G., 45 yr, female, anti-mining movement (SOS Halkidiki), Halkidiki
(I30G) G., 43 yr, male, anti-mining movement (Save Skouries), Halkidiki

2. Spain

(IS1) A., Podemos, Citizen Council, Madrid
(IS2) P., Podemos, Member of the Regional Parliament, Madrid
(IS3) L., Social Activist, Madrid
(IS4) G., Social Activist, Madrid
(IS5) J., Podemos, Circle of Culture, Madrid
(IS6) M., Podemos, Member of Europarliament, Madrid
(IS7) D., Podemos, Regional Citizen Council, Madrid
(IS8) E., Social Activist, Madrid
(IS9) M.M., Podemos, Citizen Council Leganés, Madrid
(IS10) A.G., Podemos, Citizen Council and Circle Castro-Urdiales, Cantabria
(IS11) M.B., Podemos, Circle of feminisms, Madrid
(IS12) B., Podemos, Circle of Vallecas, Madrid
(IS13) X., Podemos, Citizen Council of Basque Country and Circle of Getxo, Basque Country
(IS14) N., Podemos, Citizen Council of Getxo and Circle of Durango, Basque Country
(IS15) A.F., Podemos, Citizen Council of Cantabria and Circle Castro-Urdiales, Cantabria

(IS16) R., Podemos, Member of the Regional Parliament, Madrid
(IS17) R.M., Podemos, Circle of Alicante, Alicante

3. Italy

(I1I) R., mayoral candidate of the list 'Parma Common Good', Parma
(I2I) P., Parma Bene Comune, Parma
(I3I) A., Insurgent city, Parma
(I4I) V., activist of Indignati movement, Parma
(I5I) W., Centro Studi Movimenti Parma, Parma
(I6I) M.C., Laboratorio politico per l'alternativa, Parma
(I7I) N., spokesperson of the local committee *'niente voragini'*, Parma
(I8I) E., spokesperson of the Popolo Viola, Parma
(I9I) M., M5S city councillor, Parma
(I10I) J., Collettivo Artlab, Parma
(I11I) F., Mayor of Pomezia (M5S), Pomezia
(I12I) D., Regional Councillor of Lazio (M5S), Rome
(I13I) F., Mayor of Ragusa (M5S), Ragusa

Notes

Chapter 1. Movement Parties in Times of (Anti-)Austerity: An Introduction

1   A notable exception is the study by Serdedakis and Koufidi (2016) accounting for the relationship developed between protest and electoral politics in the crisis-ridden country from a relational and contextual approach.

Chapter 2. The Genesis of Movement Parties in the Neoliberal Critical Juncture

1   http://ec.europa.eu/public_opinion/cf/index_en.cfm.
2   However, Spain is an exception. According to the data of Van Biezen and Poguntke (2014), Spain is the only country (among the nineteen developed countries studied) in which party membership has consistently grown in the last decades.
3   This legitimacy crisis and the steady discrediting of the 'political class' allowed the emergence of multiple citizen projects oriented to scrutinize political institutions and party activities, which made Spain a kind of 'monitory democracy' (Feenstra and Keane 2014).
4   The Spanish electoral system is particularly detrimental to nationwide established minor parties (Montero et al. 1998). Izquierda Unida has never been a plausible winning choice, as its support was expected to increase from 3.77 per cent in 2008 to 5.2 per cent in 2011 (CIS barometer; No. 2885, April 2011).

5 According to Íñigo Errejón (Secretary of Political Strategy in Podemos), '15M points out to a "populist rupture" that dichotomizes the social space between "the people" (as broad as vaguely defined) and the elites or "the regime"' (Errejón 2015, 145).

6 The other 'new' successful party at the national level is Ciudadanos. However, created in Catalonia in 2006, it remained active only there. Only since 2014 has it developed a national strategy to participate in other regions and also at the national level.

7 In the Spanish case (similarly to the other countries), the electoral system for the European elections is quite different from other elections: these are proportional, with only one voting district and no entry barriers.

8 www.anticapitalistas.org.

9 For a detailed and well informed description of the origin of Podemos, see (in Spanish) the book *Podemos: Objetivo asaltar los cielos* (Rivero 2015). See also 'The Podemos revolution: how a small group of radical academics changed European politics' (*Guardian*, 31 March 2015): www.theguardian. com/world/2015/mar/31/podemos-revolution-radical-academics-changed-european-politics.

10 An English version of the manifesto is available at: https://hiredknaves. wordpress.com/2014/01/20/podemos-translated-manifesto.

11 A comparative table of both organizational models can be found here: https://dl.dropboxusercontent.com/u/3724655/Comparativa_Programas. pdf.

12 www.corriere.it/economia/11_settembre_29/trichet_draghi_inglese_304a5f1e-ea59-11e0-ae06-4da866778017.shtml.

13 The Popolo della Libertà was founded in 2008, federating the former Berlusconi's FI and the post-fascist party Alleanza Nazionale (AN, National Alliance) led by Gianfranco Fini, as well as several minor centre-right parties.

14 Meetup is an online platform created in 2001, after 9/11, to connect people with similar interests on a local scale. Its political potential emerged with the American presidential elections in 2004 when Howard Dean employed it to encourage bottom-up participation in his campaign during the Democratic primaries.

15 www.beppegrillo.it/en/2006/01/citizen_primaries_energy.html.

16 A date evoking the armistice between the Kingdom of Italy and the 'Allies' during World War II that symbolized the end of the fascist regime but also opened up a period of chaos in the country.

17 A national holiday recalling the day of liberation from Nazi-Fascism.

18 www.beppegrillo.it/en/2007/10/civic_lists.html.

19 www.beppegrillo.it/en/2008/03/political_press_release_number_3.html.

20 In Italian, 'Grillo' means 'cricket'; puns (with Pinocchio's cricket) have often been used by fake lists to capture the votes of Grillo's supporters.

21 http://video.repubblica.it/dossier/elezioni-politiche-2013/fassino-nel-2009-a-repubblica-tv–grillo-fondi-partito-vediamo-quanto-prende/120817/119302.

22 www.beppegrillo.it/en/2012/05/occupyparma.html.

Chapter 3. Organizational Repertoires of Movement Parties

1 www.syriza.gr/pdfs/katastatiko.pdf.
2 By Youth we refer mostly to the Youth of SYN, as the Youth of the Coalition of the Radical Left (Syriza) was officially constituted only in 2013 (nine years after the official formation of the electoral coalition itself).
3 No data is provided concerning the level of members' contributions or MPs' salary caps.
4 Information on the Youth section is drawn mostly from interviews with its members (I2G, I6–7G) due to scarcity of official information available.
5 See www.solidarity4all.gr/sites/www.solidarity4all.gr/files/aggliko.pdf.
6 The registration form is available at https://participa.podemos.info/es/users/sign_up.
7 https://participa.podemos.info/es (data retrieved on 18 January 2016).
8 www.eldiario.es/politica/Podemos-actualizar-censo-referendum-primarias_0_406659373.html.
9 www.tercerainformacion.es/IMG/pdf/protocolo_de_validacion_de_circulos.pdf.
10 https://www.reddit.com/r/podemos; www.appgree.com.
11 Data updated on 18 January 2016.
12 This mechanism can be promoted from Plaza Podemos (OPP, 42).
13 http://podemos.info/consulta-estatal.
14 http://podemos.info/consultasciudadanas.
15 The questions and the results of the citizens' enquiry on the local level are available at http://municipales.podemos.info/consultas-ciudadanas-2.
16 Spanish parties have an aggregate debt of 273 million euros with private banks, according to the data of the Court of Auditors (*Informe 2012*). The most indebted is the PSOE, owing 71.6 million.
17 https://participa.podemos.info/es/microcreditos/informacion.
18 https://participa.podemos.info/microcreditos.
19 The FAQ related to the party's funding model can be found at http://transparencia.podemos.info/preguntas-frecuentes.
20 http://transparencia.podemos.info/docs/codigo-etico.pdf.
21 http://podemos.info/impulsa.
22 http://transparencia.podemos.info/cuentas-claras/partido/gastos.
23 The website of the event is available at http://lamarchadelcambio.info.
24 http://euromarchas2015.net.
25 http://gente10.info/?p=53669.
26 www.publico.es/politica/lanza-ofensiva-ttip-parlamentos-autonomicos.html.
27 http://politica.elpais.com/politica/2015/09/10/actualidad/1441883658_271903.html.
28 www.beppegrillo.it/en/2009/09/political_press_release_number_18.html.
29 At the end of 2012, the Movement was forced to adopt a formal statute to present its candidates to the forthcoming general elections and to gather

(and then refuse) public reimbursements. The statute is a very standard document with a series of provisions concerning timing and rules of national assemblies and formal roles within the association (i.e. president, vice-president, and secretary) that have never been implemented. Moreover, the statute establishes a governing council formed by Grillo, his nephew, and his business consultant (probably the only ones available in Genoa when the document had to be signed).

30 Casaleggio has been the manager of *Casaleggio e Associati*, a consulting firm specializing in web strategies that manages Grillo's blog and hosts 'La Cosa' (The Thing), the official M5S web television channel. Although Casaleggio often quoted the most popular advocates of free sharing and open source, he had exclusive control over all the M5S' web infrastructures (Mosca et al. 2015a). The firm is currently managed by his son, Davide.

31 www.beppegrillo.it/movimento/codice_comportamento_parlamentare.php; www.beppegrillo.it/movimento/codice_comportamento_europee.php.

32 M5S MPs are not supposed to resign after serving half a term. The roles of coordinator and spokesperson simply rotate every three months (Passarelli and Tuorto 2015).

33 www.beppegrillo.it/2013/04/rendicontazione_delle_spese.html.

34 Last update 29 January 2016.

35 www.beppegrillo.it/en/2014/11/results_online_poll_political.html (emphasis in the original text).

36 www.beppegrillo.it/en/2014/12/online_poll_members_of_the_m5s.html.

37 www.beppegrillo.it/movimento/regolamento.

38 The regulation does not clarify who forms part of such council, but it is reasonable to expect that it is the same council established by the M5S statute formed by Grillo, his nephew, and his business consultant.

39 The committee is currently formed by two deputies, one representative in the European Parliament, and two representatives in regional assemblies.

40 According to the regulations, at least 500 certified members must sign the proposal; if at least one-fifth of all registered members support it on the blog, then the proposal can be formally put to vote (www.beppegrillo.it/movimento/regolamento/5.html). This procedure appears very difficult to implement, as at best it requires at least three months, making it impossible for the base to promptly intervene on current political issues considered important.

41 The groups were 1,264 in 1,013 cities in eighteen countries (groups of Grillo's supporters are also established in foreign countries) on 26 August 2015 (http://beppegrillo.meetup.com).

42 Suffice it to say that in about two years the coordinators of the groups have changed once in the Europarliament, twice in the Senate, and three times in the Chamber of Deputies.

43 www.beppegrillo.it/2015/11/comunicato_politico_numero_cinquantasei.html (our translation).

44 One of the September 2015 pre-electoral campaign slogans was 'On September 20th, we vote for a Prime Minister', https://www.youtube.com/watch?v=8fU_R2-G2P0.

45 www.beppegrillo.it/en/2008/12/5_star_civic_lists.html.

Chapter 4. Framing Movement Parties

1 Prime Minister G. Papandreou's Interview with Bruce Clark, *Economist* (2010), www.primeminister.gov.gr/english/2010/02/23/prime-ministers-george-a-papandreou-interview-on-the-economist.

2 During the first general strike against the austerity measures on 5 May 2010, the Party of the European Left (EL), of which SYRIZA is a member, stated the commitment of its member parties 'together with trade-unions and social movements for a social Europe' (quoted in Borreca 2015, 16).

3 https://www.youtube.com/watch?v=25YcE8TJLp8.

4 www.avgi.gr/article/4594505/suriza-i-katastrofi-stis-skouries-tha-stamatisei-apo-tin-kubernisi-tis-aristeras; for the Central Committee's support statement, see http://rproject.gr/article/anakoinosi-tmimatos-oikologias-perivallontos-horikoy-shediasmoy-syriza-mellon-den-ekviazetai.

5 https://vimeo.com/82388204.

6 www.hispantv.com/newsdetail/Espana/35848/Pablo-Iglesias-per centE2 per cent80 per cent98Traidores-a-la-patria-son-los-que-tienen-cuentas-en-Suiza per centE2 per cent80 per cent99.

7 www.publico.es/politica/iglesias-rajoy-cambia-cosas-siga.html.

8 https://www.youtube.com/watch?v=GnBqeFfomA8.

9 Academia de Pensamiento Crítico (2012). ¿Qué debe decir la izquierda? Conference of Pablo Iglesias: https://www.youtube.com/watch?v=nfK2Bl4NjGM.

10 www.tercerainformacion.es/spip.php?article63920.

11 www.canalsur.es/iglesias-ellos-llaman-al-cambio-experimento-y-caos-nosotros-democracia/531491.html.

12 www.eldiario.es/campa%C3%B1a/Programa-electoral-Podemos-Europeas_6_258334180.html.

13 www.guengl.eu/group.

14 In the words of Pablo Iglesias, 'anyone who tries to appropriate the 15M is just a snake-oil seller'. See: http://politica.elpais.com/politica/2014/05/25/actualidad/1401009854_060215.html.

15 See, for example, Iglesias' statement: www.farodevigo.es/galicia/elecciones/2015/05/14/pablo-iglesias-espacio-socialdemocracia-quedo/1239411.html.

16 http://politica.elpais.com/politica/2015/05/05/actualidad/1430837666_280083.html.

17 These documents can be consulted at http://podemos.info/propuestas.

18 See http://unpaiscontigo.es/#acuerdos.

19 http://podemos.info/foro-por-el-cambio/.

20 www.cuartopoder.es/lentesdecontacto/2015/04/25/en-directo-encuentro-de-podemos-con-los-activistas-sociales/152/.

21 Public call for the 'Forum for change'.

22 According to the 2007 Eurobarometer, 38 per cent of Spaniards tend to trust unions (48 per cent do not trust), while in 2010, 30 per cent tended to trust and 59 per cent to distrust.

23 www.infolibre.es/noticias/politica/2015/01/19/bescansa_hay_podemos_
    para_ganar_otro_para_protestar_26979_1012.html.
24 www.beppegrillo.it/en/2013/07/caste_conflict.html (emphasis in the original
    text).
25 www.beppegrillo.it/2013/01/il_m5s_non_e_di_destra_ne_di_sinistra.html.
26 www.beppegrillo.it/en/2013/02/beppe_grillos_letter_to_the_it.html.
27 www.beppegrillo.it/en/2010/12/political_press_release_number_24.html.
28 www.beppegrillo.it/en/2010/03/political_communique_number_th_3.html.
29 www.beppegrillo.it/en/2013/03/circumvention_of_voters.html.
30 As was the case in district councils in Milan and Forli, www.milanotoday.
    it/politica/toscano-lascia-movimento-5stelle.html;   www.milanotoday.it/
    politica/mozione-solidarieta-napolitano-5stelle-sfiduciato.html, and www.
    forlitoday.it/politica/dimissioni-daniele-avolio-movimento-5-stelle-reazione-
    pentastellati.html, respectively.
31 www.sona5stelle.it/wordpress/wp-content/uploads/2013/02/progetto-
    parlamento-elettronico-M5S-v011.pdf.
32 www.beppegrillo.it/en/2014/05/point_7_of_the_m5s_electoral_p.html.
33 www.beppegrillo.it/en/2014/03/in_europe_for_italy.html (emphasis in the
    original text).
34 www.beppegrillo.it/en/2014/03/in_europe_for_italy.html.
35 www.beppegrillo.it/en/2014/05/nigel_farage_the_truth.html.
36 www.efdgroup.eu/about-us/statutes?task=callelement&format=raw&item_
    id=86&element=65773f0a-221d-4b0b-95f7-c2633a21e767&method=
    download.
37 www.wumingfoundation.com/english/wumingblog/?p=1950.
38 www.youreporter.it/video_Civitavecchia_presidio_contro_il_Sindaco_5_
    Stelle_V?refresh_ce-cp.

Chapter 5. Comparing Movement Parties' Success and Failures

1 Dissolved in November 2012, it was an association of parties, with a collective leadership, made up of a 25 per cent share each by the four groups that
   composed it: Rifondazione Comunista (RC), Partito dei Comunisti Italiani
   (PdCI), the association Socialism 2000, and the association of leftist trade
   unionists 23 March Labour-Solidarity.
2 An association of Sinistra Democratica, Movimento per la Sinistra, Unire la
   Sinistra, and Associazione Ecologisti, founded in 2009.
3 According to the document 'What is Partido X?': Parties do not have to give
   us the solution, they simply have to stop obstructing the solutions that society,
   far more advanced than them, has already developed. Available here: http://
   partidox.org/que-es-x.
4 CPC Assembly 17–18 September 2005, http://www.syn.gr/gr/keimeno.php
   ?id=7225 (in Greek).

5   Another important actor in the radical left arena in Greece is ANTARSYA (Anticapitalist Left Cooperation for the Overthrow), a political and electoral coalition of the extra-parliamentary left coalescing in 2009. It has been very active in the social movement field and has even secured a few seats in the administrations of some large trade unions; despite its radical political claims and the emerging political opportunities, it has not managed to enter parliament.

6   Populism is defined as 'top-down political mobilization of mass constituencies by personalistic leaders who challenge established political or economic elites on behalf of an ill-defined pueblo, or "the people"' (Levitsky and Roberts 2011a, 6).

Chapter 6. Movement Parties: Some Conclusions

1   See the interesting debates on the blog of the Wuming Foundation (www.wumingfoundation.com/giap).

References

Accornero, G. and Ramos Pinto, P. (2015). '"Mild Mannered"? Protest and Mobilisation in Portugal under Austerity, 2010–2013'. *West European Politics*, 38(3): 491–515.

Agnantopoulos, A. and Lambiri, D. (2015). 'Variegated capitalism, the Greek crisis and SYRIZA's counter-neoliberalisation challenge'. *Geoforum*, 63: 5–8.

Aguilar Fernández, P. (2008). *Políticas de la memoria y memorias de la política. El caso español en perspectiva comparada*. Madrid, Alianza Editorial.

Albro, R. (2010). 'Confounding cultural citizenship and constitutional reform in Bolivia'. *Latin American Perspectives*, 37(3): 71–90.

Allern, E. H. (2010). *Political Parties and Interest Groups in Norway*. Essex, ECPR Press.

Allern, E. H. and Bale, T. (2012). 'Political parties and interest groups: disentangling complex relationships'. *Party Politics*, 18(1): 7–25.

Allern, E. H., D'Ippoliti, C. and Roncaglia, A. (2011). 'L'Italia: una crisi nella crisi'. *Moneta e Credito*, 64(255): 189–227.

Amador, I. B. (2013). 'Protesta Política nas Democracias da Europa do Sul (Portugal, Espanha e Grécia): uma análise comparada e longitudinal (2002–2012)'. Master's thesis in Political Science. Lisbon, ISCTE–IUL.

Andretta, M. (2016). 'Neoliberalism and its discontents in Italy: protests without movement?'. In D. della Porta, M. Andretta, T. Fernandes, F. O'Connor, E. Romanos and M. Vogiatzoglou. *Late Neoliberalism and its Discontents*. London, Palgrave: forthcoming.

Andretta, M. and Reiter, H. (2009). 'Parties, unions and movements: the European Left and the ESF'. In D. della Porta (ed.), *Another Europe*. London, Routledge, pp. 173–203.

Anria, S. (2013). 'Social movements, party organization, and populism: insights from the Bolivian MAS'. *Latin American Politics and Society*, 55(3): 19–46.

Ardanuy, M. and Labuske, E. (2015). 'El músculo deliberativo del algoritmo democrático: Podemos y la participación ciudadana'. *Revista Teknokultura*, 12(1): 93–109.

Armingeon, K. and Baccaro, L. (2012). 'Political economy of the sovereign debt crisis: the limits of internal devaluation'. *Industrial Law Journal*, 41(3): 254–75.

Arnson, C. and De la Torre, C. (2013). 'Conclusion: the meaning and future of Latin American populism'. In C. De la Torre and C. Arnson (eds.), *Latin American Populism in the Twenty-First Century*. Baltimore, Johns Hopkins University Press, pp. 351–76.

Arribas Lozano, A. (2015). 'Recordar el 15M para reimaginar el presente. Los movimientos sociales en España más allá del ciclo electoral de 2015'. *Interface: a Journal for and about Social Movements*, 7(1): 150–64.

Balafas, Y. (2012). *It Took 20 Years*. Athens, Nisos [in Greek].

Bale, T. and Dunphy, R. (2011). 'In from the cold? Left parties and government involvement since 1989'. *Comparative European Politics*, 9(3): 269–91.

Barisione, M. (2007). *L'immagine del leader. Quanto conta per gli elettori?*. Bologna, Il Mulino.

Barr, R. R. (2009). 'Populists, outsiders and anti-establishment politics'. *Party Politics*, 15(1): 29–48.

Bartels, L. (2014). 'Ideology and retrospection in electoral responses to the Great Recession'. In L. Bartels and N. Bermeo (eds.), *Mass Politics in Tough Times: Opinions, Votes and Protest in the Great Recession*. Oxford, Oxford University Press, pp. 185–223.

Bartolini, S. (2000). *The Political Mobilization of the European Left 1860–1980. The Class Cleavage*. Cambridge, Cambridge University Press.

Bassets, M. (2015). 'Spanish new patriots'. *Dissent Magazine*. Online at: www.dissentmagazine.org/article/marc-bassets-podemos-patriotism-spain.

Bellucci, P. (2014). 'Partisanship and the swing-vote in the 2010s: The Italian case'. Paper presented at the ECPR General Conference, University of Glasgow, 3–6 September.

Benedetto, G. and Quaglia, L. (2007). 'The comparative politics of Communist Euroscepticism in France, Italy and Spain'. *Party Politics*, 13(4): 478–99.

Bertolino, S. (2014). *Rifondazione Comunista*. Bologna, Il Mulino.

Biancalana, C. (2013). 'Il populismo tra malessere democratico ed esigenza partecipativa: il caso di Beppe Grillo e del Movimento 5 Stelle'. *Trasgressioni*, 1–2.

Biancalana, C. and Tronconi, F. (2014). 'Il Movimento 5 stelle: te la do io l'Europa!'. In M. Valbruzzi and R. Vignati (eds.), *L'Italia e l'Europa al bivio delle riforme. Le elezioni europee e amministrative del 25 maggio 2014*. Bologna, Istituto Carlo Cattaneo, pp. 27–40.

Bimber, B. (2003). *Information and American Democracy: Technology in the Evolution of Political Power*. Cambridge and New York, Cambridge University Press.

Biorcio, R. (2003). 'The Lega Nord and the Italian media system'. In G. Mazzoleni, J. Stewart and B. Hosfield (eds.), *The Media and Neo-populism:*

A Contemporary Comparative Analysis. Westport and London, Praeger Publishers, pp. 71–94.

— (2015a). *Gli attivisti del Movimento 5 Stelle. Dal web al territorio.* Milano, FrancoAngeli.

— (2015b). 'Partecipazione, attivismo e democrazia'. In R. Biorcio (ed.), *Gli attivisti del Movimento 5 Stelle. Dal web al territorio.* Milano, FrancoAngeli, pp. 9–28.

Biorcio, R. and Natale, P. (2013). *Politica a 5 stelle. Idee, storia e strategie del movimento di Grillo.* Milano, Feltrinelli.

Boffi, S. (2015). 'Gli attivisti del Movimento 5 Stelle a Milano'. In R. Biorcio (ed.), *Gli attivisti del Movimento 5 Stelle. Dal web al territorio.* Milano, FrancoAngeli, pp. 42–59.

Bordandini, P. (2013). 'Renewal and tradition: comparing Italian radical left parties through their middle level elites'. *South European Society and Politics*, 18(1): 61–79.

Bordignon, F. and Ceccarini, L. (2013). 'The 5 star people and the unconventional parliament'. *Studia Politica. Romanian Political Science Review*, 4: 675–92.

— (2015). 'The Five-Star Movement: a hybrid actor in the net of state institutions'. *Journal of Modern Italian Studies*, 20(4): 454–73.

Botella, J. and Ramiro, L. (2003). 'The Crisis of West European Communist parties and their change trajectories: Communists, Post-Communists, ex-Communists?'. In J. Botella and L. Ramiro (eds.), *The Crisis of Communism and Party Change. The Evolution of West European Communist Parties.* Barcelona, ed. Institut de Sciences Politiques i Socials, pp. 237–57.

Cabral, R. (2013). 'The Euro crisis and Portugal's dilemma'. *Intereconomics*, 48(1): 4–32.

Calise, M. (2000). *Il partito personale.* Roma–Bari, Laterza.

Calle-Collado, A. and Candón-Mena, J. (2013). 'Sindicalismo y 15-M'. In P. Ibarra and M. Cruells (eds.), *La democracia del futuro: Del 15M a la emergencia de una sociedad civil viva.* Barcelona, Icaria, pp. 151–86.

Calossi, E. (2007). 'Rifondazione comunista e Comunisti Italiani'. In L. Bardi, P. Ignazi and O. Massari (eds.), *I Partiti Italiani.* Milano, Università Bocconi Editore, pp. 217–46.

Calvo, K. and Álvarez, I. (2015). 'Limitaciones y exclusiones en la institucionalización de la indignación: del 15-M a Podemos'. *Revista Española de Sociología*, 24: 115–22.

Campus, D. (2006). *L'antipolitica al governo. De Gaulle, Reagan e Berlusconi.* Bologna, Mulino.

Carty, R. K. (2004). 'Parties as franchise systems: the stratarchical organizational imperative'. *Party Politics*, 10(1): 5–24.

Caruso, L. (2015). 'Il Movimento 5 Stelle e la fine della politica'. *Rassegna Italiana di Sociologia*, LVI(2): 315–40.

— (2016a). 'Oltre la destra e la sinistra? Il trasversalismo del Movimento 5 Stelle alla prova della dimensione economica e sociale'. *Quaderni di Scienza Politica*, forthcoming.

— (2016b). 'Euroscetticismo, critica dell'Unione Europea e spazio della politica. Un confronto tra Front National, Movimento 5 Stelle e L'Altra Europa con Tsipras'. *Polis. Ricerche e studi su società e politica in Italia*, forthcoming.

Casal, F., Teruel-Rodríguez, J., Barberá, O. and Barrio, A. (2014). 'The carrot and the stick: party regulation and politics in democratic Spain'. *South European Society and Politics*, 19(1): 89–112.

Casaleggio, G., Fo, D. and Grillo, B. (2013). *Il grillo canta sempre al tramonto. Dialogo sull'Italia e il movimento 5 stelle*. Milano, Chiarelettere.

Casaleggio, G. and Grillo, B. (2011). *Siamo in guerra*. Milano, Chiarelettere.

Castelli Gattinara, P. and Froio, C. (2014). 'Opposition in the EU and opposition to the EU: soft and hard Euroscepticism in Italy in the time of austerity'. EU–IED Research Report. Brussels, Institute of European Democrats.

Chalari, A. (2015). 'Re-organising everyday Greek social reality: subjective experiences of the Greek crisis'. In G. Karyotis and R. Gerodimos (eds.), *The Politics of Extreme Austerity: Greece in the Eurozone Crisis*. London, Routledge, pp. 160–78.

Chiaramonte, A. and Emanuele, V. (2014). 'Bipolarismo addio? Il sistema partitico tra cambiamento e de-istituzionalizzazione'. In A. Chiaramonte and L. De Sio (eds.), *Terremoto elettorale. Le elezioni politiche 2013*. Bologna, Il Mulino, pp. 233–62.

Chironi, D. (2014). 'Radical left-wing parties and social movements: strategic interactions'. Working Paper, Florence, EUI.

CIS (2014). *Informe del CIS Junio de 2014*. Online at: http://datos.cis.es/pdf/Es3029mar_A.pdf.

Clemens, E. S. (1996). 'Organizational form as frame: collective identity and political strategy in the American labor movement'. In D. McAdam, J. D. McCarthy and M. N. Zald (eds.), *Comparative Perspectives on Social Movements: Political Opportunities, Mobilizing Structures, and Cultural Framings*. Cambridge and New York, Cambridge University Press, pp. 205–26.

— (2005). 'Two kinds of stuff: the current encounter of social movements and organizations'. In G. F. Davis, D. McAdam, W. R. Scott and M. N. Zald (eds.), *Social Movements and Organizational Theory*. Cambridge and New York, Cambridge University Press, pp. 351–65.

Clemens, E. S. and Minkoff, D. C. (2004). 'Beyond the iron law: rethinking the place of organizations in social movement research'. In D. A. Snow, S. A. Soule, and H. Kriesi (eds.), *The Blackwell Companion to Social Movements*. Malden (MA) and Oxford, Blackwell, pp. 155–70.

Colloca, C. and Corbetta, P. (2015). 'Beyond protest: issues and ideological inconsistencies in the voters of the Movimento 5 stelle'. In F. Tronconi (ed.), *Beppe Grillo's Five Star Movement. Organisation, Communication and Ideology*. Aldershot, Ashgate, pp. 179–94.

Conaghan, C. (2011). 'Ecuador: Rafael Correa and the Citizens' Revolution'. In S. Levitsky and K. M. Roberts (eds.), *The Resurgence of the Latin American Left*. Baltimore, Johns Hopkins University Press, pp. 260–82.

Corbetta, P. and Gualmini, E. (eds.) (2013). *Il partito di Grillo*. Bologna, Il Mulino.

Cordero, G. and Montero, J. R. (2015). 'Against bipartyism, towards dealignment? The 2014 European election in Spain'. *South European Society and Politics*, 20(3): 357–79.

Cordero, G. and Torcal, M. (2015). Cómo es el votante de Podemos. *El País*, 13 February. Online at: http://elpais.com/elpais/2015/02/11/opinion/1423684763_914251.html.

Crabtree, J. (2013). 'From the MNR to the MAS: populism, parties, the state and social movements in Bolivia since 1952'. In C. De la Torre and C. Arnson (eds.), *Latin American Populism in the Twenty-First Century*. Baltimore, Johns Hopkins University Press, pp. 269–93.

Cross, W. and Blais, A. (2012). 'Who selects the party leader?'. *Party Politics*, 18(2): 127–50.

Crouch, C. (2010). 'Democracy and the Economy'. In A. Pizzorno (ed.), *La democrazia di fronte allo stato democratico*. Milano, Feltrinelli, pp. 181–92.

Cuñha, C. (2003). ' "Mais Portugal, mais CDU!" … mais PCP? The Portuguese Communist Party at the turn of the 21st century'. In J. Botella and L. Ramiro (eds.), *The Crisis of Communism and Party Change*. Barcelona, Icps, pp. 97–127.

Dal Lago, A. (2014). *Clic! Grillo, Casaleggio e la demagogia elettronica*. Napoli, Cronopio.

Dalton, R. (2004). *Democratic Challenges, Democratic Choices. The Erosion of Political Support in Advanced Industrial Democracies*. Oxford, Oxford University Press.

De la Torre, C. (2000). *The Populist Seduction in Latin America: The Ecuadorian Experience*. Athens (OH), Ohio University Center for International Studies.

— (2013a). 'In the name of the people: democratization, popular organizations, and populism in Venezuela, Bolivia, and Ecuador'. *European Review of Latin American and Caribbean Studies*, 95: 27–48.

— (2013b). 'Between authoritarianism and democracy in Latin America's re-founding revolutions'. In E. Peruzzotti and M. Plot (eds.), *Critical Theory and Democracy*. London, Routledge, pp. 152–69.

de Sousa Santos, B. (2014). 'La ola Podemos'. *Publico*, 8 December. Online at: http://blogs.publico.es/espejos-extranos/2014/12/08/la-ola-podemos.

De Waele, J.-M. and Seiler, D.-L. (eds.) (2012). *Les partis de la gauche anticapitaliste en Europe*. Paris, Economica.

della Porta, D. (1992). *Lo scambio occulto*. Bologna, Il Mulino.

— (1995). *Social Movements and Political Violence*. Cambridge, Cambridge University Press.

— (1996). *Movimenti collettivi e sistema politico in Italia. 1960–1995*. Roma–Bari, Laterza.

— (2007). *The Global Justice Movement. Cross-national and Transnational Perspectives*. Boulder, Paradigm.

— (ed.) (2009). *Democracy in Social Movements*. London, Palgrave.

— (2013). *Can Democracy Be Saved? Participation, Deliberation and Social Movements*. Cambridge, Polity.

— (2014). *Mobilizing for Democracy. Comparing 1989 and 2011*. Oxford, Oxford University Press.

— (2015a). *I partiti politici*. Bologna, Il Mulino, 1st edition.

— (2015b). *Social Movements in Times of Austerity: Bringing Capitalism back into Protest Analysis*. Cambridge, Polity.

della Porta, D. (2017). *Where Did the Revolution Go?* Cambridge, Cambridge University Press.

della Porta, D., Andretta, M., Fernandes, T., O'Connor, F., Romanos, E. and Vogiatzoglou, M. (2016). *Neoliberalism and its Discontents*. London, Palgrave: forthcoming.

della Porta, D., Andretta, M. and Mosca, L. (2003). 'Movimenti sociali e sfide globali'. *Rassegna Italiana di Sociologia*, XLIV(1): 43–76.

della Porta, D., Andretta, M., Mosca, L. and Reiter, H. (2006). *Globalization from Below. Transnational Activists and Protest Networks*. Minneapolis, University of Minnesota Press.

della Porta, D. and Chironi, D. (2014). 'Movements in Parties: OccupyPD'. *Partecipazione e conflitto*, 8(1): 59–96.

della Porta, D. and Diani, M. (2006). *Social Movements: An Introduction*. Oxford, Blackwell.

della Porta, D. and Mattoni, A. (eds.) (2014). *Spreading Protest*. Essex, ECPR Press.

della Porta, D., Mosca, L. and Parks, L. (2015). 'Subterranean politics and visible protest in Italy'. In M. Kaldor and S. Selchow (eds.), *Subterranean Politics in Europe*. London, Palgrave, pp. 60–93.

della Porta, D., O'Connor, F., Portos, M. and Subirats, A. (2017). *Referendums from Below*. Bristol, Policy Press.

della Porta, D. and Rucht, D. (1995). 'Left-libertarian movements in context: comparing Italy and West Germany, 1965–1990'. In J. C. Jenkins and B. Klandermans (eds.), *The Politics of Social Protest. Comparative Perspectives on States and Social Movements*. Minneapolis, University of Minnesota Press, pp. 229–72.

della Porta, D. and Vannucci, A. (1997). 'The "perverse effects" of political corruption'. *Political Studies*, 45(3): 516–38.

della Porta, D. and Zamponi, L. (2013). 'Protest and policing on October 15th, global day of action: the Italian case'. *Policing and Society*, 23(1): 65–80.

Diamanti, I. (2007). 'La democrazia degli interstizi. Società e partiti in Europa dopo la caduta del Muro'. *Rassegna italiana di sociologia*, 48: 387–412.

Diani, M. and Kousis, M. (2014). 'The duality of claims and events: the Greek campaign against the Troika's Memoranda and austerity, 2010–2012'. *Mobilization*, 19(4): 387–404.

DiMaggio, P. J. and Powell, W. W. (1991). 'Introduction'. In W. W. Powell and P. J. DiMaggio (eds.), *The New Institutionalism in Organizational Analysis*. Chicago and London, The University of Chicago Press, pp. 1–38.

Duverger, M. (1951). *Les parties politiques*. Paris, A. Colin.

Duyvendak, J. W. (1995). *The Power of Politics: New Social Movements in an Old Polity, France 1965–1989*. Boulder (CO), Westview.

Eleftheriou, C. (2009). 'The "uneasy symbiosis". Factionalism and radical politics in Synaspismos'. Paper presented at the 4th PhD Symposium of the LSE Hellenic Observatory, London, 25–6 June.

Eliasoph, N. (1998). *Avoiding Politics: How Americans Produce Apathy in Everyday Life*. New York, Cambridge University Press.

Ellinas, A. (2013). 'The rise of Golden Dawn'. *South European Society and Politics*, 18(4): 543–65.

EPRE (2015). *Electoral Program for Regional Elections*. Online at: http:// podemos.info/wp-content/uploads/2015/05/prog_marco_12.pdf.

Errejón, Í. (2014). 'Qué es Podemos'. *Le Monde Diplomatique*. Online at: www.Monde-diplomatique.es/?url=articulo/0000856412872168186811102294251000/?articulo=8c640f81-5ccc-4723-911e-71e45da1deca.

— (2015). 'We the people. El 15-m: ¿Un Populismo Indignado?'. *ACME: An International E-Journal for Critical Geographies*, 14(1): 124–56.

Espinoza Pino, M. (2013). 'Politics of indignation: radical democracy and class struggle beyond postmodernity'. *Rethinking Marxism: A Journal of Economics, Culture & Society*, 25(2): 228–41.

Eurostat (2015) 'Real GDP growth-volume'. Online at: http://ec.europa.eu/ eurostat/tgm/table.do?tab=table&init=1&plugin=1&language=en&pcode= tec00115.

Farinelli, A. and Massetti, E. (2015). 'Inexperienced, leftists, and grassroots democrats: a profile of the Five Star Movement's MPs'. *Contemporary Italian Politics*, 7(3): 213–31.

Feenstra, R. A. and Keane, J. (2014). 'Politics in Spain: a case of monitory democracy'. *International Journal of Voluntary and Nonprofit Organizations*, 25(5): 1262–80.

Fella, S. and Ruzza, C. (2013). 'Populism and the fall of the centre-right in Italy: The end of the Berlusconi model or a new beginning?'. *Journal of Contemporary European Studies*, 21(1): 38–52.

Fernandes, T. (2016). 'Building alliances: successful anti-austerity mobilization in Portugal'. In D. della Porta, M. Andretta, T. Fernandes, F. O'Connor, E. Romanos and M. Vogiatzoglou, *Neoliberalism and its Discontents*. London, Palgrave: forthcoming.

Fernández-Albertos, J. (2015). *Los votantes de Podemos. Del partido de los indignados al partido de los excluidos*. Madrid, Catarata.

Fernández-Albertos, J. and Manzano, D. (2012). 'The lack of partisan conflict over the welfare state in Spain'. *South European Society and Politics*, 17(3): 427–47.

Fishman, R. M. (2011). 'Democratic practice after the revolution: the case of Portugal and beyond'. *Politics and Society*, 39(2): 233–67.

Flesher-Fominaya, C. (2007). 'Autonomous movements and the institutional left: two approaches in tension in Madrid's anti-globalization network'. *South European Society and Politics*, 12(3): 335–58.

— (2014). ' "Spain is different": Podemos and 15-m'. *Open Democracy*, 29 May. Online at: https://www.opendemocracy.net/can-europe-make-it/cristina-flesher-fominaya/%E2%80%9Cspain-is-different%E2%80%9D-podemos-and-15m.

— (2015). 'Podemos' March for Change'. *Open Democracy*, 31 January. Online at: https://www.opendemocracy.net/can-europe-make-it/cristina-flesher-fominaya/ podemos%E2%80%99-march-for-change.

Floridia, A. and Vignati, R. (2014). 'Deliberativa, diretta o partecipativa? Le sfide del Movimento 5 stelle alla democrazia rappresentativa'. *Quaderni di sociologia*, 58(2): 51–74.

Font, N., Graziano, P. and Tsakatika, M. (2015). 'Economic crisis and inclusionary populism: evidence from Southern Europe'. Paper presented at the Annual APSA Conference, 3–6 September.

Fornaro, F. (2012). 'Un non-partito: il Movimento 5 stelle'. *Il Mulino*, 460(2): 253–61.

Frankland, E. G., Lucardie, P. and Rihoux, B. (eds.) (2008). *Green Parties in Transition: The End of Grass-roots Democracy?* Farnham, Surrey, Ashgate.

Franzosi, P., Marone, F. and Salvati, E. (2015). 'Populism and Euroscepticism in the Italian Five Star Movement'. *The International Spectator*, 50(2): 109–24.

Galindo, J., Llaneras, K., Medina, O., San Miguel, J., Senserrich, R. and Simón, P. (2015). *Podemos: La cuadratura del círculo*. Madrid, Debate.

Gamson, W. A. (1995). 'Constructing social protest'. In H. Johnston and B. Klandermans (eds.), *Social Movements and Culture: Social Movements, Protest, and Contention*. Minneapolis, University of Minnesota Press, pp. 85–106.

Gamson, William A. (1998). 'Social movements and cultural change'. In M. Giugni, D. McAdam and C. Tilly (eds.), *From Contention to Democracy*. Lanham (MD), Rowman and Littlefield, pp. 57–77.

Garner, R. and Zald, M. N. (1985). 'The political economy of social movement sectors'. In D. G. Suttles and M. N. Zald (eds.), *The Challenge of Social Control: Citizenship and Institutions in Modern Society*. Norwood (NJ), Ablex Publishing Corporation, pp. 119–45.

Giannone, D. (2015). 'Suspending democracy? The governance of the EU's political and economic crisis as a process of neoliberal restructuring'. In K. N. Demetriou (ed.), *The European Union in Crisis: Explorations in Representation and Democratic Legitimacy*. Heidelberg, Springer, pp. 101–22.

Goffman, E. (1974). *Frame Analysis: an Essay on the Organization of Experience*. Boston, Northeastern University Press.

Goldfrank, B. (2011). *Deepening Local Democracy in Latin America: Participation, Decentralization, and the Left*. University Park (PA), Pennsylvania State University Press.

Goldstone, J. A. (2003). 'Introduction: bringing institutionalized and noninstitutionalized politics'. In J. A. Goldstone (ed.), *States, Parties, and Social Movements*. Cambridge, Cambridge University Press, pp. 1–24.

Goretti, C. and Landi, L. (2013). 'Walking on the edge: how Italy rescued Italy in 2012'. *Intereconomics*, 48(1): 4–32.

Gualmini, E. (2013). 'Introduzione. Da movimento a partito'. In P. Corbetta and E. Gualmini (eds.), *Il partito di Grillo*. Bologna, Il Mulino, pp. 7–28.

Gunther, R. (2005). 'Parties and electoral behavior in Southern Europe'. *Comparative Politics*, 37(3): 253–74.

Gunther, R., Diamandouros, N. and Puhle, H.-J. (eds.) (1995). *Democratic Consolidation in Southern Europe*. Baltimore, Johns Hopkins University Press.

Gunther, R. and Diamond, L. (2003). 'Species of political parties: a new typology'. *Party Politics*, 9(2): 167–99.

Gunther, R., Montero, J. R. and Botella, J. (2004). *Democracy in Modern Spain*. New Haven (CT), Yale University Press.

Handlin, S. and Collier, R. B. (2011). 'The diversity of left party linkages and competitive advantages'. In S. Levitsky and K. M. Roberts (eds.), *The Resurgence of the Latin American Left*. Baltimore, Johns Hopkins University Press, pp. 139–61.

Hardiman, N. and Regan, A. (2013). 'The politics of austerity in Ireland'. *Intereconomics*, 48: 9–14.

Harmel, R. and Janda, K. (1994). 'An integrated theory of party goals and party change'. *Journal of Theoretical Politics*, 6(3): 259–87.

Harmel, R. and Robertson, J. D. (1985). 'Formation and success of new parties: a cross-national analysis'. *International Political Science Review*, 6(4): 501–23.

Haug, C., Haeringer, N. and Mosca, L. (2009). 'The ESF organizing process in a diachronic perspective'. In D. della Porta (ed.), *Another Europe*. Routledge, London, pp. 26–45.

Hawkins, K. (2010). *Venezuela's Chavismo and Populism in Comparative Perspective*. New York, Cambridge University Press.

Hazan, R. Y. and Rahat, G. (2010). *Democracy Within Parties: Candidate Selection Methods and their Political Consequences*. Oxford, Oxford University Press.

Heaney, M. (2010). 'Linking political parties and interest groups'. In L. S. Maisel, J. M. Berry and G. C. Edwards III (eds.), *The Oxford Handbook of American Political Parties and Interest Groups*. Oxford, Oxford University Press, pp. 568–87.

Hirschman, A. O. (1991). *The Rhetoric of Reaction: Perversity, Futility, Jeopardy*. Cambridge, MA, The Belknap Press of Harvard University Press.

Hug, S. (2001). *Altering Party Systems: Strategic Behavior and the Emergence of New Political Parties in Western Democracies*. Ann Arbor, University of Michigan Press.

Hutter, S. (2014). *Protesting Culture and Economics in Western Europe: New Cleavages in Left and Right Politics*. Minneapolis, University of Minnesota Press.

Iglesias, P. (2015a). 'Understanding Podemos'. *New Left Review*, 93: 7–22.

— (2015b). 'Spain on edge interview'. *New Left Review*, 93: 23–42.

— (2015c). 'El espacio de la socialdemocracia quedó vacío y lo hemos ocupado nosotros'. Interview *La Opinión de Málaga* (17 May). Online at: www.laopiniondemalaga.es/nacional/2015/05/17/espacio-socialdemocracia-quedo-vacio-hemos/766680.Html.

— (2015d). 'Qué es el cambio'. *El País*, 25 April 2015. Online at: http://elpais.com/elpais/2015/04/24/opinion/1429883919_117080.html.

— (2015e). 'Recuperar la democracia'. Speech at the Forum Nueva Economía, 27 June. Online at: www.huffingtonpost.es/pablo-iglesias/recuperar-la-democracia_b_5533727.html.

Ipsos PA (2014). *Europee 2014. Analisi del voto In Italia*. Online at: www.ipsos.it/ Voto%202014%20def.pdf.

Jasper, J. (2006). *Getting Your Way. Strategic Dilemmas in the Real World*. Chicago, The University of Chicago Press.

Jiménez, M. (2007). 'Mobilizations against the Iraq War in Spain: background, participants and electoral implications'. *South European Society and Politics*, 12(3): 399–420.

Jiménez, M. and Egea de Haro, A. (2011). *La normalización de la protesta. El caso de las manifestaciones en España (1980–2008)*. Madrid, Centro de Investigaciones Sociológicas.

Kaika, M. and Karaliotas, L. (2014). 'The spatialization of democratic politics: insights from the Indignant squares'. *European Urban and Regional Studies*. DOI:10.1177/0969776414528928

Kalogeraki, S., Alexandridis, S. and Papadaki, M. (2014). 'Exploring social support actions as alternative forms of resilience in a Greek urban community'. Paper presented at the ECPR General Conference, Glasgow, 3–6 September.

Kanellopoulos, K. and Kostopoulos, K. (2013). 'Alliance building in the Greek anti-austerity campaign, 2010–12'. Paper presented at the ECPR General Conference, Bordeaux, 3–7 September. Online at: http://ecpr.eu/filestore/paperproposal/6e60f90c-c040-4312-82de-85cf4e03ce33.pdf.

Kanellopoulos, K., Kostopoulos, K., Papanikolopoulos, D. and Roggas, V. (2016). 'Competing modes of coordination in the Greek anti-austerity campaign, 2010–2012'. *Social Movement Studies*. DOI: 10.1080/14742837. 2016.11554464

Karamichas, J. (2009). 'The December 2008 riots in Greece'. *Social Movement Studies*, 8(3): 289–93.

— (2012). 'Square politics: key characteristics of the indignant mobilizations in Greece'. Paper presented at the 62nd PSA Annual International Conference, Belfast, Northern Ireland, United Kingdom.

Katsampekis, G. (2015). 'The rise of the Greek radical left to power: notes on Syriza's discourse and strategy'. *Linea Sur*, 9: 152–61.

Katz, R. (2015). 'Party in democratic theory'. In R. Katz and W. Crotty (eds.), *Handbook of Party Politics*. London, Sage, pp. 34–46.

Katz, R. S. and Mair, P. (1995). 'Changing models of party organization and party democracy'. *Party Politics*, I: 5–28.

Kavoulakos, K. and Gritzas, G. (2015). 'Movements and alternative spaces in crisis-ridden Greece. A new civil society'. In N. G. Georgakakis and N. Demertzis (eds.), *The political portrait of Greece: Crisis and the deconstruction of politics*. Athens, Gutenberg-National Centre for Social Research, pp. 337–57.

— (2016). *Alternative Economic and Political Spaces*. Athens, Kallipos [in Greek].

Kirchheimer, O. (1966). 'The transformation of the Western European party system'. In J. LaPalombara and M. Weiner (eds.), *Political Parties and Political Development*. Princeton (NJ), Princeton University Press, pp. 177–200.

Kitschelt, H. (1988). 'Left-libertarian parties: explaining innovation in competitive systems'. *World Politics*, 40(2): 194–234.

— (1989). *The Logics of Party Formation: Ecological Parties in Belgium and West Germany.* Ithaca (NY), Cornell University Press.

— (1993). 'Social movements, political parties, and democratic theory'. *The Annals of the American Academy of Political and Social Science*, 528(1): 13–29.

— (1994). *The Transformation of European Social Democracy.* Cambridge, Cambridge University Press.

— (2006). 'Movement parties'. In R. Katz and W. Crotty (eds.), *Handbook of Party Politics.* London, Sage, pp. 278–91.

Kittilson, M. C. and Scarrow, S. E. (2003). 'Political parties and the rhetoric and realities of democratization'. In B. E. Cain, R. J. Dalton and S. E. Scarrow (eds.), *Democracy Transformed? Expanding Political Opportunities in Advanced Industrial Democracies.* Oxford, Oxford University Press, pp. 59–80.

Koelble, T. A. (1991). *The Left Unraveled: Social Democracy and the New Left Challenge in Britain.* Durham (NC), Duke University Press.

Koopmans, R. (1995). *Democracy from Below: New Social Movements and the Political System in West Germany.* Boulder (CO), Westview Press.

Kousis, M. (2012). 'Greek protests against austerity measures: a relational approach'. Paper for Session LOC03: Political Systems Crisis of Legitimacy, 22nd World Congress of the International Political Science Association, '*Reshaping Power, Shifting Boundaries*', 8–12 July, Madrid.

— (2013). 'The Greek campaign against Memoranda and austerity policies'. *Sociological Review*, 1: 33–41 [in Greek].

— (2016). 'The Spatial Dimensions of the Greek Protest Campaign against Troika's Memoranda and Austerity Measures, 2010–2013'. In M. Ancelovici, P. Dufour and H. Nez (eds.), *Street Politics in the Age of Austerity: From the Indignados to Occupy.* Amsterdam, Amsterdam University Press/University of Chicago Press (forthcoming).

Kousis, M. and Kanellopoulos, K. (2014). 'Impacts of the Greek crisis on contentious and conventional politics, 2010–2012'. In G. Tsobanoglou and N. Petropoulos (eds.), *The Social Impacts of the Eurozone Debt Crisis.* Athens, Gordios Books, pp. 443–62 [in Greek].

Kousis, M., Kalogeraki, S., Papadaki, M., Loukakis, A. and Velonaki, M. (2016). 'Alternative Forms of Resilience in Greece'. *Forschungsjournal Soziale Bewegungen*, 29(1): 50–61 [in German].

Kriesi, H. (1989). 'New Social Movements and the new class in the Netherlands'. *American Journal of Sociology*, 94(5): 1078–1116.

— (1991). 'The political opportunity structure of New Social Movements'. *Discussion Paper FS*, III: 91–103. Wissenschaftszentrum Berlin.

— (2015a). 'Party system, political system and social movements'. In D. della Porta and M. Diani (eds.), *Oxford Handbook on Social Movements.* Oxford, Oxford University Press.

— (2015b). *Party systems, electoral systems and social movements.* Working paper. Available at: www.eui.eu/Projects/POLCON/Documents/Kriesiparty systems.pdf.

Kriesi, H., Koopmans, R., Duyvendak, J. W. and Giugni, M. (1995). *New Social Movements in Western Europe: A Comparative Analysis.* London, UCL Press.

Kriesi, H., Grande, E., Lachat, R., Dolezal, M., Bornschier, S. and Frey, T. (2008). *West European Politics in the Age of Globalization*. Cambridge, Cambridge University Press.

Kriesi, H., Grande, E., Dolezal, M., Helbling, M., Höglinger, D., Hutter, S. and Wüest, B. (2012). *Political Conflict in Western Europe*. Cambridge, Cambridge University Press.

Lambrianidis, L. (2011). *Investing in Leaving: The Greek Case of International Migration of Professionals*. Athens, Kritiki [in Greek].

Lanfrey, D. (2011). 'Il MoVimento dei grillini tra meetup, meta–organizzazione e democrazia del monitoraggio'. In L. Mosca and C. Vaccari (eds.), *Nuovi media, nuova politica? Partecipazione e mobilitazione online da MoveOn al MoVimento 5 stelle*. Milano, FrancoAngeli, pp. 143–66.

Lanzone, M. E. and Tronconi, F. (2015). 'Between blogs, social networks and territory: activists and grassroots organization'. In F. Tronconi (ed.), *Beppe Grillo's Five Star Movement. Organisation, Communication and Ideology*. Aldershot, Ashgate, pp. 54–73.

Lawson, K. (1980). 'Political parties and linkage'. In K. Lawson (ed.), *Political Parties and Linkage: A Comparative Perspective*. New Haven, Yale University Press, pp. 3–24.

Leclau, Ernesto (2005). *On Populist Reason*. London, Verso.

Lello, E. and Pazzaglia, A. (2013). 'Sel: la sinistra del centro-sinistra?'. In I. Diamanti, F. Bordignon and L. Ceccarini (eds.), *Un salto nel voto. Ritratto politico dell'Italia di oggi*. Roma-Bari, Laterza, pp. 106–15.

Levitsky, S. and Loxton, J. (2013). 'Populism and competitive authoritarianism in the Andes'. *Democratization*, 20(1): 107–36.

Levitsky, S. and Roberts, K. M. (2011a). 'Latin America's "left turn": a framework for analysis'. In S. Levitsky and K. M. Roberts (eds.), *The Resurgence of the Latin American Left*. Baltimore, Johns Hopkins University Press, pp. 1–28.

— (2011b). 'Conclusion: Democracy, development, and the Left'. In S. Levitsky and K. M. Roberts (eds.), *The Resurgence of the Latin American Left*. Baltimore, Johns Hopkins University Press, pp. 399–427.

Lindekilde, L. (2015). 'Discourse and frame analysis: in-depth analysis of qualitative data in social movement studies'. In D. della Porta (ed.), *Methodological Practices in Social Movement Research*. Oxford, Oxford University Press, pp. 195–228.

Linz, J. J. and Montero, J. R. (1999). *The Party Systems of Spain: Old Cleavages and New Challenges*. Madrid, Instituto Juan March de Estudios e Investigaciones.

Lipset, S. M. and Rokkan, S. (1967). 'Cleavage structures, party systems, and voter alignments: an introduction'. In S. M. Lipset and S. Rokkan (eds.), *Party Systems and Voter Alignments*. New York, The Free Press, pp. 1–64.

Lipsky, M. (1968). 'Protest as a political resource'. *The American Political Science Review*, 62(4): 1144–58.

Lisi, M. (2012). 'Rediscovering civil society? Renewal and continuity in the Portuguese Radical Left'. *South European Society and Politics*, 18(1): 21–39.

Lobera, J. (2015). 'De movimientos a partidos. La cristalización electoral de la protesta'. *Revista Española de Sociología*, 24: 97–105.

Lobera, J. and Ferrándiz, P. (2013). 'El peso de la desconfianza política en la dinámica electoral en España'. In I. Crespo (ed.), *Partidos, medios y electores en proceso de cambio: las elecciones generales españolas de 2011*. Valencia, Tirant Lo Blanch, pp. 33–57.

Lofland, J. (1996). *Social Movement Organizations. Guide to Research on Insurgent Realities*. New Brunswick and London, Aldine Transaction.

López, I. (2012). 'Consensonomics: la ideología dominante en la CT'. In G. Martínez (ed.), *CT o la Cultura de la Transición. Crítica a 35 años de la cultura española*. Madrid, Ed. Debolsillo, pp. 77–88.

López Maya, M. (2011). 'Venezuela: Hugo Chávez and the Populist Left'. In S. Levitsky and K. M. Roberts (eds.), *The Resurgence of the Latin American Left*. Baltimore, Johns Hopkins University Press, pp. 213–38.

Lopez Maya, M. and Panzarelli, A. (2013). 'Populism, rentierism and socialism in the twenty-first century: the case of Venezuela'. In C. De la Torre and C. Arnson (eds.), *Latin American Populism in the Twenty-First Century*. Baltimore, Johns Hopkins University Press, pp. 239–68.

Lucardie, P. (2000). 'Prophets, purifiers and prolocutors: towards a theory on the emergence of new parties'. *Party Politics*, 6(2): 175–85.

Luttbeg, N. R. (1981). *Public Opinion and Public Policy: Models of Political Linkage*. Itasca (Ill.), F. E. Peacock Publishers, 3rd edn.

Lyrintzis, C. (2005). 'The changing party system: stable democracy, contested "modernisation"'. *West European Politics*, 28(2): 242–59.

Macaluso, M. (2015). 'Attivisti 5 Stelle a Palermo'. In R. Biorcio (ed.), *Gli attivisti del Movimento 5 Stelle. Dal web al territorio*. Milano, FrancoAngeli, pp. 167–81.

Madrid, R. L. (2008). 'The rise of ethnopopulism in Bolivia'. *World Politics*, 60(3): 475–508.

— (2009). 'The origins of the two lefts in Latin America'. *Political Science Quarterly*, 125(4): 1–23.

— (2011). 'Bolivia: origins and policies of the Movimiento al Socialismo'. In S. Levitsky and K. M. Roberts (eds.), *The Resurgence of the Latin American Left*. Baltimore, Johns Hopkins University Press, pp. 239–59.

Magalhães, P. (2014). 'After the bailout: responsibility, policy, and valence in the Portuguese legislative election of June 2011'. *South European Society and Politics*, 17(2): 309–27.

Maguire, D. (1995). 'Opposition movements and opposition parties'. In C. J. Jenkins and B. Klandermans (eds.), *The Politics of Social Protest. Comparative Perspectives on States and Social Movements*. London, University College London, pp. 199–228.

Mair, P. (1983). 'Adaptation and control: towards an understanding of party and party system change'. In H. Daalder and P. Mair (eds.), *Western European Party Systems: Continuity and Change*. London, Sage, pp. 405–29.

— (1994). 'Party organizations: from civil society to the state'. In R. S. Katz and P. Mair (eds.), *How Parties Organize. Change and Adaption in Party Organizations in Western Democracies*. London, Sage, pp. 1–22.

— (2009). 'Representative versus responsible government'. *Working Paper*, 09/8. Cologne, Max Planck Institute for the Study of Societies.

— (2011). 'The election in context'. In M. Gallagher and M. Marsh (eds.), *How Ireland Voted 2011: The Full Story of Ireland's Earthquake Election.* Basingstoke, Palgrave, pp. 283–97.

Mair, P. and Van Biezen, I. (2001). 'Party membership in twenty European democracies, 1980–2000'. *Party Politics*, 7(1): 5–21.

Mancini, P. (2011). *Between Commodification and Lifestyle Politics.* Oxford, Reuters Institute for the Study of Journalism.

Mansbridge, J. (1983). *Beyond adversary democracy.* Chicago, University of Chicago Press.

March, L. (2011). *Radical Left parties in contemporary Europe.* London, Routledge.

March, L. and Mudde, C. (2005). 'What's left of the radical left? The European radical left after 1989: decline and mutation'. *Comparative European Politics*, 3(1): 23–49.

Marks, G. (1989). *Union in Politics. Britain, Germany and the United States in the Nineteenth and Early Twentieth Century.* Princeton, Princeton University Press.

Marsh, M. and Mikhaylov, S. (2012). 'Economic voting in a crisis: the Irish election of 2011'. *Electoral Studies*, 30: 1–7.

Martín, I. C. (2012). 'Political disaffection revisited: the Indignant movement in Spain, or a different way of doing politics'. Paper presented at the conference 'Voting and Protesting in Europe since 2008', Georgetown University, Washington, DC, 17–18 April.

— (2015). 'Podemos y otros modelos de partido–movimiento'. *Revista Española de Sociología*, 24: 107–14.

Martínez, M. A. and Domingo San Juan, E. (2014). *Social and Political Impacts of the 15M Movement in Spain.* Online at: www.miguelangelmartinez.net/IMG/pdf/M15_impacts_v3_0_April_2014.pdf.

Masullo, J. (2017). 'Making sense of "La Salida": Challenging left-wing control in Venezuela'. In D. della Porta (ed.), *Global diffusion of protest. Riding the protest wave in the neoliberal crisis.* Amsterdam, Amsterdam University Press, forthcoming.

Mavris, Y. (2012). 'Greece's austerity election'. *New Left Review*, 76: 95–107.

Mazzoleni, G. and Schulz, W. (1999). ' "Mediatization" of politics: a challenge for democracy'. *Political Communication*, 16(3): 247–61.

McAdam, D. and Tarrow, S. G. (2010). 'Ballots and barricades: on the reciprocal relationship between elections and social movements'. *Perspectives on Politics*, 8(2): 529–42.

McCarthy, J. D. and Zald, M. N. (1987). 'Resource mobilization and social movements: a partial theory'. In M. N. Zald and J. D. McCarthy (eds.), *Social Movements in an Organizational Society. Collected Essays.* New Brunswick (NJ) and Oxford, Transaction Books, pp. 15–42.

Meguid, B. M. (2005). 'Competition between unequals: the role of mainstream party strategy in niche party success'. *American Political Science Review*, 99(3): 347–59.

Melucci, A. (1988). 'Getting involved'. In B. Klandermans, H. Kriesi and S. Tarrow (eds.), *From Structure to Action: Comparing Social Movement Research Across Cultures*. Greenwich (CT), JAI Press, pp. 329–48.

Méndez Lago, M. (2007). 'Turning the page: crisis and transformation of the Spanish Socialist Party'. *South European Society and Politics*, 11(3–4): 419–37.

Méndez, M., Morales, L. and Ramiro, L. (2004). 'Los afiliados y su papel en los partidos políticos'. *Zona Abierta*, 108–9: 153–207.

Montero, J. R. and Gunther, R. (2002). 'Introduction: reviewing and reassessing parties'. In R. Gunther, J. R. Montero and J. Linz (eds.), *Political Parties: Old Concepts and New Challenges*. Oxford, Oxford University Press.

Montero, J. R., Torcal, M. and Gunther, R. (1998). 'Actitudes hacia la democracia en España: legitimidad, descontento y desafección'. *Revista Española de Investigaciones Sociológicas*, 83: 9–49.

Montufar, C. (2013). 'Rafael Correa and his plebiscitary citizens' revolution'. In C. De la Torre and C. Arnson (eds.), *Latin American Populism in the Twenty-First Century*. Baltimore, Johns Hopkins University Press, pp. 295–321.

Morlino, L. (2005). 'Anchors and democratic change'. *Comparative Political Studies*, 38(7): 743–70.

Mosca, L. (2013). 'A year of social movements in Italy: from the No-Tavs to the five-star movement'. In A. di Virgilio and C. Radaelli (eds.), *Italian Politics. Technocrats in office*. New York, Berghahn, pp. 267–85.

— (2014). 'The Five Star Movement: exception or vanguard in Europe?' *The International Spectator*, 49(1): 36–52.

— (2015a). 'The Movimento 5 stelle and social conflicts: between symbiosis and cooptation'. In F. Tronconi (ed.), *Beppe Grillo's Five Star Movement. Organisation, Communication and Ideology*. Aldershot, Ashgate, pp. 153–77.

— (2015b). 'Problemi e limiti del modello organizzativo «cybercratico» nell'esperienza del Movimento 5 Stelle'. *Ragion Pratica*, 44(1): 37–52.

Mosca, L., Vaccari, C. and Valeriani, A. (2015a). 'An internet-fuelled party? The Movimento 5 Stelle and the web'. In F. Tronconi (ed.), *Beppe Grillo's Five Star Movement*. Aldershot, Ashgate, pp. 127–51.

Mosca, L., Valeriani, A. and Vaccari, C. (2015b). 'How to select citizen candidates: the Five Star Movement's online primaries and their implications'. In A. de Petris and T. Pogunkte (eds.), *Anti-party Parties in Germany and Italy*. Roma, Luiss University Press, pp. 114–42.

Moschonas, G. (2013). 'A New Left in Greece: PASOK's fall and Syriza's rise'. *Dissent*, 60(4): 33–7.

— (2015). 'Syriza's tremendous path to power'. *Chronos*, January. Online at: http://www.chronosmag.eu/index.php/g-moschonas-syrizas-tremendous-path-to-power.html.

Mudde, C. and Rovira Kaltwasser, C. (eds.) (2012). *Populism in Europe and the Americas: Threat or Corrective for Democracy?* Cambridge, Cambridge University Press.

Müller-Rommel, F. (1993). *Gruene Partein in Westeuropa. Westdeutscher Verlag*, Opladen.

Murillo, M. V., Oliveros, V. and Vaishnav, M. (2011). Voting for the Left or Governing on the Left?'. In S. Levitsky and K. M. Roberts (eds.), *Latin American Left Turn*. Baltimore, Johns Hopkins University Press.

Neumann, F. (1968). 'Entstehung und Entwicklung der politischen Parteien'. In W. Abendrot and K. Lenk (eds.), *Einführung in die politische Wissenschaft*. München, Francke Verlag.

Neumann, S. (1956). 'Towards a comparative study of political parties'. In S. Neumann (ed.), *Modern Political Parties*. Chicago, Chicago University Press, pp. 395–421.

O'Connor, F. (2016). 'The presence and absence of protest in austerity Ireland'. In D. della Porta (ed.), *Another Europe*. London, Routledge, pp. 173–203.

O'Neill, M. (1997). *Green Parties and Political Change in Contemporary Europe*. Aldershot, Ashgate.

Ochoa, U. D. (2014). *The Political Empowerment of the Cocaleros of Bolivia and Peru*. London, Palgrave.

Offe, C. (1985). 'New social movements: changing boundaries of the political'. *Social Research*, LII: 817–68.

Olsen, J., Koß, M. and Hough, D. (eds.) (2010). *Left Parties in National Governments*. London, Palgrave.

OPP (2014). 'Podemos' organizational principles'. Online at: http://podemos.info/wp-content/uploads/2015/06/Documento-organizativo.pdf.

Panagyiotakis, M. (2015). 'The Radical Left in Greece'. *Socialism and Democracy*, 29(3): 25–43.

Panebianco, A. (1988). *Political Parties: Organization and Power*. Cambridge, Cambridge University Press.

Panizza, F. (2013). 'What do we mean when we talk about populism'. In C. De la Torre and C. Arnson (eds.), *Latin American Populism in the Twenty-First Century*. Baltimore, Johns Hopkins University Press, pp. 85–115.

Papanikolopoulos, D. and Roggas, V. (2015). 'Syriza's electoral success as a movement effect'. Unpublished paper presented at the International conference 'Democracy Rising', Athens, 16–19 July.

Passarelli, G., Tronconi, F. and Tuorto, D. (2013). 'Dentro il Movimento: organizzazione, attivisti e programmi'. In P. Corbetta and E. Gualmini (eds.), *Il partito di Grillo*. Bologna, Il Mulino, pp. 123–67.

Passarelli, G. and Tuorto, D. (2015). 'A vote(r) like any other? Exploring the protest component in the vote for the Movimento 5 stelle'. In F. Tronconi (ed.), *Beppe Grillo's Five Star Movement. Organisation, Communication and Ideology*. Aldershot, Ashgate, pp. 179–94.

Pastor, J. (1998). 'La evolución de los movimientos sociales en el Estado español'. In P. Ibarra and B. Tejerina (eds.), *Los movimientos sociales. Transformaciones políticas y cambio cultural*. Madrid, Trotta, pp. 69–87.

Pedrazzani, A. and Pinto, L. (2015). 'The electoral base: the "political revolution" in evolution'. In F. Tronconi (ed.), *Beppe Grillo's Five Star Movement. Organisation, Communication and Ideology*. Aldershot, Ashgate, pp. 75–98.

Peruzzotti, E. (2013). 'Populism in democratic theory'. In C. De la Torre and C. Arnson (eds.), *Latin American Populism in the Twenty-First Century*. Baltimore, Johns Hopkins University Press, pp. 61–84.

Petras, J. and Veltmeyer, H. (2009). *What's Left in Latin America? Regime Change in New Times*. Surrey, Ashgate.

Piccio, D. R. (2012). 'Party Responses to Social Movements. A Comparative Analysis of Italy and the Netherlands in the 1970s and 1980s'. PhD Thesis, European University Institute.

Pinto, L. and Vignati, R. (2012). 'Il successo e i dilemmi del Movimento 5 Stelle'. *Il Mulino*, 61(4): 731–9.

Piven, F. F. and Cloward, R. A. (1977). *Poor People's Movements: Why They Succeed, How They Fail*. New York, Vintage Books.

Pizzorno, A. (1981). 'Interests and parties in pluralism'. In S. Berger (ed.), *Organizing Interests in Western Europe*. Cambridge, Cambridge University Press, pp. 247–84.

— (1997). 'Le trasformazioni del sistema politico italiano, 1976–1992'. In F. Barbagallo (ed.), *Storia dell'Italia Repubblicana*. Torino, Einaudi, pp. 303–44.

Poguntke, T. (1993). *Alternative Politics. The German Green Party*. Edinburgh, Edinburgh University Press.

— (2002a). 'Party organizational linkage: parties without firm social roots?'. In K. R. Luther and F. Müller-Rommel (eds.), *Political Parties in the New Europe: Political and Analytical Challenges*. Oxford, Oxford University Press, pp. 43–62.

— (2002b). 'Green Parties in National Governments: From Protest to Acquiescence?'. *Environmental Politics*, 11(1): 133–45.

— (2006). 'Political parties and other organizations'. In R. S. Katz and W. Crotty (eds.), *Handbook of Party Politics*. London, Sage, pp. 396–405.

Pribble, J. and Huber, E. (2011). 'Social policy and redistribution: Chile and Uruguay'. In S. Levitsky and K. M. Roberts (eds.), *The Resurgence of the Latin American Left*. Baltimore, Johns Hopkins University Press, pp. 117–38.

Psimitis, M. (2011). 'The protest cycle of spring 2010 in Greece'. *Social Movement Studies*, 10(2): 191–7.

Ramiro, L. (2003). 'Electoral incentives and organizational limits. The evolution of the communist party of Spain and the United Left'. In J. Botella and L. Ramiro (eds.), *The Crisis of West European Communist Parties and their Change Trajectories: Communists, Post-Communists, ex-Communists?*. Barcelona, Icps, pp. 71–96.

Ramiro, L. and Font, J. (2012). '¿La oportunidad de los pequeños? El voto a partidos pequeños en las elecciones al Parlamento Europeo'. In M. Torcal and J. Font (eds.), *Elecciones europeas 2009*. Madrid, Centro de Investigaciones Sociológicas, pp. 253–86.

Ramiro, L. and Vergé, T. (2013). 'Impulse and decadence of linkage processes: evidence from the Spanish Radical Left'. *South European Society and Politics*, 18(1): 41–60.

Ramiro-Fernández, L. (2005). 'The crisis of the Spanish radical left: The PCE and IU – a rejoinder'. *Journal of Communist Studies and Transition Politics*, 21(2): 302–5.

Rashkova, E. R. and Van Biezen, I. (2014). 'The legal regulation of political parties: contesting or promoting legitimacy?'. *International Political Science Review*, 35(3): 265–74.

Reif, K. and Schmitt, H. (1980). 'Nine second-order national elections – a conceptual framework for the analysis of European election results'. *European Journal of Political Research*, 8(1): 3–44.

Rendueles, C. and Sola, J. (2015). 'Podemos and the paradigm shift'. *Jacobin Magazine: A Magazine of Culture and Polemic*, 13 April. Online at: https://www.jacobinmag.com/2015/04/podemos-spain-pablo-iglesias-european-left.

Rihoux, B. and Rüdig, W. (2006). 'Analysing Greens in power: setting the agenda'. *European Journal of Political Research*, 45(S1): 1–33.

Rivero, J. (2015). *Podemos: Objetivo asaltar los cielos*. Barcelona, Planeta.

Roberts, K. M. (2013). 'Parties and populism in Latin America'. In C. De la Torre and C. Arnson (eds.), *Latin American Populism in the Twenty-First Century*. Baltimore, Johns Hopkins University Press, pp. 37–60.

— (2015). *Changing Course in Latin America: Party Systems in the Neoliberal Era*. New York, Cambridge University Press.

Rohrschneider, R. (1993). 'Impact of social movements on the European party system'. *The Annals of the American Academy of Political and Social Sciences*, 528: 157–70.

Rokkan, S. (1970). *Citizens, Elections, and Parties*. Oslo, Oslo University Press.

Romanos, E. and Sádaba, I. (2015). 'From the street to Parliament through the App: digitally enabled political outcomes of the Spanish 15M movement'. Paper presented at ESA RN 25 Midterm Conference Madrid, 19–20 February.

Rootes, C. (1995). 'A new class? The higher educated and the new politics'. In L. Maheu (ed.), *Social Movements and Social Classes*. London/Thousand Oaks, Sage, pp. 220–35.

Rüdig, W. (1990). 'Explaining green party development: reflections on a theoretical frame-work'. *Strathclyde Papers on Government and Politics*, 71. Department of Government, University of Strathclyde, Glasgow.

Rüdig, W. and Karyotis, G. (2013). 'Beyond the usual suspects: new participants in anti-austerity protest in Greece'. *Mobilization: An International Journal*, 18(3): 313–30.

— (2014). 'Who protests in Greece? Mass opposition to austerity'. *British Journal of Political Science*, 44: 487–513.

Sacchi, S. (2013). 'Social policy reform in the Italian debt crisis'. In A. di Virgilio and C. Radaelli (eds.), *Italian Politics: Technocrats in Office* 28. New York, Berghahn, pp. 207–26.

— (2015). 'Conditionality by other means: EU involvement in Italy's structural reforms in the sovereign debt crisis'. *Comparative European Politics*, 13(1): 77–92.

Sampedro, V. and Lobera, J. (2014). 'The Spanish 15-m Movement: a consensual dissent?'. *Journal of Spanish Cultural Studies*, 15(1–2): 61–80.

Sánchez-Cuenca, I. (2000). 'The Political Basis of Support for European Integration'. *European Union Politics*, 1(2): 147–71.

Santoro, G. (2014). *Breaking Beppe. Dal Grillo qualunque alla guerra civile simulata*. Roma, Castelvecchi.

Sartori, G. (1976). *Parties and Party Systems*. Cambridge, Cambridge University Press.

Scarrow, S. (2009). 'Political activism and party members'. In R. J. Dalton and H. P. Klingemann (eds.), *Oxford Handbook of Political Behaviour*. Oxford, Oxford University Press, pp. 636–54.

Scarrow, S., Webb, P. and Farrell, D. M. (2000). 'From social integration to electoral contestation'. In R. J. Dalton and M. Wattenberg (eds.), *Parties without Partisans. Political Change in Advanced Industrial Democracies*. Oxford, Oxford University Press, pp. 129–53.

Schwartz, M. A. (2005). 'Linkage processes in party networks'. In A. Römmele, D. M. Farrell and P. Ignazi (eds.), *Political Parties and Political Systems: the Concept of Linkage Revisited*. Westport (CT), Praeger, pp. 37–60.

Serdedakis, N. and Koufidi, M. (2016). 'Protest and electoral cycles: an overlooked approach in collective action studies'. *Greek Political Science Review*, forthcoming [in Greek].

Shefner, J., Pasdirtz, G. and Blad, C. (2006). 'Austerity protests and immiserating growth in Mexico and Argentina'. In H. Johnston and P. Almeida (eds.), *Latin American Social Movements*. Lanham, Rowman and Littlefield, pp. 19–41.

Silva, E. (2009). *Challenging Neoliberalism in Latin America*. New York, Cambridge University Press.

Smith, J., Karides, M., Becker, M., Brunelle, D., Chase-Dunn, C., della Porta, D., Icaza Garza, R., Juris, J. S., Mosca, L., Reese, E., Smith, P. and Vazquez, R. (2007). *Global Democracy and the World Social Forum*. Boulder (CO), Paradigm.

Snow, A. and Benford, R. D. (1988). 'Ideology, frame resonance, and participant mobilization'. In B. Klandermans, H. Kriesi and S. Tarrow (eds.), *From Structure to Action: Comparing Social Movement Research Across Cultures*. Greenwich, JAI Press, pp. 197–217.

Snow, A., Soule, S. A. and Kriesi, H. (eds) (2004). *The Blackwell Companion to Social Movements*. Oxford, Blackwell.

Spourdalakis, M. (2014). 'The miraculous rise of the "Phenomenon SYRIZA"'. *International Critical Thought*, 4(3): 354–66.

Stavrakakis, Y. (2015). 'Populism in power: Syriza's challenge to Europe'. *Juncture*, 21(4): 273–80.

Stavrakakis, Y. and Katsampekis, G. (2014). 'Left-wing populism in the European periphery: the case of SYRIZA'. *Journal of Political Ideologies*, 19(2): 119–42.

Steinberg, M. W. (1998). 'Tilting the frame: considerations on collective action framing from a discursive turn'. *Theory and Society*, 27(6): 845–72.

Stobart, L. (2014). 'Understanding Podemos 1/3: 15M and counter-politics'. *Left Flank*, 5 November. Online at: http://left-flank.org/2014/11/05/explaining-podemos-1-15-m-counter-politics.

Streeck, W. (2014). 'Taking crisis seriously: capitalism on its way out'. *Stato e Mercato*, 100: 45–68.

Strøm, K. (1990). 'A behavioural theory of competitive political parties'. *American Journal of Political Science*, 34(2): 565–98.

Subirats, J. (2015a). '¿Desbordar el "dentro"–"fuera"?'. *Revista Teknokultura*, 12(1): 161–8.

— (2015b). 'Todo se mueve. Acción colectiva, acción conectiva, Movimientos, partidos e instituciones'. *Revista Española de Sociología*, 24: 123–31.

SYN (2005). Central Political Committee Resolution. *Left and Youths: A Dynamic Relationship, a Relationship of Subversion*. Online at: http://www.syn.gr/gr/keimeno.php?id=7225.

SYRIZA (2012). *Electoral Declaration*. Online at: http://goo.gl/9gHXoM.

— (2013a). *The Statute of Syriza, the Coalition of the Radical Left*. Online at: www.syriza.gr/pdfs/katastatiko.pdf.

— (2013b). *The Political Resolution of the Founding Congress of Syriza*. Online at: http://www.syriza.gr/pdfs/politiki_apofasi_idrytikou_synedriou_syriza.pdf.

— (2014a). *The Thessaloniki Programme*. Online at: http://goo.gl/1CLTbz.

— (2014b). *We're Voting for Greece. We're Voting for Another Europe*. Online at: http://goo.gl/fcbpy6.

— (2015). *Framework of Government Programme*. Online at: http://goo.gl/hDnBCR.

Szerbiak, A. and Taggart, P. (2003). 'Theorising party-based euroscepticism: problems of definition, measurement and causality'. SEI Working Paper, No. 69 European Parties Elections and Referendums Network Working Paper No. 12. Sussex European Institute, Sussex.

Talshir, G. (2003). 'A threefold ideological analysis of Die Grünen: from ecologized socialism to political liberalism?'. *Journal of Political Ideologies*, 8(2): 157–84.

Tarchi, M. (2003). *L'Italia populista. Dal qualunquismo ai girotondi*. Bologna, Il Mulino.

Tarrow, S. G. (1989). *Democracy and Disorder: Protest and Politics in Italy, 1965–1975*. Oxford, Oxford University Press.

— (1990). 'The phantom of the opera: political parties and social movements of the 1960s and 1970s in Italy'. In R. Dalton and M. Keuchler (eds.), *Challenging the Political Order*. New Haven (CT), Yale University Press, pp. 251–73.

— (1998). *Power in Movement*. New York, Cambridge University Press.

— (2015). 'Contentious politics'. In D. della Porta and M. Diani (eds.), *Oxford Handbook on Social Movements*. Oxford, Oxford University Press, pp. 86–107.

Teperoglou, E. and Tsatsanis, E. (2014a). 'Dealignment, de-legitimation and the implosion of the two-party system in Greece: the earthquake election of 6th May 2012'. *Journal of Elections, Public Opinion and Parties*, 24(2): 222–42.

— (2014b). 'The acceleration of a slow death: political identification and the end of bipartisanship'. In Y. Voulgaris and E. Nicolacopoulos (eds.), *The Double Electoral Earthquake*. Athens, Themelio, pp. 33–60.

Teperoglou, E., Tsatsanis, E. and Nicolacopoulos, E. (2015). 'Habituating to the new normal in a post-earthquake party system: the 2014 European election in Greece'. *South European Society and Politics*, 20(3): 333–55.

Theodorikakou, O., Alamanou, A. and Katsadoros, K. (2013). ' "Neo-homelessness" and the Greek crisis'. *European Journal of Homelessness*, 7(2): 203–10.

Tilly, C. (1978). *From Mobilization to Revolution*. Reading, Addison-Wesley.

Torcal, M. (2006). 'Political disaffection and democratisation history in new democracies'. In M. Torcal and J. R. Montero (eds.), *Political Disaffection in Contemporary Democracies. Social Capital, Institutions, and Politics.* London, Routledge, pp. 157–89.

Toret, J. (2015). 'Una mirada tecnopolítica al primer año de Podemos. Seis hipótesis'. *Revista Teknokultura*, 12(1): 121–35.

Treré, E. and Barassi, V. (2015). 'Net-authoritarianism? How web ideologies reinforce political hierarchies in the Italian 5 Star Movement'. *Journal of Italian Cinema and Media Studies*, 3(3): 287–304.

Triandafyllidou, A., Gropas, R. and Kouki, H. (eds.) (2013). *European Modernity and the Greek Crisis.* New York, Palgrave Macmillan.

Tronconi, F. (ed.) (2015a). *Beppe Grillo's Five Star Movement. Organisation, Communication and Ideology.* Aldershot, Ashgate.

— (2015b). 'The organisational and ideological roots of the electoral success'. In F. Tronconi (ed.), *Beppe Grillo's Five Star Movement. Organisation, Communication and Ideology.* Aldershot, Ashgate, pp. 213–30.

Tsakatika, M. (2014). 'Syriza y la izquierda en la política griega'. In I. Martín and I. Tirado (eds.), *Grecia: aspectos políticos y jurídico-económicos de la crisis.* Madrid, CEPS, pp. 79–98.

Tsakatika, M. and Eleftheriou, C. (2013). 'Radical left's turn towards civil society in Greece: one strategy, two paths'. *South European Society and Politics*, 18(1): 81–99.

Tsakatika, M. and Lisi, M. (2013). ' "Zippin' up my boots, goin' back to my roots": radical left parties in Southern Europe'. *South European Society and Politics*, 18(1): 1–19.

Tsilimingra, E. (2011). 'Youth immigration to escape unemployment'. Online at: http://idec.gr/iier/new/metanasteusi.pdf [in Greek].

Tsipras, A. (2011). *Statement after the Meeting Between Political Leaders*, 27 May. Online at: http://goo.gl/BlFTma.

— (2015). *Speech at Athens*, 22 January. Online at: http://goo.gl/RKYrVU.

Van Biezen, I. (2000). 'Party membership in twenty European democracies, 1980–2000'. *Party Politics*, 6(3): 329–42.

— (2004). 'Political parties as public utilities'. *Party Politics*, 10(6): 702–22.

Van Biezen, I., Mair, P. and Poguntke, T. (2012). 'Going, going,…gone? Party membership in the 21st century'. *European Journal of Political Research*, 51(1): 24–56.

Van Biezen, I. and Poguntke, T. (2014). 'The decline of membership-based politics'. *Party Politics*, 20(2): 205–26.

Van Cott, D. L. (2005). *From Movements to Parties in Latin America: The Evolution of Ethnic Politics.* New York, Cambridge University Press.

— (2008). *Radical Democracy in the Andes.* New York, Cambridge University Press.

Varoufakis, Y., Holland, S. and Galbraith, J. K. (2015). *Bescheidener Vorschlag zur Losung der Eurokrise.* Munich, Kunstmann.

Vázquez-García, R. (2012). 'The Spanish party system and European integration: a consensual Europeanization'. In E. Kulahci (ed.), *The Domestic Party Politics of Europeanisation.* London, ECPR Series, pp. 109–24.

Vázquez, R., Delgado, S. and Jerez, M. (2014). 'Spanish Political Parties and the European Union: Analysis of Euromanifestos (1987–2004)'. *Perspectives on European Politics and Society*, 11(2): 201–21.

Vergé, T. (2012). 'Party strategies towards civil society in new democracies: the Spanish case'. *Party Politics*, 18(1): 45–60.

Vernardakis, C. (2012). *The Greek Left in the 2012 Elections: The Return to the Class Vote*. Online at: www.vernardakis.gr/uplmed/155_The%20Greek%20Left%20in%20the%202012%20Elections%20(1).pdf.

Verney, S. (2014). 'Broken and can't be fixed: the impact of the economic crisis on the Greek party system'. *The International Spectator*, 49(1): 18–35.

Vignati, R. (2015). 'The organization of the Movimento 5 Stelle: a contradictory party model'. In F. Tronconi (ed.), *Beppe Grillo's Five Star Movement. Organisation, Communication and Ideology*. Aldershot, Ashgate, pp. 29–52.

Voulgaris, G. and Nikolakopoulos, E. (eds.) (2014). *2012. The Double Electoral Earthquake*. Athens, Themelio [in Greek].

Wallerstein, I. (2015). 'A hora dos partidos-movimientos'. *Outras Palavras*, 15 June. Online at: http://outraspalavras.net/posts/wallerstein-limites-e-esperancas-dos-partidos-movimentos.

Weber, M. (1922). *Wirtschaft und Gesellschaft*. Tübingen, J. C. B. Mohr (P. Siebeck).

Weyland, K. (2003). 'Neopopulism and neoliberalism in Latin America: how much affinity?'. *Third World Quarterly*, 24(6): 1095–1115.

— (2013). 'The threat from the Populist Left'. *Journal of Democracy*, 24(3): 13–32.

Wolinetz, S. B. (1988). *Parties and Party Systems in Liberal Democracies*. London, Routledge.

Xenakis, S. and Cheliotis, L. (2015). 'Anger management and the politics of crime in the Greek crisis'. In G. Karyotis and R. Gerodimos (eds.), *The Politics of Extreme Austerity: Greece in the Eurozone Crisis*. London, Routledge, pp. 142–59.

Yashar, D. J. (2005). *Contesting Citizenship in Latin America: The Rise of Indigenous Movements and the Postliberal Challenge*. New York, Cambridge University Press.

— (2011). 'The left and citizenship rights'. In S. Levitsky and K. M. Roberts (eds.), *The Resurgence of the Latin American Left*. Baltimore, Johns Hopkins University Press.

Yécora, F. (2015). 'Elecciones 20-D: el análisis de los resultados'. *Debate 21*, 21 December. Online at: http://debate21.es/2015/12/21/elecciones-20-d-el-analisis-de-los-resultados.

Zald, M. N. and Ash, R. (1966). 'Social Movement Organizations: growth, decay and change'. *Social Forces*, 44(3): 327–41.

Zald, M. N. and McCarthy, J. D. (1987). 'Introduction'. In M. N. Zald and J. D. McCarthy (eds.), *Social Movements in an Organizational Society. Collected Essays*. New Brunswick (NJ) and Oxford, Transaction Books, pp. 45–7.

Zamora-Kapoor, A. and Coller, X. (2014). 'The effects of the crisis: why Southern Europe?'. *American Behavioral Scientist*, 58(12): 1511–16.

Zegada, M. T., Torrez, Y. F. and Cámara, G. (2008). *Movimientos sociales en tiempos de poder: articulaciones y campos de conflicto en el gobierno del MAS, 2006–2007*. La Paz, Centro Cuarto Intermedio/Plural Editores.

Zúquete, J. P. (2008). 'The missionary politics of Hugo Chávez'. *Latin American Politics and Society*, 50(1): 91–121.

Index